Affirmative Action and Principles of Justice

Recent Titles in Contributions in Legal Studies

Judicial Selection: The Cross-Evolution of French and American Practices
Mary Volcansek and Jacqueline Luciene Lafon

The Law School Papers of Benjamin F. Butler: New York University Law School in the 1830s
Ronald L. Brown, editor and compiler

The Civil Rights Revolution:
The Old Court and Individual Rights
John Braemen

Whom Does the Constitution Command?
A Conceptual Analysis with Practical Implications
Larry Alexander and Paul Horton

Constitutionalism: The Philosophical Dimension
Alan S. Rosenbaum, editor

Human Rights in the States: New Directions in Constitutional Policymaking
Stanley H. Friedelbaum, editor

Death by Installments: The Ordeal of Willie Francis
Arthur S. Miller and Jeffrey H. Bowman

Truman's Court: A Study in Judicial Restraint
Frances Howell Rudko

The Gladsome Light of Jurisprudence: Learning the Law in England and the United States in the 18th and 19th Centuries
Michael H. Hoeflich, editor and compiler

James Madison on the Constitution and the Bill of Rights
Robert J. Morgan

Lawyers, Courts, and Professionalism: The Agenda for Reform
Rudolph J. Gerber

John Marshall's Achievement: Law, Politics, and Constitutional Interpretations
Thomas C. Shevory, editor

AFFIRMATIVE ACTION AND PRINCIPLES OF JUSTICE

Kathanne W. Greene

Contributions in Legal Studies, Number 53

PAUL L. MURPHY, *Series Editor*

GP

GREENWOOD PRESS

New York • Westport, Connecticut • London

Library of Congress Cataloging-in-Publication Data

Greene, Kathanne W.
Affirmative action and principles of justice / Kathanne W. Greene.
p. cm. —(Contributions in legal studies, ISSN 0147–1074 ; no. 53)
Bibliography: p.
Includes index.
ISBN 0–313–26678–6 (lib. bdg. : alk. paper)
1. Affirmative action programs—Law and legislation—United States. 2. Discrimination in employment—Law and legislation—United States. I. Title. II. Series.
KF3464.G73 1989
344.73'01133—dc20 89-2121
[347.3011133]

British Library Cataloguing in Publication Data is available.

Library of Congress Catalog Card Number: 89–2121
ISBN: 0–313–26678–6
ISSN: 0147–1074

First published in 1989

Greenwood Press, Inc.
88 Post Road West, Westport, Connecticut 06881

Printed in the United States of America

The paper used in this book complies with the Permanent Paper Standard issued by the National Information Standards Organization (Z39.48–1984).

10 9 8 7 6 5 4 3 2 1

for Daneel

Contents

Preface

Affirmative action is a difficult subject to address. As this book shows, the legal issues surrounding the policy are complicated and confounding. Yet, the most difficult part of affirmative action is not understanding the philosophy or the case law of affirmative action. It is dealing with the deep emotions that continually arise among individuals confronting the issue. Whereas this book is an examination of the philosophical and legal issues, it affords an opportunity to make a brief statement about the emotional side of affirmative action.

I have been severely chastised by some members of my family because I staunchly defend affirmative action. Indeed, I have been told not to discuss the subject in their presence. I believe that this situation has arisen because these individuals, like so many others, are unwilling to face up to what any discussion of affirmative action exposes—prejudice, oppression, and injustice. Yet, those are the very reasons I have spent so many years studying and writing about affirmative action. Prejudice, oppression, and injustice do not simply go away with time. They must be recognized before they can be changed, and change requires effort. I see affirmative action as a necessary step toward change.

I would like to thank the Marriner S. Eccles Graduate Fellowship for the funds to undertake this research. Of course, none of this would have been possible without Howard Ball who gave me the opportunity to come to the University of Utah to study and work with him. He will always have my respect and admiration. Additionally, my deepest appreciation goes to Leslie Francis for her assistance, support, and encouragement. She has been both teacher and friend.

I would also like to thank my mother and father for encouragement to be whatever I wanted to be and the financial support they have given me over the years. I must also thank Chris McMahon, Nancy Hanstaad, Melanee Cherry, Debra Burrington, Mark Henkels, Greg Mendiola, the Parsons Family, R.J. Hunt, and Marge Coulam for making this dislocated southerner feel at home in Salt Lake City and for enriching my life and learning with their diverse perspectives on life and politics. Finally, I must thank my guardian angel, Charlie Seltzer, for being there when I needed his protection and his love.

Abbreviations

EEO	equal employment opportunity
EEOC	Equal Employment Opportunity Commission
EO	executive order
MBE	minority business enterprise
NAACP	National Association for the Advancement of Colored People
OFCCP	Office of Federal Contract Compliance Programs
S.Ct.	Supreme Court Reporter (in case citations)
UGESP	Uniform Guidelines on Employee Selection Procedures (also referred to as the Uniform Guidelines)
U.S.	United States Reports (in case citations)
USCCAN	U.S. Code Congressional and Administrative News

Affirmative Action and Principles of Justice

1

Affirmative Action and Principles of Justice

Affirmative action is, in no uncertain terms, a controversial policy. It has been debated by scholars, politicians, practitioners, and laypersons since its inception in the 1960s, and 20 years later it is still being debated. Much of this debate centers on whether Title VII of the Civil Rights Act of 1964, the law upon which affirmative action is based and which prohibits discrimination in employment, is compensatory or redistributive in scope. That is, is Title VII limited to providing compensation to the identified victims of discrimination, or does it permit an effort such as affirmative action, which works toward a more just distribution of women and blacks and other minorities throughout the work force?

Since 1978 the U.S. Supreme Court has been actively engaged in this debate as well. Because the Supreme Court's decisions on affirmative action help shape the implementation of the policy, the debate now centers almost exclusively on Title VII and a series of Supreme Court decisions on affirmative action. The primary question addressed by the Court is whether affirmative action is the appropriate remedy under that law. Again, is Title VII limited to compensation to the victims of discrimination or does it permit a redistributive remedy?

Before considering the elements of this debate, a definition of affirmative action is required. Employers seeking a definition can turn to the Uniform Guidelines on Employee Selection Procedures (UGESP). The UGESP contains the guidelines developed by the Equal Employment Opportunity Commission (EEOC), the Department of Justice, the Department of Labor, and the now defunct Civil Service Commission, which "... establish a uniform Federal position in the area of prohibiting discrimination in employment practices ..." (UGESP 1978: 38290). According to the UGESP, affirmative action is one part of an effort to remedy past and present discrimination and is considered essential to assuring that jobs are "genuinely and equally accessible to qualified persons, without regard to their sex, racial, or ethnic characteristics" (UGESP 1978: 38308). Affirmative action plans can be voluntary or ordered by a court.

Procedurally, affirmative action is a two-step process. The first step involves an analysis of an employer's work force: "to determine whether percentages of sex, race, or ethnic groups in individual job classifications are substantially similar to the percentages of those groups available in the relevant job market who possess the basic job related qualifications"(UGESP 1978: 38308). If the analysis shows that disparities exist, each element of the selection process (recruitment, testing, interview, recommendations for selection, hiring, promotion, etc.) is analyzed to determine which procedures are working to the detriment of these groups.

Second, if the employer finds that some or all elements of the selection process have an exclusionary effect, it is to establish "affirmative steps to remedy the situation" (UGESP 1978: 38309). These steps can be race-conscious and include the following:

1. the establishment of a long-term goal and short-range interim goals and timetables, which take into account the availability of qualified persons in the relevant job market,
2. a recruitment program to attract qualified members of the excluded groups,
3. a systematic effort to organize work and redesign jobs in ways that provide opportunities to those lacking the knowledge or skills to enter and progress in a career field,
4. validation of selection instruments such as tests according to the guidelines regulations,
5. systematic efforts to include candidates from excluded groups in the selection pool, and
6. systematic efforts to provide career advancement training to employees in dead end jobs (UGESP 1978: 38309).

As this lengthy definition shows, affirmative action is not simply the use of goals and timetables or quotas. Indeed, it is a process, only part of which involves the use of goals and timetables.

THE ISSUES

The legal debate surrounding affirmative action cannot be constructed as a simple exercise in applying the law through the judicial process. Some basic philosophical and political issues are deeply implicated as well. Indeed, the entire legal debate hinges on two principles of justice that compete with each other for status as the one principle that underlies affirmative action. These principles involve compensatory and distributive justice.[1] Distributive justice is concerned with the distribution of rights, benefits, and burdens among the members of a society (Aristotle 1925: 180). There are several different principles articulated within the realm of distributive justice. Rights and benefits can be distributed equally, on the basis of equality of opportunity, need, effort, utility, or even on the basis of a complicated calculus such as the difference principle proposed by John Rawls in his work *A Theory of Justice* (1971). There is no one "official" distributive rule in the United States.

Compensatory justice is concerned with rectifying or compensating for particular wrongs or injustices against individuals by other individuals or their government (Aristotle 1925: 180). The basic principle of compensatory justice is relatively simple. There are two parties, the victim and the perpetrator of the wrong or injustice. According to the principle, the perpetrator of the wrong is responsible for returning the victim to his or her place prior to the wrong or to pay an amount equal to fair compensation for that wrong (Goldman 1979: 32). It is generally understood that this principle applies to individuals or small, identifiable groups.

The debate on affirmative action involves issues raised in reliance on these principles of justice. The current argument against affirmative action is that Title VII of the Civil Rights Act of 1964, the statutory basis of affirmative action in private employment, was intended only to compensate those blacks and other minorities who have actually been victims of discrimination (Nickel 1975: 233–235; Goldman 1979: ch. 3). Yet, the advocates of affirmative action also use compensatory arguments when justifying the policy. One such argument is that Title VII is indeed compensatory, but that compensation is owed to all blacks or other minorities, not only those who have been the victims of an identifiable act of discrimination. Discrimination is systematic so any remedy must also be systematic (Boxill 1984: 148–169).

Distributive and utilitarian arguments are rarely used to argue against affirmative action, but they provide some of the strongest arguments for it. A distributive argument for affirmative action proceeds as follows: in the absence of discrimination (or the presence of equal opportunity) distributive inequities between whites and blacks would not be as great as they presently are and affirmative action is justified as a means toward eliminating these inequities (Nickel 1975: 235–237). A distributive argument has also been used in conjunction with arguments from utility. Such an argument holds that economic and political inequities lead to strife and resentment and a redistribution to eliminate these inequities is justified since they would promote the public welfare as well as establish a more just distribution (Nickel 1975: 237–239). The argument of the School Board of Jackson, Michigan, is that the use of affirmative action to bring more blacks and women into the professions and other white collar jobs provides role models for those who once believed such opportunities were closed to them and reduces their frustration and resentment (*Wygant v. Jackson Board of Education*, 476 U.S. 267 (1986); see also Wasserstrom, 1980:56; Dworkin, 1985:294. Often distributive and utilitarian arguments are utilized in the same justification (see Dworkin 1985; Wasserstrom 1984).

These arguments for or against affirmative action have generally been made by philosophers and others as moral arguments. Yet, when the Supreme Court of the United States considers cases involving the use of affirmative action under Title VII, it must turn to these arguments for its interpretation of the statute. This is the framework of the legal debate. If Title VII is interpreted according to a compensatory principle, Title VII relief could be limited to make-whole relief to the identifiable victims of discrimination and the concept of affirmative action could be discarded by a hostile administration. If, on the other hand, the Supreme Court interprets Title VII according to a distributive or utilitarian principle, affirmative action relief will remain appropriate. The next two sections take a closer look at this debate.

Affirmative Action as Compensation

Affirmative action as compensation is best illustrated by the Reagan administration's view of the policy. Its stand on affirmative action was simple: affirmative action is reverse discrimination and any form of discrimination is unconstitutional. The Civil Rights Division of the Justice Department, under the leadership of William Bradford Reynolds, no longer supports the use of goals or statistical formulas, the primary characteristics of most affirmative action plans. In the courts, they have argued against goals again and again. They have also argued against consent decrees and court orders that require the use of goals to redress incidents of past racial discrimination. Reynolds has argued that the Constitution and 14th Amendment are color-blind and that the only appropriate and effective means of fighting discrimination is with race-neutral policies (Allen, Days, Hooks, and Reynolds 1985: 18). Using a compensatory paradigm as guidance, Reynolds has argued that the government's policy should be to provide relief only to those individuals who have been the victims of overt discrimination. The crux of the administration's argument against affirmative action is that such programs are unjust because they do not redress specific acts of discrimination but benefit one group (nonvictims) at the expense of another group (white males) who are not themselves guilty of discrimination (Allen et al. 1985: 16).

This compensatory view of affirmative action has taken hold in the Equal Employment Opportunity Commission (EEOC) as well. Under the leadership of Clarence Thomas since 1981, the EEOC has shown a decided shift in focus. Thomas has taken an individualistic view of discrimination and the rights established under Title VII of the Civil Rights Act and has influenced the EEOC to pursue his individualistic strategy. Thomas supports bringing suit where an individual is a proven victim of discrimination, but he is opposed to cases where the plaintiffs argue that they are the victims of "historical, across-the board" discrimination citing statistical evidence to support the claim (Williams 1987: 79). The result has been that the EEOC has emphasized cases brought by individuals alleging specific acts of discrimination and avoided the use of class-action and "pattern or practice" lawsuits (U.S. Congress 1985: 9, 133–137). Williams summarizes Thomas' views on "pattern or practice" suits: "If an employer over the years denies jobs to hundreds of qualified women or blacks because he does not want women or blacks working for him, Thomas is not prepared to see a 'pattern or practice' of discrimination. He sees hundreds of local, individual acts of discrimination" (1987: 79).

There are two reasons why the EEOC has avoided class-action and "pattern or practice" suits such as those it once pressed against AT&T and General Electric. The first reason is that such suits are more likely to result in settlements involving goals and timetables (Williams 1987: 80). If such suits never reach the courts, remedial goals and timetables will not be ordered. The other reason is that avoiding such suits limits challenges to tests, job standards, and recruiting procedures which operate against blacks and women.

The failure to pursue cases based on statistical evidence as opposed to specific accusations of discrimination has resulted in a decrease in the number of cases settled by the EEOC. In 1980 the EEOC settled 32.1% of its cases but only 13.6% in 1986 (Williams 1987: 79). The number of cases where the EEOC found "no cause" increased from 28.5% in 1980 to 56.6% in 1986, and 22.3% fewer cases were filed in 1985 than in 1981 (Williams 1987: 79).

In addition to altering the form of the EEOC's enforcement efforts, Thomas and the other EEOC commissioners initiated a review of the Uniform Guidelines on Employee Selection Procedures (Williams 1987: 81; U.S. Congress 1985: 199–200). Thomas is opposed to the guidelines because they operate on the distributive premise that there would be no differences in the hiring and promotion rates of blacks, women, and other groups in the absence of discrimination (U.S. Congress 1985: 130). This is another expression of his opposition to the use of statistics to indicate the presence of discrimination. In addition, Thomas testified before Congress that he felt the guidelines were falsely premised on the inferiority of blacks and other minorities (U.S. Congress 1985: 4). Although the review of the guidelines was to have been completed in 1986, there has been no action on that report.

The EEOC's and Justice Department's shifts in their enforcement efforts indicate that the compensatory paradigm is playing a large role in the current debate over affirmative action. Moreover, it is a paradigm that focuses on compensation to individuals rather than compensation to groups. That is not to say that affirmative action is being justified under a compensatory paradigm. Instead, the paradigm is being used to argue that Title VII does not support the use of affirmative action goals and timetables but only protects individuals who are actual victims of discrimination.

This argument has been discussed by several scholars. Goldman (1979) argued that under the acknowledged principles of compensatory justice, the Reagan administration had a strong case. In compensatory justice, it is understood that there is a victim who has been injured by another individual. The governing principle states that the perpetrator of the injury must pay an amount equal to fair compensation and victims cannot demand as their right payment from unrelated or innocent third parties (Goldman 1979: 67). No one but the perpetrator can be required to make reparation and reparation must be made to the victim, not a third party. Under affirmative action, whether court ordered or voluntary, those who benefit from the policy may not have been personally discriminated against. Goldman also argued against affirmative action as compensation because those who benefit from affirmative action are those who least deserve the benefit, i.e., those individuals who are not disadvantaged and already have the skills and education necessary to qualify them for the jobs they are seeking (1979: 82). He has also argued that affirmative action does not extract reparation from the actual perpetrators of the discrimination. The burden of reparation is placed on the white male who is denied a job for which he is qualified, not the organization or individual guilty of discrimination (1979: 71). Nickel (1975) has noted these same objections to affirmative action as compensation.

Goldman justified limited affirmative action on compensatory grounds within a particular distributive framework. He incorporated a contractarian model based on Rawlsian contract theory (Rawls 1971). With regard to employment, Goldman has argued that individuals would contract for a distributive rule that requires that the most competent individuals should be hired to fill positions. He conceded, however, that hiring by competence is not a just rule until equality of opportunity is achieved. Accordingly, Goldman states: "We are therefore justified in . . . violating the distributive rule in the short run in order to make its application fairer in the long run" (1979:

199). However, Goldman will allow only for the violation of the distributive rule when it is done to compensate those who have previously been discriminated against (the actual victims of discrimation) or the chronically poor (1979: 230).

Goldman has opposed preferential treatment that is directed toward members of groups defined only by race or sex for two reasons (1979: 231). First, affirmative action directed at groups tends to benefit those who least deserve the preference. Second, such affirmative action violates the rights of the chronically poor, the actual victims of discrimination, the most qualified whites, and the public at large. It violates the rights of the poor and the actual victims because they continue to be passed over and thus do not receive the compensation to which they have a right. The most qualified whites have their rights violated because they are not liable for the past discrimination but they bear the burden of reparations. The public at large has its rights violated because it bears the administrative and efficiency costs (Goldman 1979: 231).

Segers has argued that the conditions of compensatory justice are no longer limited to individualized transactions as Goldman and Nickel seem to hold (Foster, Segers, Thornberry, and Evans 1983: 81–82). She noted that under tort law, injuries no longer need be deliberate and with malicious intent. No-fault insurance plans emphasize compensation for injuries and loss, play down individual responsibility, and spread costs among their members. Also, criminal justice victim compensation plans use taxpayer money on the ground that the state has failed to protect its citizens (Foster et al. 1983: 82). According to Segers, since the compensatory principle is no longer individualized, it is possible to attempt to justify affirmative action on compensatory grounds (see Boxill 1984).

Those who justify affirmative action on compensatory grounds have argued that Title VII and affirmative action policy are intended to compensate groups that have been the victim of both specific acts of discrimination and the effects of past discrimination. They hold that because the original discrimination was not against individuals but against groups who continue to suffer from the effects of that discrimination, compensatory justice requires that compensation be made to the group. This is actually a response to the opponent's claim that only the actual victims of discrimination should benefit from affirmative action policy. The advocates' claim is that all blacks are the victims of discrimination since discrimination is not simply isolated acts against certain individuals but is a systematic process that operates against all blacks.

Boxill (1984) has made the argument that all blacks have been the victims of discrimination. He argued that the harms of discrimination need not be economic or political but can be psychological (Boxill 1984: 151–152). Even if a particular black man or woman has not been directly discriminated against, that individual will experience a loss of self-confidence and self-respect when he or she witnesses discrimination against other blacks or women. This loss of self-confidence and self-respect can affect future opportunities by reducing the individual's expectations.

Boxill has also argued that Goldman's argument against affirmative action (it benefits those who least deserve it) is wrong. Blacks and women may differ in the extent to which they have been harmed by discrimination, but that does not lead to the conclusion that some are less deserving of compensation (Boxill 1984: 153). The compensatory paradigm does not hold that given two individuals who have been harmed by discrimination, only the individual who has suffered the most harm should be compensated.

Boxill addressed the issue of requiring white males to make reparation as well (Boxill 1984: 166–167). The argument is that affirmative action not only removes the advantages white males received under a discriminatory system, it also costs them the time and effort they have put into their education and career. Boxill states that affirmative action "does not require young white males to pay, at an additional cost to themselves, the price of their advantages . . . [but] proposes instead to compensate the injured with goods [jobs] that no one has yet to establish a right to" (Boxill 1984: 167). Boxill also argued that affirmative action does not violate a white male's right to fair competition for a job but instead affirmative action, by refusing to allow the white male a job because of an unfair advantage, actually makes the competition more fair (Boxill 1984: 167).

This discussion shows that affirmative action as compensation provides neither a conclusive justification for nor a conclusive argument against the policy. The policy does not exactly fit all articulated definitions of compensatory justice, but, at the same time, it is possible to rebut the arguments that affirmative action should be reserved only for the actual victims of discrimination and that it places an unjust burden on white males. Because of this, many scholars, including Goldman, have looked for other principles on which to justify the policy.

Affirmative Action as Distributive Justice

Conceptions of distributive justice have also been used to justify affirmative action (see Dworkin 1985; Goldman 1979; Nickel 1975; Wasserstrom 1980). A distributive argument to justify affirmative action would hold that the policy is a means for "promoting the redistribution of income and other important benefits" (Nickel 1975: 235). The redistribution itself can be justified in two ways. Keeping within the limits of distributive justice, the redistribution can be justified because it reduces distributive inequalities due to discrimination. According to Segers, ". . . the use of special opportunities to offset disadvantages stemming from past injustice may be justified as a means of achieving a society in which all individuals have more equitable shares of the benefits and burdens of American life" (Foster et al. 1983: 85).

Essential to a distributive argument for affirmative action is the premise that some distributive inequalities cannot be justified. This is not a demand for economic equality. Instead, it is an argument that it is unjust for groups such as blacks and women to be relegated to the lower end of the socioeconomic ladder because of their race or sex. A difficulty with this argument is that it is not always possible to identify which inequities are the result of discrimination and which are due to factors based on relevant distinctions. Sowell (1984) makes his case against affirmative action primarily on this ground.

Sowell disputes the claim that economic inequalities are primarily due to discrimination (1981: 65; 1984: 16). He argues that factors such as age distributions and a particular cultural inheritance can also produce economic inequalities. According to Sowell, one of the reasons that there are so few blacks, Puerto Ricans, and hispanics in high-level positions is because these groups have a younger median age than other groups such as whites and Jews and such positions are generally held by older, experienced individuals (1981: 65–66). Discrimination may not account for all economic inequalities, but, as Nickel notes, it is not speculative to suggest that many of the inequalities between blacks and whites and men and women are due to discrimination (1975: 237, n. 16).

If one is willing to accept the argument that economic inequities are the result of discrimination, the redistribution can also be justified on grounds of utility. A redistribution of benefits promotes the public welfare because it reduces poverty and inequalities and reduces the resentment, strife, and loss of self-respect attendant with economic inequality (Nickel 1975: 237; Dworkin 1985: 298; Wasserstrom 1980: 55; and Nagel 1973: 359).

Two of the most persuasive arguments in support of affirmative action have been made by Wasserstrom (1980) and Dworkin (1985). Both support affirmative action as redistribution justified by social utility. Wasserstrom justifies affirmative action as an instrumentality, a means for altering the social realities. According to Wasserstrom:

> . . . by their operation [affirmative action programs] directly alter the composition of these institutions (universities, federal, state, and local governments, corporations, the bench and bar, and state and federal legislatures) by increasing the number of nonwhites and women who in fact fill these positions of power and authority. This is desirable in itself because it is a redistribution of positions in a way that creates a new social reality—one which more nearly resembles the one captured by the good society . . . in which the places of significance will be held to a substantially greater degree than they are at present by persons who are nonwhite and female (1980: 55).[2]

Wasserstrom holds that the redistribution alone is enough to justify affirmative action since the present distribution is unjust. However, he extends the argument by holding that the redistribution alters the perception that positions of power and authority are held exclusively by white males to a perception that historically underrepresented groups can appropriately hold those positions (1980: 55–56). This is a utilitarian argument.

Dworkin (1985) makes a similar argument concerning affirmative action. He holds that the immediate goal of affirmative action is to increase the number of members of certain races in the professions, but that the long-term goal is to reduce the degree to which the United States is a racially conscious society (1985: 294). In essence, as long as whites continue to hold the positions of power and prestige to the exclusion of other groups, racial divisions will continue to exist. However, increasing the number of blacks and others in such positions will reduce the sense of frustration, injustice, and race-consciousness of blacks, who will begin to think of themselves as individuals who can succeed as well as whites can on their talents (Dworkin 1985: 294).

There are, of course, problems with utilitarian justifications of the redistribution. The most significant problem is that the redistribution has costs as well as benefits. These costs include resentment on the part of those who are better qualified but passed over and by the individuals who benefit from the policy. Other costs are threats to the self-esteem of those who benefit and the possibility that such programs only increase racial consciousness and racial tensions (Segers in Foster et al. 1983: 79; Dworkin 1985: 297). Another important problem with such justifications is that there is inevitably a trade-off between utility and individual rights (Segers in Foster et al. 1983: 80).

Dworkin's argument for affirmative action considered this trade-off between utility and individual rights. Dworkin noted that all arguments for a utilitarian-type justification of affirmative action must fail if the policy violates an individual's constitutional or moral rights

(Dworkin 1985: 298).[3] According to Dworkin, there are three possible violations of rights that can result from affirmative action: it can violate a person's right to be judged on merit, it can violate a person's right to be judged as an individual instead of as a member of a group, and it can violate a person's right not be excluded from an opportunity simply because of race (1985: 298). With regard to merit, Dworkin notes that there is no acceptable definition of merit upon which to base a right (1985: 299). Additionally, there are no educational institutions or employers who judge individuals solely on the basis of merit. With regard to a person's right to be judged as an individual, Dworkin notes that it is impossible for administrators and managers to judge each person solely on individual characteristics. Instead, some statistical generalizations must be made in order to eliminate some members of the applicant pool (e.g., employment tests, ACT scores, etc.) (1985: 299). This being the case, it is wrong to conclude that a generalization based on race (when that generalization is not based on contempt or prejudice) violates the rights of persons, whereas generalizations based on test scores do not.

With regard to an individual's right not be excluded from benefits on the basis of race, Dworkin notes that this right only exists when the exclusion is not based simply on race, but when an individual's race is the object of prejudice or contempt (1985: 300–301). As a human characteristic, race is no different from intelligence, age, or skills; it is a factor that is simply beyond the control of the individual. It is not a violation of a right to be denied admission to a university or offered a certain job because an individual is not intelligent enough. Similarly, it is not a violation of a right to be denied a benefit on the basis of race as long as the denial is not because of racial prejudice or a belief that certain races are inferior to others (Dworkin 1985: 301).

Interpreting Title VII

Scholars who have sought to justify or condemn affirmative action in terms of principles of justice have not done so in a vacuum. As noted previously, these justifications are the framework for the legal debate. The Supreme Court must interpret Title VII when applying it to specific cases and this process of interpretation requires a search for the underlying principle or principles behind the statute. This is done through a judicial tool of statutory interpretation: theories of legislation. These theories, which may involve a search for legislative intent or a search for coherence, guide justices in the interpretation of statutes by identifying the legal rights and duties that Congress established when it enacted the legislation (Dworkin 1985: 319). Theories of intent interpret the law through an examination of the words of the statute and/or the legislative history of the law as found in the committee hearings, reports, and congressional debates. The coherence theory interprets the law in terms of the political justification of the statute. In either case, the Court must determine whether Title VII is based on compensatory or distributive justice before it can apply the law to the facts of the case.

Equally important to the Court's interpretation of Title VII with respect to affirmative action is its own early employment discrimination cases. Congress did not define discrimination, but left the task to the Court. Thus these early interpretations of the statute that defined discrimination will shape the Court's later interpretation of it in relation to affirmative action. These early interpretations do not stand alone, however. They must be viewed in the context of amendments that were subsequently made to Title VII by Congress. Thus the legal debate surrounding affirmative action is not the simple application of a law to different sets of facts. Instead, it also involves accounting for the political reactions to these decisions in later applications.

The aim of this book is to provide a comprehensive examination of the legal debate over affirmative action through a case study of the Supreme Court's affirmative action decisions. By combining a policy analysis and a doctrinal analysis with a philosophical foundation, the philosophical, political, and legal aspects of the debate over affirmative action will be brought together. The emphasis is on the Court's justification of the policy in terms of justice. The Court, of course, must couch its decisions in legal terms only, but this analysis should show that the philosophical and political aspects of the policy are present in the Court's decisions as well.

NOTES

1. Affirmative action has been justified using a variety of principles of justice (see Boxill 1984; Dworkin 1985; Fullinwider 1980; Goldman 1979; Nickel 1975; Wasserstrom 1980). Fullinwider (1980) examined theories of rights, social utility, and compensatory and distributive principles as possiblities for justifying affirmative action. Goldman (1979) found affirmative action unjustifiable on compensatory grounds but defended it with distributive principles. Boxill (1984) and Nickel (1975) have also noted that affirmative action has been justified on compensatory, distributive and utilitarian grounds. Dworkin (1985) and Wasserstrom (1980) have justified affirmative action on redistributive grounds.
2. For another approach to discrimination law which argues for redistribution as a remedy, see Catherine A. MacKinnon, *Sexual Harassment of Working*

Women: A Case of Sex Discrimination, New Haven: Yale University Press, 1979, p. 127.

3. Dworkin notes that there are no rights in the Constitution or the words of Title VII that are violated by affirmative action. Therefore, the rights that are violated must involve some fundamental principle of political morality (1985:298). Moreover, since no rights are violated, Dworkin would leave the questions of utility (policy) to the legislature, not the courts.

2

The Legislative History of Title VII

The term "affirmative action" originated in a bill presented to the House of Representatives in 1950, which required that employers not discriminate and that they take "affirmative action" to provide back pay and reinstatement to those who had been discriminated against (Burstein 1985: 30). However, affirmative action as it is defined today was not articulated as a policy until President Lyndon Johnson issued Executive Order (EO) 11246, which required that federal contractors take affirmative action to ensure the hiring of qualified blacks, women, and other minorities in their work forces.[1] The use of affirmative action was never limited to federal contractors. Most challenges to affirmative action have been brought by private or public employers either under the Equal Protection Clause of the Fourteenth Amendment, Title VII of the Civil Rights Act of 1964, or both.[2] These challenges have been to affirmative action programs that have been undertaken voluntarily by the employer, were agreed to in a consent decree, or that were implemented after a court ordered the employer to establish an affirmative action program after a finding of discrimination.

The Supreme Court cases that are the main focus of this work have generally been challenges brought under Title VII of the Civil Rights Act of 1964, as amended, and the legal debate over affirmative action arises from the Court's interpretation of this title. With regard to affirmative action, §706(g) of Title VII states only that after a finding of discrimination a court may order an employer "to take such affirmative action as may be appropriate . . . ." The section as it was originally written goes on to state that such action "may include, but is not limited to reinstatement or hiring of employees, with or without backpay." In 1972 this section was amended to include the phrase "or any other equitable relief as the court deems appropriate." This definition is somewhat unclear as to whether it includes affirmative action as it is defined in the Uniform Guidelines on Employee Selection Procedures and it applies only to court-ordered affirmative action. This section does not address the additional questions of whether Title VII permits voluntary affirmative action or affirmative action undertaken in compliance with a consent decree. Thus the Supreme Court has had to make the determination of whether affirmative action is acceptable under the prohibitions and requirements of the statute.

Statutory interpretation is one of the primary functions of the Supreme Court (Ball 1987: 34). When Congress passes legislation, especially comprehensive and controversial legislation such as the Civil Rights Act, it is often unable or unwilling to address all the possible issues and problems that will arise when the statute is implemented. This may be a function of the complexity of the issues being addressed or it may result from the need to negotiate and compromise in order to satisfy the various interests in Congress needed to pass the legislation. The responsibility for filling in the gaps not addressed in the resulting statute is that of the federal courts and ultimately the Supreme Court.

The interpretation of statutes by the courts requires the use of a theory of legislation as a guide. There is no single theory of legislation utilized by the federal courts. Indeed, Ronald Dworkin, a prominent legal philosopher, refers to such theories as "contested" concepts whose authority derives solely from their persuasive force (Dworkin 1985: 320). Different judges and justices prefer different theories. There are three main theories of legislation used today. Two of these theories involve identifying the "intent" of the legislature: institutionalized intention and collective understanding. Institutionalized intention assumes that a policy or principle is enacted so that it becomes part of the legislation by express legislative decision and is generally discernable from a statute's legislative history. Collective understanding takes intent to be "some combination of beliefs of particular congressmen who draft, advocate, oppose, lobby for or against, and vote to pass or reject a particular statute" (Dworkin 1985: 322; see also Landis 1930). Legal Realists have long accepted the idea that statutory interpretation cannot rely on a simple reading of the words, but they have rejected the idea that this problem can be resolved through identifying legislative intent (Radin 1930: 866, 870). Radin argued that the legislative history of a statute will not assist in the identification of legislative intent because the legislative process involves negotiation and compromise among many members of Congress, each of whom may hold different ideas and beliefs regarding a statute (1930: 871–873).

Dworkin has developed a theory of interpretation that is not dependent on legislative intent. The coherence theory holds that a statute should be interpreted to advance the policies or principles that furnish the best political justification for the statute (Dworkin 1985: 327). However, there can be disagreement on what principles or policies provide the justification of a statute. It may be that there are two justifications for a statute, both of which fit equally well with the words of the statute and the political climate of the time but are not attached to the statute by some convention (Dworkin 1985: 328). If this is the case, then a court must choose between the principles or policy on the basis of which justification is superior in terms of political morality (Dworkin 1985: 328–329).

Because the Supreme Court has been required to interpret Title VII in its affirmative action cases, any analysis of its decisions requires an in-depth examination of the title and its legislative history. This chapter provides that legislative history.[3] However, it does not seek to divine the intent of the statute. It, instead, examines both the policymaking process and the statute itself in order to highlight the major elements of the policy and the principles it represents. Emphasis is also placed on identifying any justification or justifications of the statute, particularly compensatory or redistributive justifications.

EQUAL EMPLOYMENT OPPORTUNITY AND CIVIL RIGHTS: SETTING THE AGENDA

The first federal action regarding equal employment opportunity (hereafter EEO) was the signing of Executive Order 8802 by Franklin Roosevelt in 1941 (Burstein 1985: 13). This order banned discrimination in employment by the federal government and defense contractors. Prior to this time there had been no movement on EEO legislation because few people believed the Supreme Court would hold such legislation constitutional. Before the New Deal, the Supreme Court had limited the power of the federal government to regulate private employment practices, and thus discrimination (Burstein 1985: 15–17). However, by the late 1930s the Court had begun to show signs of change that made the legislative environment more conducive to EEO legislation. In particular, the Court began reversing its stance on federal regulation of the economy and employment relations by holding the New Deal legislation constitutional in cases such as *National Labor Relations Board v. Jones and Laughlin Steel Corporation*, 301 U.S. 1 (1937) and *United States v. Darby*, 312 U.S. 100 (1940) (Ball 1980: 145–146). At the same time, the Court was showing a greater concern for individual constitutional rights (Berger 1968: 90). In *U.S. v. Carolene Products Corporation*, 304 U.S. 144 (1938), Justice Stone wrote his famous footnote #4 suggesting that state legislation involving rights in the Bill of Rights might require closer scrutiny than the rational basis presumption of constitutionality required.[4] Strict scrutiny was not articulated as a standard of review until several years later, but the standard is based on Stone's note. Also, the Court began showing a greater willingness to hear cases involving civil rights issues and foreshadowed later trends in the case of *Chambers v. Florida*, 309 U.S. 227 (1940) where they ruled that forcing a confession from four black men accused of murdering a white denied them due process under the Fourteenth Amendment (Berger 1968: 90).

Once the environment became more hospitable to EEO legislation, several bills were presented in Congress. In 1941 a bill was introduced to give Executive Order 8802 the force of law and in 1942 a bill was introduced to prohibit discrimination by private employers and labor unions as well as the federal government and defense contractors (Burstein 1985: 17). No such legislation was passed until Title VII of the Civil Rights Act of 1964, but between 1942 and 1964 hundreds of EEO bills were introduced in Congress (Burstein 1984: 19). Thus it seems that the EEO agenda began during the New Deal.

According to Burstein in his analysis of EEO legislation, each bill presented to Congress since 1941 exhibited certain elements dealing with which groups the legislation protected, who was prohibited from discriminating, what employment practices were unlawful, how the law was to be enforced, and what penalties to which violators were subject (1985: 19–20). All the legislation prior to 1964 prohibited discrimination on the basis of race, religion, and national origin. Gender discrimination was not considered until 1964 (Burstein 1985: 20–21). The first EEO bills dealt only with the federal government, defense contractors, and private employers. By 1955 the list was expanded to include labor unions and employment agencies as well (Burstein 1985: 23). In 1972 state and local governments were added to this list (Burstein 1985: 24).

The practices prohibited under EEO legislation have changed only slightly since the 1940s. In general, employers were prohibited from refusing to hire, to discharge, or otherwise discriminate with respect to the terms, conditions, and privileges of employment (Burstein 1985: 26). The changes that were made in these provisions were not significant. The enforcement provisions of these bills differed primarily in two respects. Some bills called for administrative enforcement with the agency having the power to issue enforceable orders whereas others preferred to leave enforcement up to the courts (Burstein 1985: 30). This was a major point of contention during the consideration of Title VII by Congress.

Finally, the EEO bills offered three alternatives for penalties.[5] The first option was criminal penalties, but this was never seriously considered. Another option was that the victim be returned to her rightful place by giving her the job, promotion, or of whatever she had been deprived (Burstein 1985: 31). The third option was to return the individual to her rightful place in addition to awarding damages in the amount of pay lost and expenses incurred. According to Burstein, the third option was the most widely considered (1985: 31–32) and was first expressed in a bill passed by the House (but not the Senate) in 1950: discriminators were to "cease and desist from such unlawful employment practice and to take such affirmative action, including reinstatement or hiring of employees, with or without backpay, as will effectuate the policies of the Act" (1985: 30). The interpretation of the remedial provision of Title VII, which was slightly altered by the 1972 amendments, is one of the major issues to be considered below and in the following chapter.

Burstein concluded from his analysis that the major provisions of EEO legislation were decided early in the agenda-setting process (1985: 32). Yet, whereas the basic structure of EEO legislation was established early, the fact remained that no such legislation was passed until 1964. It thus seems that some consideration must be given to the social, economic, and political changes and events that made the passage of Title VII possible.

The social, economic and political changes and events that culminated in the passage of the Civil Rights Act of 1964 are all part of the protest movement for civil rights that began to take shape in 1956. One day Rosa Parks refused to give up her seat to a white man on a Montgomery, Alabama, bus resulting in the successful Montgomery bus boycott. However, this event only signifies a major shift in strategy on the part of blacks working for civil rights. Since its inception around the turn of the century, the National Association for the Advancement of Colored People (NAACP) had been working for black civil rights but had chosen to concentrate their efforts in the courts via litigation (Kluger 1980). This was a slow and difficult strategy, but the NAACP had a series of successes before the Supreme Court in higher education cases, the goal of which was systematically to break down the separate but equal doctrine that the Supreme Court had expounded in *Plessy v. Ferguson*, 163 U.S. 537 (1896).

The first success came in the state courts—the Maryland Court of Appeals—in the case of *Pearson v. Murray*, 182 A. 590 (1936). In that case a black was denied admission to the University of Maryland School of Law but was offered an out-of-state scholarship to cover his legal education elsewhere. The court ruled that under the separate and equal doctrine, the equality afforded by this policy was deficient and the state could only meet the standard by admitting the student to the white law school (Barker and Barker 1982: 399). Two years later in *Missouri ex rel. Gaines v. Canada*, 305 U.S. 337 (1938), the Supreme Court made a similar ruling regarding out-of-state scholarship arrangements. The Court held that in order for there to be equal treatment as required by the separate but equal doctrine, the students must be provided an education within the state.

The result of the *Gaines* decision was the creation of separate black professional schools by many southern states. In 1950 new litigation reached the Court on this issue. In *Sweatt v. Painter*, 339 U.S. 629 (1950), the Supreme Court addressed the issue of whether the black law school established in Texas was equal to the white law school in terms of facilities, faculty, and other educational opportunities. They found that the schools did not meet the standard of equality required by the separate but equal doctrine (Barker and Barker 1982: 399). On the same day, the Court struck down a University of Oklahoma Graduate School policy of internally segregating a black student in the case of *McLaurin v. Oklahoma State Regents for Higher Education*, 339 U.S. 637 (1950) (Abraham 1983: 117).

In the meantime, the NAACP was working on segregation in secondary and primary education. In 1952 the Supreme Court heard arguments in a series of cases from Kansas, South Carolina, Virgina, and Delaware, which were consolidated as *Brown v. Board of Education of Topeka, Kansas*, 347 U.S. 483 (1954). The Court first heard arguments in this case in 1952 and rearguments in 1953. On May 17, 1954 the Supreme Court ruled that segregated schools were "inherently unequal." The separate but equal doctrine was overturned.

Brown brought an end to the separate but equal doctrine, but it did not bring equality to blacks. The South moved slowly toward school desegregation and many times the federal government had to intervene to force the states to desegregate. Similarly, blacks were still subject to segregation in public accommodations and public transportation and were still subject to discrimination in employment and voting rights. When the expected gains from *Brown* did not materialize, the blacks became frustrated and moved toward another strategy—protests and nonviolent direct action (Oberschall 1973: 206–207). This movement crystallized with the Montgomery bus boycott, which began after Rosa Parks was arrested for refusing to give up her seat (Schulke and McPhee 1985: ch. 3).

The mobilization of blacks after the Montgomery bus boycott has been attributed to two primary factors (Oberschall 1973: ch. VI). The first factor, of course, was the *Brown* decision, which showed blacks that the federal government, at least the judiciary, was supportive of civil rights efforts. Another major factor was the emergence of new leadership in the black community. These leaders came primarily from the black church organizations. A study by E. Franklin Frazier indicated that black churches were one institution least controlled by whites and the church leaders were the least likely to suffer sanctions by whites since they were supported by blacks themselves (Frazier

1974: 43–44). Hence, with little to lose, the black church leaders began organizing protest activity.

Once blacks became organized, the Civil Rights movement, which was no longer limited to the courts and a litigation strategy, began to take on a new shape. The activities of the movement in the late 1950s and early 1960s took two forms: protests and nonviolent direct action. Nonviolent direct action is commonly referred to as civil disobedience. In his study of the Civil Rights Movement, Dye (1971) provided a description of nonviolent direct action: "The political purpose of nonviolent direct action and civil disobedience is to call attention or 'to bear witness' to the existence of injustices. Only laws regarded as unjust are broken, and these laws are broken openly without hatred or violence. Punishment is actively sought rather than avoided since punishment will further emphasize the injustices of the law" (1971: 119). According to Dye, the purpose of civil disobedience is "to stir the conscience of an apathetic majority" in an effort to change the unjust policy (1971: 119). A person can demonstrate sincerity by accepting the punishment for violating the unjust law and thus "shame the majority" and make it consider "how far it will go to protect the status quo" (Dye 1971: 119).

It was primarily the nonviolent direct action movement headed by Martin Luther King, Jr. and the Southern Christian Leadership Conference (SCLC) and the Student Non-violent Co-ordinating Committee that provided the impetus for the passage of the Civil Rights Act of 1964. Throughout the early 1960s, blacks staged sit-ins at segregated lunch counters, wade-ins at segregated public swimming pools, and kneel-ins at segregated churches (Dye 1971: 120). The most significant direct action activity took place in Birmingham, Alabama, in 1963. For a week in May, blacks of all ages boycotted the downtown Birmingham merchants and staged protest activities at city hall and at other public facilities (Schulke and McPhee 1986: ch. 8).

The object of these protests, as in all direct action activity, was to fill the jails of Birmingham. The protesters succeeded in this task and those not jailed continued the protests. Finally, frustrated by the large numbers of blacks still protesting, the police chief of Birmingham, "Bull" Conner, and his men met the blacks with hoses and dogs. All this took took place in front of the cameras of the television networks and America watched as the blacks bravely faced the blasts of fire hoses and the jaws of police dogs (Schulke and McPhee 1986: ch. 8).

Following the events in Birmingham, civil rights activists converged on Washington, D.C., for a protest march. Through the streets of the capital in August 1963 (Dye 1971: 121–122) peacefully marched 200,000 people, both black and white. The marchers demanded a civil rights law that prohibited discrimination in voting, public accommodations, and employment. Civil rights was clearly on the public agenda.

By 1963 civil rights was not only on the public agenda but the congressional agenda as well. Both the public and Congress had come to believe that the federal government should and legitimately could act on civil rights. As noted above, in 1963 several hundred civil rights bills had been introduced in Congress. The next step was the actual formulation of the policy.

It should be noted that Congress had 20 years of EEO legislative activity to work with when it began formulating the employment discrimination title of the Civil Rights Act. The possibilities for coverage, prohibited practices, enforcement and penalties were already on the table, so the task was really to decide whether to develop a strong bill with extensive coverage and prohibitions, enforcement by an administrative agency, and strong penalties; a weak bill with limited coverage and prohibitions, enforcement by the courts, and minor penalties; or some moderate form. Hence, the formulation stage was primarily a political activity involving compromise and negotiation. The next sections examine the formulation of Title VII beginning with President John F. Kennedy's civil rights proposal and following it through the House and Senate. In addition, the formulation of the 1972 amendments to Title VII are examined.

KENNEDY'S CIVIL RIGHTS PROPOSALS

In early 1963 President Kennedy presented a mild civil rights bill to Congress which was intended to broaden existing protections of black voting rights and extend the life of the U.S. Commission on Civil Rights (Dye 1971: 125). However, after the events in Birmingham and the March on Washington, Kennedy began to feel pressure to present stronger legislation. In June he sent a message to Congress calling for legislation that guaranteed voting rights, equal access to public accommodations, equality in employment practices, nondiscrimination in federally assisted programs, and authority for the Justice Department to file suit in desegregation cases.

In his message to Congress, Kennedy stressed the importance of the link between social and politicial rights and liberties and the economic distress of blacks: "Employment opportunities . . . play a major role in determining whether the rights described above [voting, access to public accommodations and facilities, desegregated schools] are meaningful. There is little value in a Negro's obtaining the right to be admitted to hotels and restaurants if he has no cash in his pocket and no job" (U.S. Congress 1963: 11177). Kennedy went on to say that progress was needed in three areas if unemployment among blacks was to be lessened. First, he called for the creation of new jobs for blacks and other poor citizens through greater economic growth. Kennedy also called for more education and training programs to raise the level of skills among blacks, and finally for the elimination of discrimination in employment. In his message to Congress, Kennedy repeatedly stressed these three areas where progress was necessary to relieve black unemployment: (1) job creation through economic growth, (2) increased education and training to raise the level of skills, and (3) the elimination of racial discrimination in employment (U.S. Congress 1963: 11177–11178).

Kennedy placed the need for more education and training to increase the skill levels of blacks first in priority. In his message, he requested more federal funding for all levels of education, from grade school to graduate school, and the enactment of several measures that would provide an expansion of job training and experience programs (U.S. Congress 1963: 11177). Only then did the president approach the issue of racial discrimination: " . . . even the complete elimination of racial discrimination in employment—a goal toward which this nation must strive—will not put a single unemployed Negro to work unless he has the skills required . . . —and thus the passage of this legislation . . . is essential if the objectives of this message are to be met" (U.S. Congress 1963: 11178).

There is some evidence to suggest that Kennedy was aware of the redistributive aspects of fair employment practices legislation. He cited employment and education statistics that showed that blacks were twice as likely to be unemployed as whites and that in general blacks had much lower levels of educational attainment than whites (U.S. Congress 1963: 11177). By citing these statistics, Kennedy identified the issue as being more than discrimination in employment but as a need to eliminate economic disparities between blacks and whites. Kennedy also recognized that nondiscriminatory employment policies were not enough to eliminate these disparities (U.S. Congress 1963: 11177–11178). However, it would be hasty to conclude that Kennedy would have endorsed affirmative action as it is conceived today. Instead, he endorsed what might be considered an extremely weak form of affirmative action where such disparities would be eliminated through expanding the job market and increasing the availability of job training programs and educational opportunities.

Regarding the elimination of racial discrimination, Kennedy identified in his message some proposed and previously implemented plans toward this goal. First, he recommended that the Committee on Equal Employment Opportunity be given "a permanent statutory basis, assuring adequate financing and enforcement procedures" (U.S.

Congress 1963: 11178). He proposed an executive order extending the Committee on Equal Employment Opportunity to include construction programs through grant-in-aid programs. He also noted that he had previously directed that all federal construction programs be reviewed to prevent racial discrimination. He had also directed the Secretary of Labor to assure that apprenticeship programs did not discriminate and that the federal-state employment service not discriminate but assured equal opportunity for blacks in job placement and counseling activities. Kennedy indicated that the Justice Department had intervened in a NLRB case involving charges of racial discrimination in unions. He articulated a new federal policy that only nondiscriminating employee organizations would be recognized. He also stated that 118 AFL-CIO unions had signed nondiscrimination agreements with the Committee on Equal Employment Opportunity.

Kennedy's legislative proposals for equal employment opportunity were relatively weak compared to the final version of Title VII in that they applied only to federal contractors and not private employers (Whalen and Whalen 1985: 35). Yet, his position on equal opportunity probably reflected the prevailing view on the issue, i.e., with improved education and training and the elimination of blatant racial discrimination, blacks would surely begin to move up the economic ladder on their own merit. Indeed, it will become clear with the analysis of the Senate debate that it was always assumed the final criterion in any employment decision would be merit.

The weakness of Kennedy's employment proposals may have been due to political considerations. He had been forced to act on civil rights legislation, but at the time his main priority was his proposed tax reform bill, which was already before the Congress. He feared that if his civil rights legislation were too strong, the House Ways and Means Committee might retaliate by not letting his tax measure out of committee. Indeed, at the president's request, the House Judiciary Subcommittee No. 5 that held hearings on the Kennedy bill (HR7152) delayed reporting it to the full committee until after the House Ways and Means Committee had acted on the tax bill (Whalen and Whalen 1985: 22–23). In fact, the proposals for improving the employment situation of blacks fit nicely with his tax reform measure, which he hoped would stimulate the economy and create more jobs.

Yet, whatever the reasons for the weakness of Kennedy's employment proposals, the fact remains that they did give some consideration to the distribution of political and social rights and benefits. Kennedy believed that equal opportunity and the education and training opportunities that are essential to it are important not only in themselves, they also serve to further other civil rights such as the right to vote and the right to enjoy public accommodations. He believed that when these rights are shared equally and economic benefits are distributed on the basis of nonracial criteria, justice will be served for all citizens, black and white.

However, at the same time, Kennedy recognized the need for legal remedies for the denial of individual rights: "The growing and understandable dissatisfaction of Negro citizens with the present pace of desegregation, and their increased determination to secure for themselves the equality of opportunity and treatment to which they are rightfully entitled, have underscored what should already have been clear: the necessity of the Congress enacting this year . . . legislation providing *legal remedies for the denial of certain individual rights* [emphasis supplied]" (U.S. Congress 1963: 11175). Legal remedies for the denial of individual rights more closely represent compensatory values than redistributive ones. That is, the denial of rights can be viewed as an injury for which the victim should be compensated. The form of compensation may vary depending on the right involved. In the case of discrimination in employment, compensation may take the form of a monetary reward. As shown below, Congress specifically included an award of back pay in the remedies available to those who have been discriminated against.

Thus both redistributive and compensatory principles seem to play a role in fair employment practices legislation. The redistributive principles are evidenced by the fact that Kennedy suggested that one of the justifications of the legislation was the need to eliminate economic inequality between blacks and whites. However, he did not emphasize this point. The compensatory aspects are evidenced by the principle of nondiscrimination in employment and legal remedies for violation of that principle.

HR7152 IN THE HOUSE OF REPRESENTATIVES: A STRATEGY OF STRENGTH AND COMPROMISE

Following Kennedy's message to Congress, the proposed legislation was sent to the House of Representatives where it was introduced by Emanuel Celler (D-NY), given the label HR7152, and sent to the House Judiciary Commitee. Celler, who was the chairman of the Judiciary Committee, assigned HR7152 to Subcommittee No. 5, which he also chaired, and hearings began soon thereafter.

At Kennedy's request, the hearings in the Judiciary subcommittee were extended in an effort to get the tax reform bill onto the floor of the House. It was not until September 1963 that the subcommittee finally began the mark-up of the bill. Outside the committee room, reporters filled the hall anxiously awaiting any word that might indicate what was happening. These were unusual proceedings because Celler told the subcommittee that all the changes made would be tentative until the committee had had time to analyze the bill thoroughly.

As the mark-up was progressing, a bomb exploded in a black church in Birmingham, Alabama, killing four little girls and injuring many other children (Whalen and Whalen 1985: 33–34). The nation and the Congress were shocked by this and a move was quickly made by Celler to strengthen the Kennedy bill. The Civil Rights leaders, who were always in close contact with Celler and continued to make their views known, had asked for a stronger employment title, and after the bombings the members of Celler's subcommittee were willing to give it to them (Whalen and Whalen 1985: 34). The Democrats on the subcommittee began offering strengthening amendments including a much stronger fair employment practices title, which created an Equal Employment Opportunity Commission with strong investigatory and enforcement powers (Whalen and Whalen 1985: 35). Kennedy's employment title had dealt with discrimination only by federal contractors and relied on persuasion rather than the force of law (Whalen and Whalen 1985: 35). At the same time, Republican amendments were easily rejected.

On October 2 Celler called for a voice vote on HR7152 and then announced that the revised bill would be reported favorably to the full Judiciary Committee (Whalen and Whalen 1985: 37). In this strengthened version, the EEOC would be established by law instead of at the president's discretion and was empowered to investigate charges of discrimination in all firms having more than 25 employees. These changes were retained in the full committee version (Whalen and Whalen 1985: 37).

Having angered the Republicans with the strong revision of the bill, Celler faced a much more difficult job getting it out of the full committee, where nothing went according to plan. The strategy had been to have a strong subcommittee bill that would be weakened in the full committee in order to get it through the House. Unfortunately, before any real compromise could take place, Arch Moore (R-WV) moved that the weak version of the subcommittee bill be reported favorably to the House in its present form (Whalen and Whalen 1985: 49). Celler was able to avoid a vote on the motion only because the House had been called to order and all committee work was required to end.

The committee did not meet again for several days and in the meantime a great deal of lobbying took place. Even Kennedy was busy lobbying for some kind of compromise. A compromise bill was developed that only slightly weakened the bill (Whalen and Whalen 1985: 58). When the committee met again, Celler had enough votes to defeat Moore's motion. Following the defeat, Celler moved to replace the subcommittee bill with the compromise developed in conjunction with the Justice Department. After a reading of the compromise, a motion was passed to prevent any more discussion and then a vote was taken on the compromise. Just seconds before the House was called to order, the compromise bill was accepted by the committee by a vote of 20–14 (Whalen and Whalen 1985: 64–66).

The primary differences between the subcommittee bill and the full committee recommendation for Title VII were as follows:

1. In the subcommittee bill, the Equal Employment Opportunity Commission was composed of an "Equal Employment Opportunity Board" and an "Office of the Administrator of the Equal Employment Opportunity Commission." The full committee bill did not divide the commission this way.
2. The subcommittee bill established procedures for hearings by the EEOC to be followed by judicial review in the district courts. The full committee bill provided the EEOC with investigatory powers. If after an investigation the commission had reasonable cause to believe the employer was guilty of discrimination, the commission was authorized to use conciliation and persuasion to halt the discriminatory practices. If the conciliation procedures did not stop the discriminatory practices, the bill stated that the commission "shall" bring suit against the employer in the district court.
3. In the full committee bill the courts were authorized to grant injunctive relief and to use masters for the hearing of issues of fact (*U.S. Code Congressional and Administrative News* 1965: 2475) (hereafter cited as USCCAN).

The bill accepted by the committee was recommended for passage in House Report No. 914. The House report included both the majority recommendation for passage and additional views of committee members opposed and in favor of the legislation.[6] The majority report did little to indicate the thinking that went into the bill. It began with a short legislative history indicating the movement of the bill through the Judiciary subcommittee and then in a general statement it made a sweeping appeal concerning the need to eliminate discrimination through federal action. There was no discussion relating to the need to improve the economic status of blacks or relating to the need to compensate for discrimination. Instead, the report simply laid out the provisions of the bill in a title by title analysis. Analysis is a misnomer, however, for the report was nothing more than a description of each title, section by section.

There were eight additional views included in the House report. Several of these additional comments were written by the opponents of the legislation. These discussions generally indicated the opponent's displeasure with particular aspects of the bill. Almost every addition protested the manner in which the bill was handled in committee, particularly in the subcommittee (*USCCAN* 1965: 2429, 2432, 2462). Also, several of the comments argued against specific provisions of the bill. Particular emphasis was given to the opposition's view that many of the provisions would eventually be held unconstitutional (*USCCAN* 1965: 2476–2477). Title VII was also challenged on the grounds that it was an excessive extension of the authority and power of the executive branch (*USCCAN* 1965: 2429, 2432–2433, 2459).

The first additional view included in the House report was by Robert Kastenmeier (D-WI) (*USCCAN* 1965: 2409–2412). He recommended passage of HR7152 but felt it was necessary to record the different views on the contents of the bill. His primary concern was with reporting the differences between the bill that came out of the full committee and the bill he preferred from the subcommittee. Kastenmeier preferred Title VII of the subcommittee bill, which allowed the EEOC to issue enforceable orders on a finding of discrimination. He believed that the use of the courts was slower and more cumbersome for the individual(s) seeking relief (*USCCAN* 1965: 2411).

The second additional view was submitted by George Meader (R-MI), an opponent of the bill (*USCCAN* 1965: 2412–2428). Meader plainly objected to the way the bill was handled in the subcommittee and the full committee. In addition, he argued that the bill was nothing more than extending the already prevalent "government by injunction" that threatened individual rights (*USCCAN* 1965: 2415–2419). Meader also held that the bill was an unwarranted expansion of federal power based on an overly broad interpretation of the commerce clause and the Fourteenth Amendment's equal protection clause. Meader concluded his addition with a list of amendments he proposed to offer for each title. Regarding Title VII, Meader stated that the title contained "onerous provisions for recordkeeping, inspection, and reporting" and would be an "ill-advised limitation" on the discretion of businesses and workers (*USCCAN* 1965: 2426). He went on to propose an amendment that would limit the legislation to cover only employment by the federal government or the execution of federal contracts as in Kennedy's original bill. He held that the enforcement power for nondiscrimination in federal employment could be placed in the Civil Service Commission and the enforcement in federal contracts could be achieved "by requiring them to enter into an enforceable undertaking and relying upon the body of law providing remedies for the violation of contracts . . . " (*USCCAN* 1965: 2427).

The third additional view was submitted by Carleton King (R-NY) (*USCCAN* 1965: 2428–30). King stated that there was a need for civil rights legislation by Congress but that he was dismayed at the way the bill was "steamrolled" through the subcommittee and committee. He expressed a need for careful consideration of the bill by the House and a careful consideration of all amendments presented on the floor of the House (*USCCAN* 1965: 2430). The fourth additional view by Arch Moore, Jr. (R-WV) echoed the same view (*USCCAN* 1965: 2430).

The fifth addition to the House report was a "Minority Report upon Proposed Civil Rights Act of 1963, Committee on Judiciary Substitute for HR7152," signed by E. E. Willis (D-LA), E. L. Forrester (D-GA), William Tuck (D-VA), Robert Ashmore (D-SC), John Dowdy (D-MS), and Basil Whitener (D-NC) (*USCCAN* 1965: 2431–2462). This addition began by expressing dissatisfaction with the handling of the bill in the subcommittee and committee. The report held that the committee bill was not "moderate" or a "compromise" but like the subcommittee bill was "extreme" and "vicious" (*USCCAN* 1965: 2432). The report went on to argue that the bill would seriously impair the civil rights of those who fell within the scope of the legislation. It listed several rights violated by Title VII including the right of an employer to hire whomever it chose, seniority rights, the rights of unions to choose members, and the right of schools to determine their teaching staff (*USCCAN* 1965: 2433). It went on to add that the bill would equate "racial imbalance" with discrimination, a definition that was held to be the true intent of the Kennedy administration (*USCCAN* 1965: 2436).

The next section of the minority report examined the supposed effects of the legislation on farmers, homeowners, banks and bankers, labor unions and members, individual workers, hotels, restaurants and theaters, the press, teachers and schools, and veterans benefits and social security (*USCCAN* 1965: 2437–2443). The report held that Title VII would lead to the destruction of seniority systems and result in "blacklisting" of unions that discriminated or would require the hiring of unqualified minorities to avoid such practices (*USCCAN* 1965: 2440).

The minority report went on to highlight the differences between the full committee bill and the subcommittee bill (*USCCAN* 1965: 2445–2447). The difference the report noted with regard to Title VII was that the president is given unlimited enforcement powers by section 711(b), which provided the president with the authority "to take such action as may be appropriate" to prevent the continuation of an unlawful employment practice in the performance of a federal contract. The report concluded with a lengthy discussion of the unconstitutionality of the legislation.

The sixth addition was provided by Richard Poff (R-VA) and William Cramer (R-FL) (*USCCAN* 1965: 2462–2480). This addition analyzed the bill in terms of subject matter. In the discussion of employment discrimination, it argued that the bill was unconstitutional on the grounds that it included an unreasonably broad definition of the commerce power and that it could not be justified under the Fourteenth Amendment's privileges and immunities clause since much of the action covered by the act involved individuals and not states (*USCCAN* 1965: 2475–2476).

This addition also addressed the question of what constituted "reasonable cause" for a finding of discrimination. It argued that it was possible with the wording of the committee bill for "racial disparity" to constitute discrimination. Poff and Cramer believed that this would shift the burden of proof to the employer. In addition, they argued that the use of a master to hear the evidence, as the committee bill allowed, would deny the employer the right to trial by jury (*USCCAN* 1965: 2477).

The seventh addition was provided by William Cramer (R-FL) (*USCCAN* 1965: 2480–2487). He began with a description of the administration's bill, the subcommittee bill, and the full committee bill to show that the latter was much stronger than the one originally proposed by Kennedy (*USCCAN* 1965: 2483–2485).

All but one of the first seven additional views in the House report were opposed to the bill for at least one of four reasons: (1) it was an unconstitutional use of the commerce power or violated the Fourteenth Amendment, (2) it would lead to the destruction of seniority systems, (3) it violated the property rights of employers, and (4) it would allow evidence of racial imbalance to constitute evidence of discrimination. This fourth reason, echoed later in the Senate debate, is important to the Court's employment discrimination and affirmative action decisions since the Court did accept racial imbalance as evidence of discrimination.

The final additional view included in the report was submitted by seven advocates of the bill: William McCulloch (R-OH), John Lindsey (R-NY), William Cahill (R-NJ), Garner Shriver (R-KS), Clark MacGregor (R-MN), Charles Mathias (R-MD), and James Bromwell (R-IA) (*USCCAN* 1965: 2487–2519). This comprehensive addition was intended as a supplement to the committee report and it made the affirmative case for the bill (*USCCAN* 1965: 2488). Using statistics and an examination of previous legislation and court decisions, this comment proceeded with a title by title analysis. The discussion of Title

VII echoed the sentiments expressed concerning nondiscrimination in employment in President Kennedy's message to Congress.

The comments on Title VII began with a table showing the unemployment rates of 1963 by color, age, sex, and occupational grouping (*USCCAN* 1965: 2513). The table showed that blacks suffered from an employment rate twice that of whites. It also showed that black employment was concentrated in semiskilled and unskilled jobs. Also included was a table indicating the "unbalanced occupational distribution" (*USCCAN* 1965: 2514).

The text of this additional viewpoint also stressed the need to eliminate this maldistribution:

> National prosperity will be increased through the proper training of Negroes for more skilled employment together with the removal of barriers for obtaining such employment. Through toleration of discriminatory practices, American industry is not obtaining the quality of skilled workers it needs. With ten percent of the workforce under the bonds of racial inequality, this stands to reason. . . . [T]his country is not making satisfactory use of its manpower. Consider how our shortage of engineers, scientists, doctors, plumbers, carpenters, technicians, and the myriad of other skilled occupations could be overcome in due time if we eliminate job discrimination (*USCCAN* 1965: 2515).

These passages indicated again that the advocates of Title VII believed that fair employment involved more than simple nondiscrimination in employment but also required positive action to bring blacks into all employment categories, including skilled, white-collar, and professional occupations. This was a redistributive goal and was used over and over again as a justification for Title VII. The emphasis here was that there was a need to eliminate a serious injustice—employment discrimination—which had relegated blacks to low-skilled, low-paying jobs and the solution should not only eliminate the injustice but should move toward improving the economic position of blacks. It should also be noted that the discussion lacked any reference to compensating individual blacks for the discrimination inflicted upon them as the primary justifcation for the policy.

The House report indicated that the split between the advocates and the opponents of the bill was distinct. The advocates tended to emphasize the severity of the situation of the blacks, particularly regarding their position in the work force. The opponents all emphasized the unconstitutionality of the legislation as too broad an interpretation of the commerce clause and too great an expansion of federal power. These different emphases are essentially a matter of justification. The advocates stressed the need to eliminate economic disparities between blacks and whites, whereas the opponents felt the bill was constitutionally unjustifiable.

In terms of the House report, Title VII seemed to be justified primarily in redistributive terms. The disadvantaged group, although based on race, was a socioeconomic minority and the injury to that group was more systematic than specific. The primary goal of Title VII, at least from the advocates' perspective, was to establish a policy which would lead to the elimination of socioeconomic disparity in the distribution of jobs. This can be seen by the emphasis on employment statistics showing that blacks were concentrated in low-paying, low-skilled jobs.

There is no discussion of compensating blacks for past discrimination. However, the compensatory aspects are evident in the words of the statute. That is, an individual who is discriminated against can seek relief through the EEOC and the courts and the employer must make reparation through the hiring of the individual, possibly with back pay and retroactive seniority. The exact nature of the remedy was left to the courts.

Following the Judiciary Committee's favorable report, HR7152 was sent to the House Rules Committee where it languished for the remainder of the year despite attempts to get it to the floor (Whalen and Whalen 1985: 84–85). In the meantime, President Johnson began courting civil rights leaders and publicly expressing his support of the bill, even stating that it would be his first priority in the new year (Whalen and Whalen 1985: 78–84). When 1964 came and the 88th Congress began, the Rules Committee began hearings on the bill. The hearings continued over three weeks and on January 30, 1964, the Rules Committee voted to send the bill to the House floor for debate (Whalen and Whalen 1985: 90–99).

The debate on the House floor continued in the same vein as the House report. That is, the opposition opposed the legislation on the grounds that it was unconstitutional and too broad a grant of power to the executive branch. The advocates also continued their arguments for the constitutionality of the bill on the grounds that prior laws, particularly laws regulating labor relations, trade regulations, and antitrust, and court decisions supported the provisions of the bill (Schwartz 1970: 1124). They also argued that provisions allowing the federal government to intervene on behalf of individuals being denied rights and liberties was necessary in light of the fact that many states, businesses, and individuals continued to remain recalcitrant toward desegregation and fair employment practices (Schwartz 1970: 1125).

In the House, 124 amendments were offered but only 34 were written into the bill and these were primarily technical revisions, which did not alter any of the major provisions of the bill (Whalen and Whalen 1985: 121). One significant change to Title VII made at this time was the addition of "sex" as one of the categories of illegal discrimination. This amendment was offered by a southerner who felt that the addition of gender would make the bill unacceptable. He was, to his dismay but to the joy of others, mistaken. HR7152 passed by a vote of 290 to 130.

The major provisions of the House version of HR7152 were as follows:

1. Coverage. Title VII covered all employers and labor unions with 25 or more employees, all federal, state, and commercial employment agencies, and any training apprencticeship program by employers, labor unions and joint labor-management committees.
2. Prohibited practices. Employers, etc. were prohibited from discriminating in any phase of employment or union membership on the basis of race, sex, religion, color, and national origin.
3. Enforcement. Title VII created the Equal Employment Opportunity Commission. The EEOC would investigate charges of discrimination, attempt conciliation, and if conciliation failed could then file suit in federal district court. If the Commission failed to file suit, the individual retained the right to file suit in district court with permission of one member of the commission (§706(g)).
4. Penalties. If the court found that the accused had engaged in an unlawful employment practice, the court could enjoin the accused from continuing such practice and order the accused to take affirmative action, including the reinstatement of employees with or without back pay. No order of the court could require the admission or reinstatement of an individual to a labor organization or the hiring, reinstatement, or promotion of an individual by an employer if the labor organization or employer took action for any reason other than discrimination on account of race, color, religion, or national origin (Schwartz 1970: 1442–1445).

This analysis suggests that in the House debate Title VII was justified primarily on redistibutive grounds. In other words, in the presence of equal opportunity, blacks would not be relegated to the lower end of the socioeconomic ladder and this inequality should be eliminated. The principle involved is equality of opportunity. There is also a recognition by the advocates that nondiscrimination in employment would not be enough to assure equal opportunity. On the other hand, the bill itself did not expressly consider the redistributive aspects but only calls for nondiscrimination and compensation for acts of discrimination in the form of injunctive relief and the hiring of the victim with the possibility of additional relief such as back pay.

HR7152 IN THE SENATE: AN ECONOMIC DISCUSSION OF TITLE VII

The bill that passed the House was significantly stronger than the one presented by Kennedy seven months earlier, and the leaders of the House who had worked so hard for it informed the Senate leaders that they expected the bill to remain strong if it was to become law. The Senate leaders knew, however, that getting HR7152 through the Senate was not going to be an easy task. Their first problem was avoiding the Senate Judiciary Committee, which was chaired by a southerner, James Eastland (D-MS). Yet, even if the bill was not sent to the committee, they knew they would also have to find a way to end a certain filibuster by the southerners. To end a filibuster, the Senate leaders would have to try to invoke cloture, but to do so they needed the support of Senate minority leader Everett Dirksen (R-IL). This became their strategy (Whalen and Whalen 1985: 148).

Immediately following the introduction of HR7152 to the Senate, Majority Leader Mike Mansfield (D-MT) moved to bypass the committee hearings and report and place the bill directly on the Senate calender. This motion was strongly opposed by many senators, particularly the southern senators, who argued that such an important bill should be carefully considered and not rushed through the Senate. Mansfield's motion was approved, however, and HR7152 was placed directly on the Senate calendar (Schwartz 1970: 1089).

At this point the lengthy debate/fillibuster began. The advocates of the bill were prepared. They established bipartisan teams led by Hubert Humphrey (D-MN) and Thomas Kuchel (R-CA), the majority and minority whips. Humphrey and Kuchel's roles were to present the affirmative case for the bill and much of their presentation represents, as much as anything, a committee report on HR7152. Humphrey and Kuchel also spent a great deal of time questioning the opponents of the bill and attempting to expose the fallacy of their arguments (Schwartz 1970: 1090).

Because Title VII was one of the most controversial titles in the Civil Rights Act of 1964 (along with Title II, public accommodations), it stimulated a great deal of debate. The Senate debate mirrored the House's in many respects: the opponents viewed the title as an unconstitutional intrusion of the federal government into business activities and too large a grant of power to the executive branch because the EEOC could institute suits against an employer. The advocates of Title

VII centered their arguments around the need to improve the economic position of blacks. Yet, the Senate debate, as would be expected, dealt with the issues surrounding Title VII in greater detail.

Beginning the debate on Title VII, Humphrey emphasized the problems of blacks in the economy. He cited the same statistics used in the House report showing that blacks had an unemployment rate twice that of whites. He also cited statistics indicating that blacks lacked meaningful job opportunities: ". . . [S]eventeen percent of non-white workers have white collar jobs; among white workers the figure is 47 percent. On the other hand, only four percent of whites who are employed work at unskilled jobs in non-agricultural industries, among the nonwhites the figure is 14 percent" (Schwartz 1970: 1223). Humphrey also indicated that among those citizens with professional and technical skills, the rate of blacks who are employed in positions using those skills was 10 percent less than the rate for whites (Schwartz 1970: 1224). The Senator also showed that blacks were further discriminated against with respect to earnings. According to Humphrey, a black man with a college degree earned less in his lifetime than a white with an eighth-grade education and that black college graduates had only half the lifetime earnings of white college graduates (Schwartz 1970: 1224). Yet, Humphrey held that he did not cite statistics for statistics sake but "to emphasize the plight of the Negro in the economy" (Schwartz 1970: 1225). Humphrey continued: "The crux of the problem is to open employment opportunities for Negroes in occupations which have been traditionally closed to them. This requires both an end to discrimination which now prevails and an upgrading of Negro occupational skills through education and training" (Schwartz 1970: 1225).

These remarks suggest that the advocates of Title VII felt a strong need to show that nondiscrimination in employment alone was not enough to solve the economic problems of blacks, but that any solution had to work toward a redistribution of blacks throughout the job market. This is a clear reference to a redistributive goal. Humphrey indicated, however, that these other actions included education and training, the same ideas articulated by Kennedy in his address to Congress. There is no suggestion of affirmative action types of programs.

A year earlier Humphrey had introduced in the Senate an Equal Employment Opportunities bill (S1937), which suggested more detailed requirements for the achievement of equal opportunity (Field in Sutherland 1971: 160). This bill called for a strong administrator in the Department of Labor and recognized the need for job finding and placement agencies, manpower training programs, technical analysis of employment trends, inspection personnel, and related farm labor services (Field in Sutherland 1971: 160). When introducing this bill, Humphrey noted that overt discrimination was not the only factor leading to disparities in black and white employment but that often recruitment practices and other institutional practices also operated to the disadvantage of blacks. He also noted that the traditional concept of enforcing nondiscrimination in employment by providing relief only to those individuals who brought charges against the employer should be *"broader and more comprehensive"* if equal employment opportunity was to be promoted (U.S. Congress 1963: 12532). This statement seems to suggest that Humphrey approved of affirmative action-type relief.

Humphrey's remarks on Title VII throughout the debate seem somewhat cautious in comparison to the remarks he made when introducing S1937. In the latter, he recognized the systematic nature of employment discrimination. He was aware of the ways in which recruitment and selection procedures operated to the disadvantage of blacks. Indeed, those remarks seem to suggest one of the major characteristics of affirmative action: the use of more comprehensive search procedures which work to bring more blacks into the selection pool. Yet, there is no evidence of similar remarks in the debate on Title VII. This may be a result of the role Humphrey played in that debate. When Humphrey introduced S1937, he was presenting a strong bill dealing only with employment discrimination. As the floor leader of HR7152, his task was to assure the passage of a much more comprehensive civil rights law. To suggest a need to alter the recruitment and selection procedures of employers would have played into the hands of the opponents of Title VII who continually argued that Title VII was an unconstitutional intrusion of the federal government into the business activities of employers.

In his contributions to the debate on HR7152, Senator Kuchel addressed the specific provisions of Title VII. Like Humphrey, Kuchel began with a discussion of the difficulties faced by blacks in the economy and the inefficiency of discrimination. Regarding the specific provisions, Kuchel sought to diffuse the arguments of the opponents. He stressed the use of voluntary compliance prior to an EEOC-initiated suit for relief and denied that Title VII would affect seniority systems or require racial quotas or racial preferences (Schwartz 1970: 1252). Humphrey later echoed these same sentiments with regard to the Dirksen substitute provisions for Title VII.

When the Senate debate began, Washington was already filled with hundreds of groups and activists following the progress of the bill. After the debate had been going on for a month, thousands more arrived. Catholic, Protestant, and Jewish seminarians descended on Washington in April and began 24-hour vigils at the Lincoln

Memorial, vowing not to stop until HR7152 passed the Senate; other groups organized daily rallies (Whalen and Whalen 1985: 157, 164). Outside the Capitol, the press waited anxiously for news. They were making a series of daily reports on the debate and television cameras greeted the Senators as they left each day (Whalen and Whalen 1985: 149). And each day the Senate gallery was filled with activists mentally recording the day's events. The visibility of the proceedings was like none other.

After two-and-one-half months of debate on HR7152, it seemed that the bill was going nowhere. Yet, during this time a great deal of maneuvering and compromise had taken place behind the scenes. Everett Dirksen had been working with the majority leadership and representatives of the attorney general (with some input from Celler and others in the House) on a substitute for HR7152. These activities shadowed the bargaining that went on in the House Judiciary Committee several months before. Whereas the floor debate was highly visible, the real work was taking place behind closed doors.

In late May, Mansfield agreed to go along with the substitute, and on May 26 Dirksen introduced the Dirksen-Mansfield substitute to the Senate. The substitute, which essentially made cloture possible, took away the power of the EEOC to initiate suits in the courts and gave it to the attorney general, strengthened the voluntary compliance mechanism, clarified the relationship of federal to state antidiscrimination laws, and included a section stating that racial preferences would not be required by the act (§703(j)). From that point on the Senate was no longer debating HR7152 but was debating the Dirksen-Mansfield substitute.

Following the introduction of the substitute, Senator Clark (D-PA) spoke first. He expressed his dissatisfaction with the changes but said that he reluctantly decided to support the substitute because he recognized that it was better than no bill at all (Schwartz 1970: 1327–1329). In particular, Clark did not favor the subordination of federal power to the states and localities. He felt that it made the individual's task more difficult and time-consuming and it provided an opportunity for states and cities to pass antidiscrimination laws and ordinances with no federal standards for guidance (Schwartz 1970: 1330).

Clark also felt that the substitute was defective because it removed the EEOC's power to initiate suits. He approved of the new provision that allowed the attorney general to initiate suits when it has found an employer involved in a "pattern of discrimination," but he expressed concern that this provision's enforcement would depend on the political philosophy of the administration in power at the time (Schwartz 1970: 1331). Indeed, the use of "pattern or practice" suits was an issue that would arise later in the debates over the amendments to Title VII and is still an issue today.

Clark was followed by Edmund Muskie (D-ME), whose discussion of Title VII emphasized the role of economics in civil rights:

> The foundations upon which other necessary freedoms for the Negro must be built is economic freedom. The chance to hope; the chance to dream of a fair chance at a good job; to have things so many Americans take for granted.
>
> Again the facts are shocking. Here are but a few:
>
> First. The unemployment rate among nonwhites is double the rate among whites.
>
> Second. Forty-seven percent of all white workers hold white-collar jobs; for nonwhites the figure is seventeen percent.
>
> Third. Twenty percent of all Negro women who graduate from high school can find only domestic work. For whites the figure is two percent.
>
> Fourth. Finally, the average Negro with fours years of college will earn less in his lifetime than a white man who quit school after the eighth grade (U.S. Congress 1964: 12614).

The emphasis on the economic plight of blacks by Muskie is another example showing that the advocates felt the real justification for Title VII was the need to eliminate the maldistribution of the workforce.

Muskie then engaged in an exchange with Sam Ervin (D-NC). Ervin argued that there were four times as many whites unemployed as blacks and the reasons for that unemployment were a lack of education and skills, economic conditions, and automation. Ervin then asked Muskie if blacks and whites did not suffer from the same economic effects. Muskie responded by pointing out to Ervin that blacks not only had to deal with "economic factors that may produce unemployment," but they must also face "the factor of discrimination which reduces his possibility for getting employment opportunities" (U.S. Congress 1964: 12615).

This type of exchange, which occurred throughout the Senate debate on Title VII, highlights the emphasis placed on the maldistribution of jobs between blacks and whites. In fact, at this point in the debate, all the advocates had strongly emphasized economic disparities between blacks and whites. If the justification of Title VII was based on such disparities, then it seems reasonable to conclude that the major emphasis of Title VII should be on the elimination of these disparities, which is blatantly a redistributive goal. Yet, to expressly make such a claim would surely have added to the opposition to the title. As a result, Muskie and the others strongly expressed the conviction that the bill provided only for equal opportunity, not racial balance (U.S. Congress 1964: 12617).

Because the issue of racial balance was a major point of contention for the opponents, the substitute directly addressed the issue. When Humphrey took the floor again to provide a title by title analysis of the substitute he made this statement concerning racial balance:

> A new subsection 703(j) is added to deal with the problem of racial balance among employees. The proponents of the bill have carefully stated on numerous occassions that Title VII does not require an employer to achieve any sort of racial balance in his workforce by giving preferential treatment to any individual or group. Since doubts have persisted, subsection (j) is added to state this point expressly. This subsection does not represent any change in the substance of the title. It does state clearly and accurately what we have maintained all along about the bill's intent and meaning (U.S. Congress 1964: 12721–12722).

This statement is often quoted by Supreme Court justices who oppose affirmative action.

One provision of Title VII that also suggests that the title was intended to deal with discrimination on a systematic basis was the provision allowing the attorney general to initiate "pattern and practice" suits. This provision was the result of a compromise between those who wanted the EEOC to be able to initiate suits and those who did not. The opponents of Title VII were adamantly against granting this power to the EEOC, whereas the advocates felt that this power was necessary if Title VII was to be of any value at all. The compromise eliminated the power of the EEOC to initiate suits, but granted the attorney general the authority to fight discrimination systematically. According to Humphrey: "Section 707 is a new section, authorizing suits by the attorney general . . . It provides that the attorney general may institute suit on behalf of the United States when he has reasonable cause to believe that there is a pattern or practice of intentional resistance to the full enjoyment of any of the rights secured by Title VII" (U.S. Congress 1964: 12724).

Later in the debate Humphrey was asked to explain the meaning of "pattern or practice" as used in Titles II and VII: "[A] pattern or practice would be present only when the denial of rights consists of something more than an isolated, sporadic incident, but is repeated, routine, or of a generalized nature . . . The point is that single, insignificant, isolated acts of discrimination by a single business would not justify a finding of a pattern or practice . . . " (U.S. Congress 1964: 13776).

These remarks by Humphrey are cautious as well. Whereas not expressly admitting the systematic nature of discrimination, they, too, suggest a recognition of it. By being cautious in this manner, Humphrey did not alarm the opponents to the true potential for fighting discrimination that this provision contained (though some might still argue that this potential has yet to be realized). Still, of all the provisions of Title VII, this compromise best highlights the advocates' desire to attack discrimination by means other than isolated punches at individual acts of discrimination where only the individual who sued would benefit.

Following Humphrey's analysis of the bill, the debate on the substitute version of Title VII became a battle of amendments. One of them, an amendment introduced by Sam Ervin to delete all of Title VII, provided an important and lengthy discussion of all major aspects of the title. Ervin began the discussion of his amendment by arguing that there were already a variety of statutes and a long list of court cases where blacks were granted equal rights, hence Title VII was unnecessary (U.S. Congress 1964: 13075). He went on to hold that "the purpose of the bill is to rob all Americans of some of their basic economic, personal, and property rights, for the sole benefit of one segment of the population . . ." (U.S. Congress 1964: 13075). This might be construed as opposition to the redistributive aspects of the policy.

Later Ervin yielded the floor to Sparkman (D-AL) to allow him to discuss the effects of Title VII on seniority systems. According to Sparkman, Title VII would be detrimental to seniority and merit systems and impair the free choice of employers, unions, and union members. He went on to argue that although the Dirksen substitute had added §703(h),[7] which protected seniority systems, the addition of the attorney general's power to initiate "pattern or practice" suits offset any gain. Sparkman also spoke out on the lack of any effort to deal with the question of "racial balance" and whether statistics showing a racial imbalance could be presented as evidence of discrimination. He concluded by charging that Title VII was directed primarily at the South (U.S. Congress 1964: 13076). Sparkman's remarks on seniority systems and racial balance seem to indicate that the opponents were aware of the redistributive aspects of the bill and that it was these aspects to which they were so strongly opposed.

Ervin then made this indictment of Title VII:

> The bill would give the federal government the power to go into any business or industry in the United States having as many as 25 employees and affecting interstate commerce and tell the operator of that business whom he had to hire . . . whom the

> employer had to promote . . . whom he should lay off and whom he should retain in times of fiscal adversity . . . how he should fix the rates of compensation as between employees . . . what the workload of his employees should be . . . and how many employees he should have . . . (U.S. Congress 1964: 13077–13078).

These statements by Ervin and Sparkman are essentially a summary of the opponent's arguments against Title VII. There is only one brief mention of the attorney general's power to initiate suits in Sparkman's address on the effects of Title VII on seniority systems. There he criticized the power as being unlimited. One might interpret Sparkman's criticism of that power as an expression of a desire to limit the use of suits to individual acts of discrimination. However, these comments were made in the context of a debate on deleting Title VII altogether.

Clark, the reluctant supporter of the Dirksen substitute, responded vigorously to Ervin's case against Title VII: "This title would not deprive any one of any rights . . . The bill does not make anyone higher than anyone else. It establishes no quotas. It leaves the employer free to select whomever he wishes to employ. It enables a labor union to admit anyone it wishes to take in. It tells an employment agency that it can get a job for anyone that it wishes to get a job" (U.S. Congress 1964: 13079–13080). Clark continued his defense of Title VII by stating why he felt Title VII was so important: "[T]he most important civil right for disadvantaged citizens is the right of equal job opportunity . . . . The second reason . . . is that of great economic need. Economics is at the heart of the racial situation. The Negro has been condemned to poverty because of a lack of equal job opportunities. This poverty has kept the Negro out of the mainstream of American life. This is the issue that confronts us on the economic side" (U.S. Congress 1964: 13080). Once again, the advocates emphasized the economic side of discrimination and the need to eliminate the socioeconomic disparities between blacks and whites.

Just prior to the vote on the Ervin amendment, Humphrey summarized the proponents' view of Title VII. This comment is quite conservative and seems to go against all that has been suggested above by emphasizing the securing of individual rights. According to Humphrey: "The leadership group of Senators that worked on the substitute attempted to find a way and a means on the one hand of enabling an individual to secure its own rights through the courts of law; and second, these Senators wanted to encourage State and local government action in this area. The goal was to see to it that people were employed on the basis of merit rather than on false standards such as color or race" (U.S. Congress 1964: 13082). The fact that this statement by the primary spokesman for the bill seems to contradict the discussion above by Clark is not fatal to the redistributive justifications for the bill. Humphrey himself had utilized a redistributive justification. As has also been shown above, Humphrey was consistently cautious in his statements on Title VII and would have been required to be even more so when debating an amendment to delete the title from the bill. But more importantly, the issue of individual rights is inherent in any antidiscrimination bill, whether dealing with voting, public accommodations, segregated schools, or employment practices. Civil rights are individual rights and the ultimate goal of any antidiscrimination statute would be to secure those rights. The real question is whether the means to secure those rights is based on eliminating individual acts of discrimination alone or eliminating a widespread practice. In this case, it seems that both bases came into play. The Ervin amendment to delete Title VII was soundly defeated on a vote of 33–64.

On June 10, 1964 the Senate finally invoked cloture by a vote of 71–29. At this point movement on the substitute proceeded at a rapid pace. Amendment after amendment was offered and the opponents requested quorum call after quorum call. Just as quickly the Senate voted down almost all those amendments, including an amendment to include age in Title VII, an amendment making it legal to use professionally developed ability tests, an amendment nullifying any collective bargaining agreement that required union membership in a union that discriminates, and an amendment permitting the hiring of an employee of a particular race when hiring that individual would be more "beneficial" to the normal operations of the business (U.S. Congress 1964: 13500–14000). Senator Tower (R-TX), who introduced the amendment on ability tests, did manage to get an amendment passed that permitted the use of professionally developed ability tests provided that the test, its administration, or actions based on its results were not designed, intended, or used to discriminate (U.S. Congress 1964: 13724).

On June 17, 1964 the Senate voted on the Dirksen substitute and it passed 76–18. All that was left was a third reading of the bill. However, before that occurred, many Senators used their debate time remaining after the invocation of cloture to express their support or opposition to the bill. Some of these opinions provide some insight into the Senate's view of the bill.

Senator Gruening called for "vigorous" enforcement of the act:

> More is needed to wipe away the century old inequalities and inequities than the passage of this much needed bill. There must be vigorous enforcement of its provisions.

> But more is called for than vigorous enforcement. Inequalities have come about through lack of educational opportunities. Much more in the way of educational facilities must be made available. Negroes who cannot compete in the employment market because of missed educational opportunities must have readily available such training as is necessary to permit them to catch up (U.S. Congress 1964: 14251).

Senator Fong (R-HA) began his final speech by once again citing the unemployment and wage statistics cited so often during the debate. He also lamented the loss in productivity from discrimination: "Such is the high cost of intolerence revealed by these disturbing figures. How can a legislative program undo generations of discrimination against the non-white worker? How can such a deep-rooted problem be adequately met, if at all? These questions underscore the urgent need for a beginning in the lawful redress of discriminatory practices, the necessity of ending these tragically wasteful discriminatory practices, if the country is to continue its economic growth" (U.S. Congress 1964: 14297). Even with passage of the bill assured, the advocates continued to emphasize the need to improve the economic status of blacks.

Once the Senate passed the Dirksen substitute, procedure required that the bill be sent to the House to be reconsidered. Advocates wanted to bypass the Rules Committee and a conference committee in order to prevent further debate and another possible Senate filibuster on the conference report, so the bill was referred to the House Judiciary Committee, and Celler immediately directed it to the floor (Whalen and Whalen 1985: 219). To prevent too much dissent to this procedure, only 40 minutes of debate was allowed, no amendments could be offered, and a two-thirds vote was required for passage (Whalen and Whalen 1985: 219). On July 2, 1964 the House passed the bill by a vote of 289–126. That evening Johnson signed the bill into law.

The Senate debate on Title VII confirms the conclusion that the title was justified primarily in redistributive terms. The expressed problem that the title was designed to remedy was not just employment discrimination but also the maldistribution of blacks in the work force. The goal was to open opportunities and occupations to blacks that they had been denied by white society, or, in other words, to provide that rights and opportunities were no longer distributed primarily to whites but to all persons on the basis of merit.

However, this was not the final word on employment discrimination or Title VII. The next sections examine the years leading up to the amendments to Title VII and their enactment.

INITIAL IMPLEMENTATION OF TITLE VII: 1965 – 1971

Following the passage of the Civil Rights Act of 1964, President Johnson signed EO11246, which prohibited discrimination in federal employment and by federal contractors and subcontractors. EO11246 called for federal contractors to take "affirmative action" to increase the number of blacks employed. Enforcement responsibilities were given to the Civil Service Commission (now the Office of Personnel Management (OPM)) and the Office of Federal Contract Compliance Programs (OFCCP) in the Department of Labor, respectively. With this executive order the shape of employment discrimination policy was complete for the next seven years.

Title VII and EO11246 established the following system of enforcement agencies. The EEOC was given the responsibility of enforcing nondiscrimination by private employers. The Department of Justice was given the responsibility of dealing with "pattern and practice" suits and bringing suit against private employers upon the recommendation of the EEOC. The OFCCP was given responsibility for eliminating discrimination by federal contactors and subcontractors, and the Civil Service Commission was authorized to oversee the employment activities of the federal government. There was no provision for coordination of the activities of these agencies, although it was assumed that the Department of Justice and the EEOC would coordinate their activities (U.S. Commission on Civil Rights 1971: 136).

The U.S. Commission on Civil Rights had been making yearly reports on enforcement efforts, and by the early 1970s there was mounting evidence to show that the enforcement activities of these agencies were not meeting expectations. In 1971 the commission's annual report presented statistics showing the lack of progress and detailing the various problems that had been identified in the enforcement effort.

The statistics showing the failure of the effort were numerous.[8] The conclusions reached by the commission on the basis of these numbers were summarized in the report: "Despite these provisions against employment discrimination, the problem of unequal opportunity remains severe.... [W]hile there has been some overall minority employment gains in the general private labor market, discrimination continues largely unabated 6 years after Congress ordained equal employment opportunity as organic law" (U.S. Commission on Civil Rights 1971: 18). This lack of progress suggested a need for some change in the policy.

In order to identify alternative courses of action, the commission addressed the problems faced by each of the enforcement agencies. The report noted that the Civil Service Commission was making greater efforts to fight discrimination, but that it still suffered from a lack of adequate data to determine the status of equal employment opportunity in individual agencies (U.S. Commission on Civil Rights 1971: 133). The review of the OFCCP was dismal and cited four major problem areas. First, the report concluded that the OFCCP had still failed to explain in detail the meaning of affirmative action and therefore was having difficulty enforcing the policy. Second, the report stated that the monitoring of enforcement was haphazard and the agency needed to develop procedures. Third, the agency had never used any of the sanctions (termination of the contract or debarring the company from receiving contracts) it was empowered to use to enforce the policy. Finally, the agency had failed to collect adequate ethnic and racial data to facilitate an evaluation of the enforcement effort (U.S. Commission on Civil Rights 1971: 134).

The EEOC did not fare much better than OFCCP in the report. First, the report cited two major problems that seemed to be crippling the EEOC's enforcement efforts: lack of enforcement power and "grossly inadequate" staff and budget resources (U.S. Commission on Civil Rights 1971: 135). According to the report:

> The Commission believes its [the EEOC] lack of enforcement power is the principal reason its attempts at conciliation have been frustrated. As evidence it cites the fact that conciliation has been achieved in less than half the cases in which reasonable cause has been found. [note omitted] (U.S. Commission on Civil Rights 1971: 109–110).

The report also noted:

> [that the] EEOC has been crippled in its formative years by organizational and personnel problems . . . Particularly damaging have been the inordinately rapid turnover of Chairmen, commissioners, and key supervisory personnel; long vacancies in major operational posts; an exceedingly high rate of attrition among field compliance personnel; inadequate training programs, especially for investigative and conciliation staff; insufficient coordination among the various central offices and between headquarters and the field; and failure to establish clear lines of direction for supervision of the field and for liaison with other federal agencies (U.S. Commission on Civil Rights 1971: 135).

The report concluded that these and other problems resulted in the EEOC taking a passive role in the implementation of Title VII, i.e., the agency waited for complaints to be brought to them instead of systematically dealing with discrimination (U.S. Commission on Civil Rights 1971: 135). The commission went on to cite five consequences of these organizational problems and the agency's passive role: (1) the complaint process usually took an average of two years and in half the cases where the agency found "reasonable cause" they had been unable to secure relief, (2) no pattern or practice suits had been filed, (3) complainants had not been provided adequate legal assistance to initiate pattern or practice suits, (4) the EEOC had not been cooperating with state and local antidiscrimination agencies, and (5) the EEOC had failed to hold public hearings in conjunction with the enforcement agencies such as the OFCCP and the Justice Department (U.S. Commission on Civil Rights 1971: 135–136).

With regard to the Justice Department, the report concluded that there were three major problems in enforcement efforts. The first was that the Civil Rights Division was much too small to contend with the volume of litigation that would be required to adequately deal with discrimination. Second, the Justice Department devoted all its efforts to cases involving discrimination against blacks to the detriment of other groups, particularly women. Finally, the Justice Department had also failed to coordinate its activities with the EEOC and the OFCCP (U.S. Commission on Civil Rights 1971: 136).

This commission report plainly showed that the federal government's efforts at eliminating job discrimination were inadequate and required some reformulation of the law if the effort was to succeed. Of particular concern was the ability of the EEOC to carry out its mandate without adequate enforcement power and budgetary and staff resources, changes only Congress could make. Yet, whereas the strong pressures of the Civil Rights movement that had brought about the passage of Title VII were no longer present, the evidence of the U.S. Commission on Civil Rights was strong enough to move Congress to act.

THE EQUAL EMPLOYMENT OPPORTUNITY ACT OF 1972: SYSTEMATIC DISCRIMINATION AND THE NEED FOR CHANGE

In 1971, seven years after the passage of Title VII, Congress considered several bills that, among other things, would extend enforcement power over Title VII to the EEOC. The first such type of bill had been intoduced in 1965 and was passed by the House but not the Senate (Bureau of National Affairs 1973: 156). In 1970 a bill was passed by the Senate but never debated in the House (Bureau of National Affairs 1973: vii). However, in 1972 the House and Senate reached a compromise on the 1971 bills, and the Equal Employment Opportunity Act of 1972 was passed in March (Bureau of National Affairs 1973: 107).

The 1972 amendments made significant changes in Title VII involving coverage of and exemptions to the title, enforcement power, and administrative changes in the EEOC (Bureau of National Affairs 1973: 1–4). Coverage was extended to employers and labor unions with 15 or more employees or members, state and local governments, federal employees (under the Civil Service Commission, now the Office of Personnel Management), and advertising notices of joint labor-management committees (Bureau of National Affairs 1973: 1–2). Exemptions were eliminated for educational activities of educational institutions but expanded for religious corporations and associations (Bureau of National Affairs 1973: 2). Administratively, the general counsel of the EEOC was made a presidential appointee and established the Equal Employment Opportunity Coordinating Council to coordinate the activities of the various agencies of the government with responsibility for equal employment opportunity, which included the Labor and Justice departments, the EEOC, the Civil Service Commission, and the Civil Rights Commission (Bureau of National Affairs 1973: 3–4).

The most fundamental changes in Title VII involved the enforcement power. Under the 1964 version of Title VII, the EEOC could only investigate charges of discrimination, attempt to eliminate the discriminatory practices through conciliation and negotiation, and if conciliation failed, recommend that the attorney general bring suit in federal district court. Under the amendments, the EEOC was authorized to bring suit in court unless the case involved a state or local government in which case the attorney general was authorized to bring suit (Bureau of National Affairs 1973: 2–3). If the EEOC or the attorney general was not able to process a complaint quickly enough or if the aggrieved party found any conciliation agreement unacceptable, the individual retained the right to seek relief in the courts (Bureau of National Affairs 1973: 3). The EEOC was also granted jurisdiction over "pattern or practice" suits. In addition, the EEOC or the attorney general was permitted to bring action for preliminary or temporary injunctive relief pending final resolution of the charge when it was deemed that prompt judicial action was required to carry out the purposes of Title VII (Bureau of National Affairs 1973: 3).

Unlike the Civil Rights Act of 1964 which never went to conference, the Equal Employment Opportunity Act of 1972 resulted from a compromise worked out in conference committee (Bureau of National Affairs 1973: 107). Hence, along with debate from the floor, the legislative history of the bill includes the committee reports of both houses of Congress and a conference report. In addition, following the passage of the legislation, a section by section analysis was published in the Congressional Record (Bureau of National Affairs 1973: 127).

The conference report consisted of two parts: the report presenting the compromise version of the bill and a joint explanatory statement by the bill's managers. In the explanatory statement, the conferees described the differences between the Senate and House versions of the bill and the version that was accepted. Of particular interest were the differences in the scope of relief that could be granted in the district court (Bureau of National Affairs 1973: 122). First, the Senate required a finding that the respondent engaged in an unlawful employment practice and the House required a finding of "intentional" discrimination (Bureau of National Affairs 1973: 122). The conference version required a finding of intentional discrimination. Second, the Senate version added the phrase "or any other equitable relief that the court deems appropriate" to the description of relief that could be provided. The House version did not include such language. The conference version authorized the court to enjoin the respondent from unlawful employment practice, order such affirmative action as may be appropriate, and any other equitable relief as may be appropriate.

The third difference involved the question of back pay relief. The compromise provided that back pay liability was limited to that which accrued from the date not more than two years prior to the filing of the charge (Bureau of National Affairs 1973: 122–123). Fourth, the House bill restated the prohibition of court-ordered remedies based on any adverse action except unlawful employment practices (part of §706(g)). The Senate version did not restate this prohibition, but it was retained in the conference version (Bureau of National Affairs 1973: 122–123). Finally, only the House bill prohibited class action law suits, but this was eliminated in the conference version.

Both the House Committee on Education and Labor Report and the Senate Committee on Labor and Public Welfare Report contained large sections describing the need for the legislation (Bureau of National Affairs 1973: 157–159, 228–232). The House Labor Committee Report began by holding that "the machinery created by the Civil Rights Act of 1964 [was] not adequate" to the task of the congressional goal of equal employment opportunity (Bureau of National Affairs 1973: 157). The report went on to note that statistics indicated that after six years of Title VII enforcement, there was still evidence of discrimination and the only way to reaffirm the "policy of equal opportunity in employment" and reduce discrimination was to provide the EEOC with effective enforcement powers (Bureau of National Affairs 1973: 157). Of particular concern were the data that indicated that the number of charges filed had increased over the six years but that the ability of the EEOC to achieve voluntary compliance was limited to approximately half the cases (Bureau of National Affairs 1973: 157–158).

According to the report: "The impact of the commission's inability to obtain relief from employment discrimination is reflected in an examination of the statistics showing the distribution of minorities in occupational groups. While the tables show some improvement since 1964, minority groups are not obtaining their rightful place in our society" (Bureau of National Affairs 1973: 158). The report then went on to discuss the same statistics for women, a concern largely ignored in 1964. These statements show a continuing if not growing concern with the redistributive goal of Title VII. The primary justification for changing the title is based on the perception that the redistributive goal had not yet been reached.

As in the original debates over Title VII in 1964, the primary justification for the changes in Title VII was the poor economic position of blacks, and now women, in the labor force. That is, Title VII was judged in terms of how well it had met the goal of eliminating the maldistribution of blacks and women throughout the labor force.

In its explanation of the proposed changes in the enforcement provisions of Title VII, the House report included the following remarks on discrimination:

> During the preparation and presentation of Title VII of the Civil Rights Act of 1964, employment discrimination tended to be viewed as a series of isolated and distinguishable events, due, for the most part, to the ill-will on the part of some identifiable individual or organization. It was thought that a scheme which stressed conciliation rather than compulsory processes would be more appropriate for the resolution of this essentially "human" problem. Litigation, it was thought, would be necessary only on an occasional basis in the event of determined recalcitrance. Experience, however, has shown this to be an oversimplified expectation, incorrect in its conclusions.
>
> Employment discrimination, as we know it today, is a far more complex and pervasive phenomenon. Experts familiar with the subject generally describe the problem in terms of "systems" and "effects" rather than simply intentional wrongs . . . The forms and incidences of discrimination which the commission is required to treat are increasingly complex . . . (Bureau of National Affairs 1973: 162).

This statement is the first expression by Congress of the view that discrimination is a systematic problem not limited to isolated acts of individuals. Humphrey's remarks on discrimination when he introduced S1937 provided some evidence that Congress recognized that discrimination was not solely a matter of individual acts, but this is the first time that that view was openly expressed in a debate over Title VII. This recognition of the systematic nature of discrimination further points toward Title VII being redistributive since the policy seeks to remedy a societal injustice in addition to providing relief to specific victims of injustice.

Having recognized the systematic nature of discrimination, the House report discussed "pattern or practice" discrimination:

> Pattern or practice discrimination is a pervasive and deeply imbedded form of discrimination. Specific acts or incidences of discrimination within the commission's jurisdiction are frequently symptomatic of a pattern or practice which Title VII seeks to eradicate. The Commission has the basic responsibility to achieve the objectives of Title VII. Since the Commission is being vested with cease-and-desist enforcement authority [in the form of preliminary or temporary injunctive relief], it is imperative that it be empowered also to deal with "pattern or practice" discrimination in order to deal comprehensively with systematic discrimination (Bureau of National Affairs 1973: 168).

This statement that Title VII was designed to eradicate the pattern and practice of discrimination is another example of the expression of the redistributive goal of the title. The title was not intended solely to provide relief for specific acts of discrimination but to address the entire system of injustice.

This link between systematic discrimination and the use of "pattern or practice" suits suggests somewhat of a change in the thinking of Congress. That is, having recognized the true complexity of discrimination, Congress began to recognize the true potential of the "pattern or practice" suit. If discrimination was systematic, then it should be addressed systematically. Although never actually expressed in the 1964 debates, it would seem unlikely that the advocates of Title VII did not already recognize this relationship when they traded the EEOC's power to initiate suits for "pattern or practice" suit authority. It seems likely that they did not make this link for fear that it would lessen the likelihood of getting Title VII passed.

In addition to the majority report, there was an additional minority view and several individual views of the House bill. The minority view was opposed to legislation on the grounds that granting the EEOC enforcement powers further complicated the relief process by interposing the EEOC before the courts, involving a massive expansion of jurisdiction at a time when the EEOC was just getting itself established. It also failed to provide due process protections (Bureau of National Affairs 1973: 220). Representative Edith Green (D-OR) opposed the section of the bill that transferred to the EEOC the authority granted to the Office of Federal Contract Compliance under EO11246 (Bureau of National Affairs 1973: 221–222). The other individual views opposed the bill primarily on their objection to the granting of the EEOC of any enforcement power (Bureau of National Affairs 1973: 222–224).

The Senate Committee on Labor and Public Welfare Report concerned a somewhat different version of the House bill. With some modification, this was the bill accepted by the conference committee and the Congress as a whole (Bureau of National Affairs 1973: vii). In the report, there is extensive discussion of the need for the bill. According to the report the "pervasiveness" and "tenacity" of employment discrimination required a strong enforcement role for the EEOC. The report concluded that the major problem with the 1964 Act was that the EEOC did not have "the authority to issue judicially enforceable orders to back up its findings of discrimination" (Bureau of National Affairs 1973: 228). According to the report:

> . . . unless the Department of Justice concludes that a pattern or practice of resistance to Title VII is involved, the burden of obtaining enforceable relief rests upon each individual victim of discrimination, who must go into court as a private party, with the delay and expense that entails, in order to secure the rights promised him under the law. Thus, those persons whose economic disadvantage was a prime reason for enactment of equal employment opportunity provisions find that their only recourse in the face of unyielding discrimination is one that is time consuming, burdensome, and all too often, financially prohibitive (Bureau of National Affairs 1973: 228).

These remarks hint at a conclusion expressly stated in an analysis of the amendments printed in the Congressional Record: the individual should have to seek redress from the courts only as the last resort. This suggests further recognition of a broader purpose to Title VII than simply the compensation of individual victims.

The Senate report cannabalized the House report views on discrimination. It suggested that the need for stronger EEOC enforcement power stemmed from the large number of charges filed with the EEOC and the commission's ability to obtain relief in only half the cases brought before it. The report continued:

> The impact of this inability to obtain relief from employment discrimination surfaces in another, more indictative set of facts—economic disparities which presently affect this Nation's minorities and women.
>
> In a special report released this year by the Bureau of the Census, "The Social and Economic Status of Negroes in the United States," the evidence is clear that while some progress has been made toward bettering the economic position of the Nation's black population, the avowed goal of social and economic equality is not yet anywhere near a reality. For example, the report shows that the median family income for Negroes in 1970 was $6,279, while the median income for whites during the same period was $10,236. This earnings gap shows that Negroes are still far from reaching their rightful place in society (Bureau of National Affairs 1973: 230).

Once again, the justification of Title VII and the amendments was based on economic disparities between white males and blacks and women.

The debates on the floor of each house reiterated the same views as expressed in the two committee reports. However, unlike in 1964, the 1972 debates directly addressed the role of affirmative action under Title VII and Executive Order 11246. In the Senate, Sam Ervin proposed two amendments that would have prohibited affirmative action. The first would have prohibited any department, agency, or officer of the United States (thereby including the courts) from practicing "discrimination in reverse" (U.S. Congress 1972: 1664). Arguing against this amendment, Senator Javits (R-NY) noted that the courts had already rejected the argument that all preferential treatment was inconsistent with §703(j) and that Congress should reject that argument as well (U.S. Congress 1972: 1665). Javits placed two lower court opinions that upheld affirmative action in the record, *Contractors Association of Eastern Pennsylvania v. Schultz*, 442 F.2d. 159 (CA3) (1971) and *U.S. v. Iron Workers Local No. 86*, 443 F.2d. 544 (CA9) (1971). According to Javits, Ervin's amendment would "undercut the whole concept of affirmative action" as developed by the Department of Labor under Executive Order 11246 and would deprive the courts of the opportunity to order affirmative action when necessary to correct "a history of unjust and illegal discrimination in employment" and thus would undermine efforts to correct these injustices (U.S. Congress 1972: 1665). Ervin's amendment was defeated by a substantial margin.

A month later, Ervin proposed another amendment that would have prohibited the EEOC and the OFCCP from ordering the use of preferential treatment (U.S. Congress 1972: 4917). Once again Javits called for a rejection of the amendment for essentially the same reasons given above. It was rejected by a vote of 60–30.

There is also evidence in the debates that the Senate recognized the redistributive aspects of affirmative action. In his closing statements, Cranston (D-CA) discussed the application of Title VII to the federal government via the amendments. According to Cranston, the amendments would:

> [require] that federal Agencies make a special effort to employ and promote qualified minority persons according to their relative proportions in the population of the area surrounding agency field offices. Although statistics available to me show that there has been some recent improvement, the situation is by no means satisfactory. In many instances, federal minority employment remains disgracefully low. There is a national pattern of disproportionately low employment of certain minorities and a definite pattern of exclusion of minorities, when they are employed, from the higher, better-paying Government position (U.S. Congress 1972: 4929).

Following the passage of the conference bill, a section-by-section analysis of the legislation was printed in the *Congressional Record,* which provided some commentary on the legislation's provisions (Bureau of National Affairs 1973: 127–136). Of interest in this analysis are the commentary on private actions and class action lawsuits. Regarding private action, the analysis commented: "It is hoped that the recourse to the private lawsuit will be the exception and not the rule, and that the vast majority of complaints will be handled through the offices of the EEOC or the attorney general, as appropriate. However, as the individual's right to redress are paramount under the provisions of Title VII it is necessary that all avenues be left open for quick and effective relief" (Bureau of National Affairs 1973: 131). This comment suggests that Title VII does have a compensatory purpose in the sense that individual's right to redress for discrimination is an important part of the policy. Yet, as was noted earlier, the securing of individual rights is always compensatory to some degree.

Regarding class action lawsuits, the analysis stated:

> In establishing the enforcement provisions . . . it is not intended that any of the provisions contained therein shall affect the present use of class action lawsuits under Title VII . . . The courts have been particularly cognizant of the fact that claims under Title VII involve the vindication of a major public interest, and that any action under the Act involves considerations beyond

> those of the individual claimant. As a consequence the leading cases in this area are necessarily class action complaints and that, accordingly, it is not necessary that each individual entitled to relief be named in the original charge or in the claim for relief. A provision limiting class actions was contained in the House bill and specifically rejected by the Conference Committee (Bureau of National Affairs 1973: 131).

This comment supports the argument that Title VII is both redistributive and compensatory. That is, Congress sought to retain the class action lawsuit because the nature of discrimination is such that it cannot be attacked simply by addressing isolated acts of discrimination. Indeed, even during the debates in 1964, it was noted that injunctive relief benefitted not only those individuals seeking relief, but all future applicants as well (Schwartz 1970: 1228). Yet, because relief is sought through the courts, a case will center on the claims of a particular individual.

THE REAGAN EEOC AND THE IMPLEMENTATION OF TITLE VII

By 1977 the EEOC was still faced with major management difficulties, including case backlogs, an average charge processing time of two years, and an ineffective systemic case investigation and litigation program. Under the leadership of chair Eleanor Holmes Norton, a major reorganization was made and the charge intake and processing system was improved. Emphasis was also placed on the negotiation of settlements. A systemic charge processing system was also introduced to initiate broad-based actions to produce large-scale benefits for the minorities and women who continued to face systematic discrimination (U.S. Congress 1986: 4). These changes all corresponded with the apparent desires of Congress when it passed the 1972 amendments to Title VII.

In 1982 Clarence Thomas was appointed chair of the EEOC by Ronald Reagan. Immediately he began to institute major policy changes in line with the administration's views on fighting employment discrimination (U.S. Congress 1986: 4). These changes primarily involved the enforcement policies of the agency. The new policies weakened the enforcement efforts in systematic discrimination and placed the emphasis on make-whole relief for individual victims of discrimination. (These changes are discussed in greater detail in the last chapter.)

TITLE VII AND THE SUPREME COURT

From the words of Title VII, the goal of Congress seemed to be little more than a requirement of nondiscrimination. The debates, however, indicate a much more comprehensive goal. That is, the simple elimination of discrimination would not fix the injustice that Congress continously identified as the real problem that needed fixing: the exclusion of blacks and women from the upper reaches of the socioeconomic ladder. Time and again, in 1964 and 1972, Title VII was justified on the basis of the need to eliminate economic disparities between the races. There was no other clearly expressed justification for the title.

As noted at the beginning of this chapter, the responsibility for interpreting Title VII falls to the Supreme Court. There were two interpretive problems for the Court. First, it needed to provide a definition of discrimination. Second, with regard to affirmative action, the Court has had to deal with this dilemma: should it interpret Title VII according to the plain words of the statute, which provides no more than a nondiscrimination principle, or should it interpret the title according to the intent of Congress, which provides both compensatory and distributive principles as justifications for the statute. The Court's response to the first problem is discussed in the next chapter.

NOTES

1. See *Contractors Association of Eastern Pennsylvania v. Schultz*, 442 F.2d. 159 (CA3), in which the court of appeals held that EO11246 was constitutional. The Supreme Court denied certiorari.
2. The Equal Protection Clause of the Fourteenth Amendment states that "No state may deny any person . . . the equal protection of the laws." The Fifth Amendment Due Process Clause has been held to include an equal protection component that is applicable to Congress. Title VII of the Civil Rights Act of 1964, as amended, prohibits discrimination in employment by private and public employers.
3. For a complete legislative history of the Civil Rights Act of 1964, see Whalen and Whalen, 1985.
4. According to Justice Stone:

   There may be a narrower scope for operation of the presumption of constitutionality when legislation appears on its face to be within a specific prohibition of the Constitution, such as those of the first ten amendments, which are deemed equally specific when held to be embraced within the Fourteenth . . .

   It is unnecessary to consider now whether legislation which restricts those political processes which can ordinarily be expected to bring about repeal of undesirable legislation, is to be subjected to more exacting judicial scrutiny under the general prohibitions of the Fourteenth Amendment than are most other types of legislation . . .

Nor need we enquire whether similar considerations enter into the review of statutes directed at particular religious or national or racial minorities . . . whether prejudice against discrete and insular minorities may be a special condition, which tends seriously to curtail the operation of those political processes ordinarily to be relied upon to protect minorities, and which may call for correspondingly more searching judicial inquiry (304 U.S. 144 1938).

5. Penalties involve the violator, in this the employer, and remedies involve the victims of discrimination.
6. If this was an attempt to discover the intent of Congress, this report would be of little value since the provisions of the bill were radically altered in the Senate. However, an examination of the report is essential for developing an understanding of the principles involved in and the justification for the statute.
7. Section 703(h) was added to satisfy the strongest opponents of Title VII. It protects the operation of bona fide seniority systems, i.e., those not intended to discriminate, though the effects of its operation might be perceived as discrimination.
8. The report examined the efforts to fight employment discrimination in three areas: the federal government (CSC/OPM), federal contract compliance (OFCCP), and private employment (EEOC and Justice Department). With regard to federal employment, the commission found that from 1962 to 1967, black employment increased only 1% and Hispanic employment increased only .4% and most blacks and Hispanics were still concentrated in low-skilled, low-paying grades (U.S Commission on Civil Rights 1971:22). The statistics on contract compliance were only from specific examples. The worst example was that of the Bay Area Rapid Transit system, which expected $80 million in federal funds and employment of 8,000 people, but as of 1967 there were no blacks at all employed in the construction of the system (U.S. Commission on Civil Rights 1971: 43). The report on private employment emphasized the backlog of cases in the EEOC and the small number of "pattern or practice" suits brought by the Justice Department, but it noted that whereas there was some improvement in minority employment, most minorities remained in low-skilled, low-paying jobs (U. S. Commission on Civil Rights, 1971: 94).

3

Early Title VII Employment Discrimination Case Law

The legislative history of Title VII shows that Congress was concerned with both distributive and compensatory principles when it enacted the policy. This chapter analyzes the role of these principles in the Supreme Court's early employment discrimination cases. These cases outline the statutory and constitutional frameworks used by the Court in its Title VII cases. (The affirmative action cases are examined in the next chapter.) This analysis shows that both compensatory and distributive principles were present in the development of Title VII case law.

Affirmative action has been challenged on both constitutional and statutory grounds. The constitutional challenges are based on the Equal Protection Clause of the Fourteenth Amendment, which states that "No State shall . . . deny to any person within its jurisdiction the equal protection of the laws." The Equal Protection Clause applies to state action that includes action taken by local governments and other public employers or agencies. Because the Court has also held that the Due Process Clause of the Fifth Amendment contains norms of equal protection that are indistinguishable from those of the Fourteenth Amendment (Tribe 1988: 1437, see *Bolling v. Sharpe,* 347 U.S. 497 (1954)), actions of the federal government are also subject to equal protection challenges.

Equal protection can be violated in two ways: the government can establish classifications that distinguish among people who should be considered similarly situated or the government can fail to classify individuals who should be considered differently situated (Tribe 1988: 1438). Before 1938 the Court analyzed all classifications in terms of a rational basis test. This test required only that the classification be rationally related to a legitimate governmental purpose. Few classifications were found to violate equal protection under this test, for the Court generally deferred to the government's legislative purpose as legitimate (Goldman 1987: 50–51).

Since 1938, when analyzing government classifications in terms of equal protection, the Court has established different levels of review. The critical legal language was the footnote written by Justice Harlan

Fiske Stone in the case of *United States v. Caroline Products Co.,* 304 U.S. 144 (1938). The footnote distinguished cases burdening fundamental rights or walling off discrete and insular minorities as worthy of stricter scrutiny or closer analysis than ordinary equal protection cases. Fundamental rights include, inter alia, those related to the political process, the right to travel, Fifth Amendment rights, and, according to some liberal scholars, the right to privacy (Tribe 1988: 1454–1465). In the case of *Korematsu v. United States,* 323 U.S. 214 (1944), the Court held that racial classifications are inherently suspect and should be subject to strict scrutiny. Strict scrutiny has come to require that a classification serve a compelling governmental interest or purpose and that the means chosen to serve that interest or purpose be narrowly tailored (see *Shapiro v. Thompson,* 294 U.S. 618 (1969) and *Fullilove v. Klutznick,* 448 U.S. 448 (1980)). Although the Court upheld the racial classification in *Korematsu,* which permitted the deportation of Japanese-Americans from the West Coast during World War II, very few racial classifications survive strict scrutiny (Tribe 1988: 1467). Other suspect classifications are those based on alienage or legitimacy (Tribe 1988: 1544–1561).

There is also an intermediate level of equal protection analysis that has been utilized recently for classifications based on gender and age. This intermediate level of review is not as developed as strict scrutiny or the rational basis test and the courts have utilized at least five standards. Tribe identifies these as (1) assessing importance, (2) demanding close fit, (3) requiring current articulation, (4) limiting afterthought, and (5) permitting rebuttal (1978: 1082). The first and second tests have been utilized by a minority of the Court to examine benign racial classifications in affirmative action decisions. The first test requires that the objectives served by the classification are "important" though not compelling. The second test requires that the means chosen to effectuate a governmental purpose must be "substantially related" to the achievement of the articulated objectives (Tribe 1978: 1082–1083).

Although affirmative action goals and quotas benefiting blacks are a racial classification, they are considered a benign racial classification since they are intended to benefit blacks rather than to disadvantage them. This has been troubling for the courts in equal protection cases because strict scrutiny, which is fatal to most racial classifications, does not distinguish between benign and invidious classifications. The Court has been and is still divided over whether benign classifications based on an affirmative action plan should be subject to the strict scrutiny/compelling interest test or to an intermediate test. The equal protection challenges to affirmative action considered below center on this debate. None of the decisions has a clear majority definitively applying either test. However, affirmative action has been upheld under the strict scrutiny test on the grounds that remedying past discrimination is a compelling governmental interest. When the Court has found that the purpose of affirmative action is to remedy past discrimination, the main question has been whether the goals or quotas are narrowly tailored to serve that purpose. There is also some debate on whether there must be a judicial, legislative, or administrative finding of discrimination to justify affirmative action as a remedy for past discrimination. In addition, the Court has addressed but not completely resolved the question of whether there are other compelling interests that might justify affirmative action.

Whereas the constitutional challenges to affirmative action establish the broad parameters for the justification of the policy, the statutory challenges under Title VII of the Civil Rights Act of 1964, as amended, establish even stricter limits on the policy. The Equal Protection Clause is concerned only with the acceptability of racial classifications; it does not prohibit such classifications outright. Indeed, it *permits* such classifications under certain circumstances. Title VII, however, *prohibits* discriminatory classifications or actions in employment.

Title VII is not a blanket prohibition of discrimination in employment. It applies to specific parties, on specific bases, in specific areas of employment, and it contains exceptions. Title VII applies to private employers of at least 15 persons, public employers, employment agencies, and labor organizations. Under §703 of Title VII, it is an unlawful employment practice for these parties:

> to fail or refuse to hire, to discharge or otherwise discriminate against an individual with respect to his compensation, terms, conditions, or privileges of employment . . . to limit, segregate, or classify his employees or applicants for employment in any way which would deprive or tend to deprive any individual of employment opportunities or otherwise adversely affect his status as an employee . . . on the basis of race, color, religion, sex, or national origin . . . [and] to discriminate against any individual because of his race, color, religion, sex, or national origin in admission to, or employment in, any program established to provide apprenticeship or other training.

Section 703 also prohibits employment agencies from refusing or failing to refer individuals on the basis of race, color, religion, sex, and national origin. Labor organizations are also prohibited under this section from excluding or expelling from its membership an individual on the basis of race, color, religion, sex, or national origin.

Section 703 also contains exemptions. It is not unlawful for an employer, employment agency, or labor organization to hire, classify, etc. on the basis of religion, sex, or national origin when religion, sex, or national origin is a bona fide occupational qualification (§703(e)). Section 703(h) provides that it is not unlawful for an employer "to apply different standards of compensation, or different terms, conditions, or privileges of employment pursuant to a bona fide seniority or merit system . . . ."

In order to satisfy the opponents of Title VII who argued that the Title would require an employer to achieve a particular racial balance in its work force, §703(j) was added in the Senate in 1964. Section 703(j) reads as follows:

> Nothing contained in this title shall be interpreted to *require* any employer, employment agency, labor organization, or joint labor-management committee subject to this title to grant preferential treatment to any individual or to any group . . . on account of an imbalance which may exist with respect to the total number or percentage of persons of any race, color, religion, sex, or national origin employed . . . in comparison with the total number of persons of such race, color, religion, sex, or national origin in any community, State, section, or other area, or in the available work force in any community, State, section, or other area [emphasis supplied].

The definition of discrimination is not found in Title VII; that task was left to the courts. Schlei and Grossman (1983:2) identify three types of discrimination recognized by the courts as actionable under Title VII: disparate treatment, adverse impact, and the present effects of past discrimination. Disparate treatment exists when an employer "treats some people less favorably than others because of their race, color, religion, sex, or national origin" (Schlei and Grossman 1983: 13, citing *Teamsters v. United States*, 431 U.S. 324, 335–336 n.15 (1977)). Adverse impact is discrimination due to employment practices such as testing, interviewing, and educational requirements, which disproportionately eliminate minorities from consideration in hiring, promotion, transfer, and eligibility for training programs (Schlei and Grossman 1983: Part 3). A third type, the present effects of past discrimination, has been recognized by the Court but has been limited in later decisions. The present effects of past discrimination is discrimination that results from the application of seniority systems and other actions. That is, the employment practices or seniority systems may be neutral on their face, but their application perpetuates the exclusion of blacks and other minorities. The operation of seniority systems is the most obvious example of this type of discrimination; last-hired, first-fired layoff rules can seriously erode gains made by blacks and other minorities. However, the Court has held that bona fide seniority systems do not violate Title VII even if they perpetuate the past effects of discrimination.

Whereas the courts have been responsible for defining discrimination, Title VII does provide a means for and specifies the available relief in §706. An individual or class of individuals may file a complaint with the Equal Employment Opportunity Commission (EEOC). The EEOC then investigates and determines if cause exists for action. If it is determined that cause exists, the EEOC first will attempt to eliminate the unlawful employment practice informally through conference, conciliation, or persuasion. If informal methods fail, the EEOC can bring suit on behalf of the individual or class unless the employer is a government, governmental agency, or political subdivision, in which case the EEOC will refer the case to the Attorney General (Schlei and Grossman 1983:1541–1542). Section 707 grants the Attorney General and the EEOC the authority to bring civil action in a district court against any person or group of persons engaged in a pattern or practice of discrimination.

When an individual, the Attorney General, or the EEOC brings suit under Title VII, the case begins in a federal district court, the trial court of the federal system. The case can be brought either as an individual challenge to an employment practice or a class-action lawsuit, where an individual sues for herself and all others similarly situated. The process begins with the filing of a complaint by the plaintiff and the issuance of a summons to the defendant (Ball 1987: 244). The complaint is presented to the court in the pleadings. The pleadings consist of arguments by the plaintiff regarding the nature of the court's jurisdiction to hear the case, the type of relief sought by the plaintiff, and the defendant's response to the complaint (Ball 1987: 244).[1]

Before a case proceeds to trial, there is a period of discovery where both parties engage in a review of the facts and an examination of witnesses to determine the nature of the dispute (Ball 1987: 244–245). There is then a pretrial conference between the judge and attorneys in an effort to determine if the dispute can be settled prior to trial. It is also possible at this point for pretrial motions by either side. Sometimes the litigants will ask the judge for a summary judgment on the basis of the facts revealed during discovery. If summary judgment is granted, there is no trial and the court enters its order in the case. Either party may then appeal. If the judge does not grant summary judgment the case goes to trial (possibly with a jury), and a verdict is reached.

Section 706(g) specifies the relief a court may order:

> ... the court may enjoin the respondent from engaging in such unlawful employment practice, and order such affirmative action as may be appropriate, which may include, but is not limited to, reinstatement or hiring of employees, with or without backpay ..., or any other equitable relief as the court deems appropriate ... No court shall require the admission or reinstatement of any individual as a member of a union, or the hiring, reinstatement, or promotion of an individual as an employee, or the payment to him of any back pay, if such individual was refused admission, suspended, or expelled, or was refused employment or advancement or was suspended or discharged for any reason other than discrimination on account of race, color, religion, sex or national origin .... .

The phrase "any other equitable relief as the court deems appropriate" was added to §706(g) in 1972 and grants the courts broader relief authority.

After the verdict has been reached and the remedy specified (when the verdict is in favor of the plaintiff), the parties are permitted to make Motions After Verdict including motions necessary to start the appeals process (Ball 1987: 245). If the case is appealed, it goes to the appropriate court of appeals. Here the parties submit briefs to the court specifying the particular challenges to the district court's decision and the arguments for how the case should be decided. The court of appeals judges (who sit on three-judge panels) then hear oral arguments from both sides. After conference, the judges report their decision (Ball 1987: 250). If there are further appeals, the next possible step is the Supreme Court.

To reach the Supreme Court, one of the parties must file a petition for a writ of certiorari.[2] The Court has complete discretion over the issuance of such a writ. If the case is accepted, the Court grants certiorari and jurisdiction is noted (Ball 1987: 269). Within 45 days from the time the writ is issued, the parties to the case submit written briefs. This is followed by oral arguments. The Court then discusses the case in conference and votes. The Justices then write their opinions and the judgment is announced (Ball 1987: 269).

The affirmative action cases examined below involve all three types of discrimination: disparate treatment, present effects of past discrimination, and adverse impact. However, the cases do not all involve court-ordered relief as provided under Title VII. Several of the cases involve voluntary affirmative action, i.e., the employer developed an affirmative action program on its own initiative in an effort to remedy its own perceived past discrimination. The statutory analysis for these two types of affirmative action, voluntary and court-ordered, is different. When examining court-ordered affirmative action, the question is whether §706(g) requires affirmative action as a remedy. In the cases involving voluntarily adopted plans, the question is whether the plan is discriminatory, analyzed in terms of whether the employer had engaged in discrimination that justifies the use of affirmative action as a remedy, and whether §703(j)'s ban on preferential treatment permits an employer to utilize affirmative action to remedy its perceived discrimination. A third type of affirmative action is that adopted in conciliation agreements and consent decrees. The Court has been inconsistent in its analysis of settlements and consent decrees. In some cases it has considered whether the settlement or decree could be ordered by a court after a finding of discrimination and in other cases the Court has analyzed the settlement or decree in terms of what an employer can do voluntarily.

Affirmative action is only one part of employment discrimination law developed under Title VII. Much of the early case law centered on the definition of discrimination and the appropriate remedies available under §706(g). Remedies first took the form of relief to the identified victims of discrimination, but in the 1970s almost every circuit court had approved of race-conscious remedies. Thus the Supreme Court first heard cases involving relief to the victims of discrimination and later heard the affirmative action decisions.

EARLY CASES: DEFINING DISCRIMINATION AND THE SCOPE OF MAKE-WHOLE RELIEF

Defining Discrimination

One of the first tasks of the Court was to define discrimination under Title VII. Although Title VII clearly forbade disparate treatment, the Court needed to decide whether Title VII covered other categories of discrimination. It decided that Title VII included two further forms of discrimination, adverse impact and the perpetuation in the present of the effects of past discrimination.

The Court established adverse impact as a type of discrimination covered by Title VII in the case of *Griggs v. Duke Power Co.*, 401 U.S. 424 (1971). The category of the present effects of past discrimination was relied on by the lower courts for almost 10 years as a type of discrimination forbidden by Title VII, but when the Court addressed the issue in *Teamsters v. United States*, 431 U.S. 324 (1977), it limited this doctrine with respect to bona fide seniority systems.

Griggs v. Duke Power involved the requirement of a high school diploma or passing scores on a standardized intelligence test as a qualification for a job. The question before the Court was whether this was prohibited by Title VII when it was not significantly related to job performance, as it disqualified blacks at a higher rate then whites and the jobs had previously been reserved for whites (401 U.S. at 425–426). The district court found the company had ceased its discriminatory conduct and held that Title VII did not cover the impact of prior inequities (401 U.S. at 426–427). The court of appeals felt that the present effects of past discrimination were covered by Title VII and could be remedied, but it considered the question of intent as controlling and found no violation since there had been no showing that the requirement involved a discriminatory purpose (401 U.S. at 428–429).

Chief Justice Burger, writing for the Court, noted the congressional objective behind Title VII:

> The objective of Congress in the enactment of Title VII is plain from the language of the statute. It was to achieve equality of employment opportunities and remove barriers that have operated in the past to favor an identifiable group of white employees over other employees. Under the Act, practices, procedures, or tests neutral on their face, and even neutral in terms of intent, cannot be maintained if they operate to "freeze" the status quo of prior discriminatory employment practices (401 U.S. at 429–430).

This statement summarized the position by the Court, which was that the employment practices that operated to exclude blacks were prohibited by Title VII unless that practice or requirement could be shown to be related to job performance (401 U.S. at 432). In addition, the Court held that the absence of discriminatory intent did not protect employment practices that operated to exclude blacks (401 U.S. at 432).

Distributive values are implicit in the adverse impact theory of discrimination. Adverse impact is identified by racial imbalances in employment categories, i.e., the absence of minorities in relation to their percentages in the labor market. Therefore, it is clearly concerned with the distribution of workers through the work force. This concern with distribution when identifying discrimination is followed by a concern with redistribution when considering remedies for that discrimination. Affirmative action is a natural outgrowth of adverse impact theory since adverse impact is based on racial imbalances and affirmative action is a means of remedying those imbalances.

A broad reading of *Griggs* might also suggest that Title VII prohibited employment practices that perpetuated in the present the effects of past discrimination. Indeed, the lower courts had accepted this reading of the title beginning with *Quarles v. Phillip Morris, Inc.*, 279 F.Supp. 505 (1968) (Schlei and Grossman 1983: 2). However, the Court severely limited this doctrine in *Teamsters v. United States.*

International Brotherhood of Teamsters v. United States, 431 U.S. 325 (1977), involved a Title VII action against a trucking company (T.I.M.E.-D.C., Inc.) and the Teamsters union. The government argued that the company had discriminated in employment by refusing to hire blacks and Hispanics to higher paying line driver positions. It also argued that the seniority system that was part of the collective bargaining agreement between the company and the union violated Title VII because it perpetuated the effects of past and present discrimination (431 U.S. at 324). The government sought injunctive and "make-whole" relief.

The district court found the company and union in violation of Title VII in both instances and enjoined the company and union from further violations (431 U.S. at 324). The district court also granted individual relief by dividing the class into three subclasses and applying a different formula to each for the filling of line driver positions and the establishment of seniority. One class of those who were "severely injured" were granted retroactive seniority to the effective date of Title VII (431 U.S. at 325). The court of appeals eliminated the three subclasses and held that each driver could apply for line driver jobs on the basis of their company seniority, limited by a "qualification" formula (431 U.S. at 325).

With respect to the employment discrimination, the Court held that the use of statistical proof was an appropriate, though not an irrefutable, basis for a finding of discrimination (431 U.S. at 340). The Court held that the Government had made a prima facie case of employment discrimination on the basis of both statistics and witnesses and upheld the lower courts on this issue (431 U.S. at 342–343).

With respect to the seniority system, the Court stated that if the employer had violated Title VII in terms of hiring, promotion, and transfer, then those injured could receive relief in the form of retroactive seniority following *Franks v. Bowman Transportation Co.*, (431 U.S. at 347–349). However, the Court held that §706(h) of Title VII immunized a bona fide seniority system even if it operated to perpetuate the effects of past discrimination (431 U.S. at 350–356). In this case, the Court held that the seniority system was bona fide because it applied equally to all groups (it discouraged all individuals, black, white, or Hispanic, from transferring, i.e., there was no disparate treatment), the seniority system "did not have its genesis in racial discrimination, and that it was negotiated and had been maintained without an illegal purpose" (431 U.S. at 355–356).

Justices Marshall and Brennan dissented from this particular holding of the Court and argued that §703(h)'s protection of bona fide seniority systems made §703(j)'s prohibition against preferential treatment inapplicable. That is, Justice Marshall argued the different privileges of employment in the petitioner's seniority system were the result of an intention to discriminate and that in the absence of this discrimination the blacks and Hispanics would not be disadvantaged by the seniority system (431 U.S. at 381–382).

Justice Marshall continued:

> I [cannot] believe that the Congress that enacted Title VII would have agreed to postpone for one generation the achievement of economic equality. The backers of the Title viewed economic equality both as a practical necessity and a moral imperative. [note omitted] ... They sought ... "to eliminate those discriminatory practices and devices which have fostered racially stratified job environments to the disadvantage of minority citizens," *McDonnell Douglas Corp. v. Green*, 411 U.S. 792, 800 ... ; and "to make persons whole for injuries suffered on account of unlawful discrimination," [*Albemarle*]. In short, Congress wanted to enable black workers to assume their rightful place in society (431 U.S. at 387–388).

Justice Marshall also argued that when Congress had enacted the 1972 amendments to Title VII, it noted and approved of the lower court decisions invalidating seniority systems that perpetuated discrimination. Whereas Congress took action with respect to court opinions with which it was not satisfied, it did not attempt to overrule seniority cases and actually endorsed the "perpetuation principle" in the Committee Reports (431 U.S. at 391).

Teamsters did not entirely reject a theory of discrimination based on the present effects of past discrimination. Instead, it limited that definition only with regard to seniority systems. Just as the definition of discrimination as adverse impact affects the types of remedies available, this limitation also affects the development of remedies with respect to seniority systems. This is not only considered in *Teamsters*, it is also essential to the affirmative action cases.

Developing Remedies

As noted above, *Teamsters* involved the next task of the Court in the development of Title VII case law: establishing the scope of make-whole relief under Title VII. Make-whole relief is tangible relief such as an award of backpay, retroactive seniority, or a position or promotion to an individual who has shown that the employer has discriminated against him or her. Make-whole relief is intended to place the victim of discrimination in the economic and/or hierarchical position she would have been in absent the employer's discrimination. It is, of course, based on the principle of compensation for injury.

The make-whole relief cases were the first type of Title VII case heard by the Court and they represent a distinct period in the development of affirmative action case law. When these decisions were brought down, the lower courts had already upheld race-conscious affirmative action, but the Court had not yet ruled on any of these cases.[3] The only questions raised in these cases were the type of compensation available under Title VII and who should receive it. Yet, as shown below, these decisions included holdings that are essential to the shift away from compensation taken by the Court in its later affirmative action decisions. The make-whole cases examined are *Albemarle Paper Company v. Moody*, 422 U.S. 405 (1974), *Franks v. Bowman Transportation Company, Inc.*, 424 U.S. 747 (1976), and *Teamsters.*

Albemarle Paper Company v. Moody, 422 U.S. 405 (1975), was a class-action Title VII suit seeking injunctive relief and backpay relief against Title VII violations in "any policy, practice, custom, or usage" at the paper plant (422 U.S. at 405). The district court found that a collectively bargained reorganization "locked" black employees into lower paying job classifications and ordered Albemarle to implement a system of plant-wide seniority. It refused, however, to order backpay on the grounds that the violation of Title VII had not been in "bad faith" and backpay was not requested until five years after the complaint was filed (422 U.S. at 409–410). The district court also refused to enjoin Albemarle's testing program, which had been shown to have an adverse impact on blacks and was not related to job performance, on the grounds that it had been professionally validated (422 U.S. at 410–411).

The Supreme Court rejected the district court's argument that the testing program had been adequately validated and remanded that particular issue to the lower court for reconsideration (422 U.S. at 435–436). The Court also reversed the denial of backpay on the "lack of bad faith" theory of the district court. The Court held that the district court's decision must be measured against the purposes of Title VII as articulated in *Griggs v. Duke Power Company* (422 U.S. at 417). *Griggs* had held that the purposes of Title VII were "to achieve equality of employment opportunities and remove barriers that ha[d] operated in the past to favor an identifiable group of white employees over other employees" (*Griggs*, 401 U.S. at 429–430 (1971)) and "to make persons whole for injuries suffered on account of unlawful employment discrimination" (422 U.S. at 418).

In *Albemarle,* the Court held that backpay had an "obvious connection" with the purpose of equality of employment opportunity and the removal of barriers (422 U.S. at 417). The Court stated: "If employers faced only the prospect of an injunctive order, they would have little incentive to shun practices of dubious legality. It is the reasonably certain prospect of a backpay award that 'provide[s] the spur or catalyst which causes employers and unions to self-examine and to self-evaluate their employment practices and to endeavor to eliminate, so far as possible, the last vestiges of an unfortunate and ignominious page in this country's history' [cite omitted](422 U.S. at 417–418).

The Court then cited legislative history in support of the "make-whole" purpose of Title VII (422 U.S. at 419–422). According to the Court: "Title VII deals with legal injuries of an economic character occasioned by racial or other anti-minority discrimination. The terms 'complete justice' and 'necessary relief' have acquired a clear meaning in such circumstances. Where racial discrimination is concerned, 'the [district] court has not merely the power but the duty to render a decree which will so far as possible eliminate the discriminatory effects of the past as well as bar like discrimination in the future'" *Louisiana v. U.S.,* 380 U.S. 145, 154 (1965) (422 U.S. at 418).

The Court held that against these standards the denial of backpay on the grounds that the employer had not acted in bad faith was unacceptable. Such a remedy would be "punishment for moral turpitude, rather than a compensation for workers' injuries," which would essentially void the make-whole purpose of Title VII (422 U.S. at 422). In addition, the Court stated: " . . . Title VII is not concerned with the employer's "good intent or absence of discriminatory intent" for 'Congress directed the thrust of the Act to the *consequences* of employment practices, not simply the motivation.'" *Griggs v. Duke Power Co.,* 401 U.S. at 432 (422 U.S. at 422–423). With regard to the fact that the district court denied backpay because of the delay in requesting it, the Court remanded to the district court for further consideration.

Another aspect of make-whole relief considered by the court was retroactive seniority. *Franks v. Bowman Transportation Company* was a class-action suit brought by blacks who had been denied employment as over-the-road drivers. Bowman was found in violation of Title VII, but the district court denied retroactive seniority relief to the plaintiffs. The court of appeals denied retroactive seniority to those blacks who had never been hired by Bowman but granted seniority relief for those who were employed by Bowman but who had been denied positions as over-the-road drivers (424 U.S. at 751).

The first question the Court addressed was whether §703(h) limited the type of relief a court could order under §706(g). The Court examined the legislative history of §703(h) and concluded that that section was essentially a definition of what constitutes discrimination when a seniority system is challenged as perpetuating the effects of past discrimination (424 U.S. at 761). The Supreme Court held that §703(h) was not intended to limit or modify the type of relief available after a finding of discrimination, whether in hiring or promotion (424 U.S. at 761–762).

The Court then addressed the question of whether seniority relief was appropriate under the remedial provisions of Title VII. It held that the legislative history of Title VII indicated that §706(g) gave the courts "wide discretion in exercising their equitable powers to fashion the most complete relief possible" (424 U.S. at 764) and that because seniority can have significant effects on the economic security of individuals, particularly in this case where it affected layoffs, recall, potential earnings, vacations and pensions, to deny seniority relief would fall short of making the victims whole (424 U.S. at 766–767).

The Court refused, however, to hold that an award of seniority was appropriate under all circumstances (424 U.S. at 770). It held that seniority relief "must be reviewed in terms of its effect on the attainment of the Act's objectives under the circumstances presented . . . " (424 U.S. at 771). The Court held that the court of appeals had erred in denying relief because the unnamed class members had not filed administrative charges with the EEOC. The Court also summarily rejected the district court's denial of seniority relief because such claims "presuppose a vacancy, qualification, and performance by every member" (424 U.S. at 771–772).

The Court noted that this second reason for the denial of seniority was based on a concern that some of the class members were not actual victims of discrimination (424 U.S. at 772). They held that nonvictim status would be material when individual class members sought positions and that at that time Bowman would be required to demonstrate that individuals who reapplied were not the victims of discrimination. The use of seniority relief was appropriate because there had already been a finding of discrimination (424 U.S. at 772). The matter of who was entitled to seniority was simply a question to be decided by the district court.

The Court also rejected the claim that relief could be denied to identifiable victims simply because "such relief diminishes the expectations of other, arguably innocent employees" since to do so would "frustrate the central 'make-whole' objective of Title VII" (424 U.S. at

774). The Court stated: "We are of the view . . . that the result we reach today—which, standing alone, [note omitted] establishes that a sharing of the burden of the past discrimination is presumptively necessary—is entirely consistent with any fair characterization of equity jurisdiction . . . " (424 U.S. at 777). This sharing of the burden issue is also raised in the affirmative action cases. When relief is awarded to identified victims, the sharing of the burden is not a serious problem. When the relief is awarded in the form of affirmative action, the sharing of the burden becomes more significant. Generally, the Court has allowed a burden upon whites when the remedy is directed at a hiring violation and the burden is spread among a broad group of individuals or society as a whole, but the Court has limited the burden that whites can be made to bear when it involves the seniority rights of particular individuals.

Franks is not a seniority case but a disparate treatment case. That is, the question before the Court was not whether the seniority system was bona fide but whether a court could order seniority relief to the victims of discrimination upon a finding of disparate treatment in hiring and promotion. In *Albemarle,* backpay relief was not in doubt as a remedial device in disparate treatment cases since the title specifically mentioned backpay in §706(g). However, seniority relief was not mentioned in §706(g). Additionally, §706(h) protected bona fide seniority systems. *Franks* held that such seniority relief was appropriate in a disparate treatment case, though only for the actual victims of discrimination. Thus the Court included seniority relief in the category of "other appropriate relief" available under §706(g) in disparate treatment cases despite §703(h)'s protection of seniority systems. When necessary to restore identified victims to their hierarchical status, retroactive seniority was an appropriate remedy.

Teamsters also involved the question of individual relief after a finding of a pattern or practice of discrimination. The Court held in *Teamsters* that every postact minority applicant was presumptively entitled to relief (431 U.S. at 362) and that incumbent employees who failed to apply were not inexorably barred from an award of retroactive seniority. Nonapplicant employees must show that they should be treated as applicants to obtain relief (431 U.S. at 363–364). This latter holding was based on two arguments: (1) the courts could fashion the most complete relief possible and (2) the assertion that a person who had not actually applied could never be rewarded relief cannot have force when a consistently enforced discriminatory policy deters job applications by those aware of the discrimination (431 U.S. at 364–365). However, nonapplicants were required to show that they would have applied but for the discriminatory practice (431 U.S. at 367–

368).[4] Thus *Teamsters* limited seniority relief to the identified victims of discrimination, but expanded the definition of a victim.

These cases establish the foundation of Title VII case law before the Court's affirmative action decisions. Violations of Title VII could be based on disparate treatment or adverse impact, but §703(h) limited violations based on the operation of seniority systems to non-bona fide seniority systems. The disparate treatment theory of discrimination emphasized compensation of the identified victims of discrimination, but the adverse impact theory emphasized work force distributions. This opened the door to affirmative action remedies. In this early period, court-ordered remedies under §706(g) after a finding of disparate treatment or adverse impact could include hiring, reinstatement, promotions, and awards of backpay and retroactive seniority to the actual victims of discrimination. It was only when the Court began to hear affirmative action cases, that affirmative action as a remedy under §706(g) was considered.

Affirmative action added two new dimensions heretofore not considered by the Court: a remedy not directed at the actual victims of discrimination and voluntary remedial action by employers. The question of relief not directed to the victims of discrimination was first addressed by the Court as an equal protection challenge in *Regents of the University of California v. Bakke*, 438 U.S. 265 (1978). The next section examines *Bakke* both for its articulation of the level of review for examining affirmative action in terms of the Equal Protection Clause and for the presence of distributive and compensatory principles in the opinions. The section also briefly examines the case of *Fullilove v. Klutznick*, 448 U.S. 448 (1980), for its holding on the level of review of affirmative action in terms of the Equal Protection Clause.

GOALS AND QUOTAS CONSIDERED UNDER EQUAL PROTECTION: *BAKKE* AND *FULLILOVE*

Regents of the University of California v. Bakke

The decision in *Regents of the University of California v. Bakke*, 438 U.S. 265 (1978), which has been the subject of much debate and analysis since it was handed down, was not the definitive decision on affirmative action many thought it would be. Yet *Bakke* is very important to this analysis because it provided a framework for equal protection challenges to affirmative action. In addition, *Bakke* was the first major Supreme Court decision that did not directly involve issues of judicial remedies for identifiable victims of discrimination. Therefore, it is in this decision where the question of affirmative action and not make-whole relief is first addressed by the Court.[5]

Allan Bakke is a white male who was denied admission to the medical school at the University of California at Davis in two consecutive years. Bakke sought both declaratory and injunctive relief (his admission to medical school) in the superior court of Yolo County, California. He alleged that the medical school admissions program, which reserved 16 of 100 places in each year's class to members of minority groups, discriminated against him in violation of the Equal Protection Clause of the Fourteenth Amendment, a provision of the California constitution, and Title VI of the Civil Rights Act of 1964.[6] The trial court found that the special admissions program operated as a quota and held (1) that the school could not take race into account in making admission decisions, (2) that the program violated the federal and state constitutions and Title VI, but (3) Bakke had failed to show that he would have been admitted except for the special admissions program, therefore he was not entitled to be admitted to the school.

The California Supreme Court heard the case on direct appeal. It affirmed the trial court's judgment that the program was invalid under the Equal Protection Clause. It reversed the court's refusal to admit Bakke on the grounds that the university was required to show whether Bakke would have been admitted in the absence of the special admissions program. The university had conceded that it was unable to make such a showing.

On writ of certiorari, the U.S. Supreme Court affirmed in part and reversed in part in a plurality opinion, delivered by Justice Powell. Five members of the Court (Justices Powell, Stevens, Stewart, and Rehnquist, and Chief Justice Burger) held that the California Supreme Court judgment must be affirmed to the extent that the special admissions program was unlawful and Bakke must be admitted to the medical school. Five members (Justices Powell, White, Marshall, Brennan, and Blackmun) also agreed that the California court's judgment should be reversed to the extent that it prohibited the university from giving any consideration to race in its future admissions process.

Justice Powell first addressed the question of whether the Court should consider whether there was a right to private action under Title VI that prohibited discrimination in federally funded programs. Because the lower courts had not considered that question, Justice Powell held that they need not address the issue (438 U.S. at 283). He went on to state that Title VI proscribed only those racial classifications that violate the Equal Protection Clause or the Fifth Amendment (438 U.S. at 287). With respect to equal protection analysis, Powell considered the university's argument that the lower court had incorrectly applied strict scrutiny because such scrutiny should be reserved for classifications that disadvantage "discrete and insular minorities" (438 U.S. at 287). Justice Powell held that whereas the Fourteenth Amendment was originally intended to protect freed slaves and guarantee their rights, during the amendment's dormancy following the *Slaughterhouse Cases*, 16 Wallace 36 (1873), the United States became a nation of minorities. Therefore, the Fourteenth Amendment now protected all ethnic groups including whites (438 U.S. at 292). According to Justice Powell: "It is far too late to argue that the guarantee of equal protection to all persons permits the recognition of special wards entitled to a degree of protection greater than that accorded others. The Fourteenth Amendment is not directed solely against discrimination due to a 'two-class theory'— that is, based upon differences between 'white' and 'Negro'" (438 U.S. at 295). Thus Powell held that all racial classifications, even benign racial preferences, must be subject to strict scrutiny analysis. He rejected the university's contention that the Court had approved preferential classifications without applying strict scrutiny (438 U.S. at 300). Additionally, he argued that in all these cases involving racial classifications, the preferences were designed as remedies for "the vindication of constitutional entitlements" after a judicial finding of discrimination (438 U.S. at 300).

Justice Powell sought to determine whether any of the purposes that the special admissions program purported to serve were compelling (438 U.S. at 305–306). The university stated these purposes as follows: (1) to reduce "the historic deficit of traditionally disfavored minorities in medical schools and in the medical profession" (quoting Brief of Petitioner 32, 438 U.S. at 306), (2) to counter the effects of societal discrimination, (3) to increase the number of physicians who will practice in communities presently underserved, and (4) to obtain the benefits that result from an ethnically diverse student body (438 U.S. at 306).

Powell found that reducing the effects of past discrimination with preferences is a compelling interest only after a government body with the authority to establish such a preference has made a finding of discrimination. Additionally, the classification must directly serve the purpose of remedying discrimination, i.e., be narrowly tailored (438 U.S. at 307). According to Justice Powell: "We have never approved a classification that aids persons perceived as members of a relatively victimized groups at the expense of other innocent individuals in the absence of judicial, legislative, or administrative findings of constitutional violations . . . [cites omitted] After such findings have been made, the governmental interest in preferring members of the injured groups at the expense of others is substantial, since the legal rights of the victims must be vindicated" (438 U.S. at 307). Thus, whereas Justice Powell found that a racial classification designed to remedy the effects of past discrimination after a finding of discrimination serves a compelling interest, he held that the university was not a body capable of making a finding of discrimination (438 U.S. at 309).

Powell also held that whereas the purpose of "facilitating the health care of . . . citizens" may be sufficiently compelling to support the use of a suspect classification, there was no evidence in the record that the special admissions program was designed to promote that goal (438 U.S. at 310). However, he found that the purpose of attaining an ethnically diverse student body is a constitutionally permissible goal of a university in view of the First Amendment's special concern for academic freedom. However, the university's use of racial classification was not necessary to promote this goal since there is evidence that other universities such as Harvard were able to achieve this goal without the use of a quota (438 U.S. at 315–316).

Because there were alternatives to the university's special admissions program to achieve those goals deemed compelling by the Court, Justice Powell held that the university's use of a racial classification violated the Fourteenth Amendment since it disregarded the individual rights guaranteed by that amendment (438 U.S. at 320). However, he reversed the lower courts' holdings that the university was prohibited from considering the race of an applicant. The university had a substantial interest that could be legitimately served by a properly devised admissions program (438 U.S. at 320). Powell ordered Bakke's admission to the medical school since the university could not show that he would not have been admitted absent the special program (438 U.S. at 320).

Justices Brennan, White, Marshall and Blackmun submitted a joint opinion in which they concurred in Justice Powell's judgment that the university was not prohibited from considering race in its admissions program but dissented from the judgment that the program was unlawful. Brennan began with the question of whether Title VI barred recipients of federal funds from giving preferential treatment to disadvantaged members of racial minorities as part of a program designed to enable these citizens to overcome the obstacles created by past discrimination (438 U.S. at 328). Like Justice Powell, Justice Brennan found that Title VI prohibited only those uses of racial criteria that would violate the Fourteenth Amendment if employed by a state or its agencies, but it did not prohibit the use of preferences as a means of remedying past societal discrimination "to the extent that such action is consistent with the Fourteenth Amendment" (438 U.S. at 328). Justice Brennan argued that the legislative history of Title VI, administrative regulations interpreting the statute, and the Court's own decisions did not lend support to the proposition that Congress intended to bar race-conscious efforts to "extend the benefits of federally financed programs to minorities . . . " (438 U.S. at 328).

Justice Brennan also addressed the issue of whether it was necessary to use strict scrutiny when examining a racial preference (438 U.S. at 356). He held that because the case does not involve a fundamental right and because whites do not as a class have any of the "traditional indicia of suspectness," (quoting *San Antonio v. Rodriguez*, 411 U.S. 1 (1973)), the proper standard would be that racial classifications designed to further remedial purposes "must serve important governmental objectives and must be substantially related to the achievement of those objectives," an intermediate level of review (438 U.S. at 359).

According to Justice Brennan, the university's articulated purpose of remedying the effects of past societal discrimination was sufficiently important to justify the use of a race-conscious admissions program if it could be shown that minority underrepresentation was substantial and chronic and that the handicap of past discrimination was impeding access of minorities to the medical school (438 U.S. at 362). According to Justice Brennan:

> Congress can and has outlawed actions which have a disproportionately adverse and unjustified impact upon racial minorities and has required or authorized race-conscious action to put individuals disadvantaged by such impact in the position they otherwise might have enjoyed. See *Franks v. Bowman*, 424 U.S. 747 (1976); *Teamsters v. United States*, 431 U.S. 324 (1977). Such relief does not require as a predicate proof that recipients of preferential advancement have been individually discriminated against; it is enough that each recipient is within a general class of persons likely to have been the victims of discrimination (438 U.S. at 363).

This is clearly a movement away from the view that affirmative action is limited to the identified victims of discrimination and hence compensatory only.

Justice Brennan found that the university had shown that the failure of minorities to qualify was due primarily to the effects of past discrimination (438 U.S. at 369). Justice Brennan also found that the special admissions program did not stigmatize either the nonminorities such as Bakke since he would not be relegated to the status of a second-class citizen by his rejection (438 U.S. at 375) nor the minorities who were admitted since they were still required to meet the same standards as the nonminorities while in school (438 U.S. at 376).

Finally, Justice Brennan found that the special admissions program did not violate the Constitution "simply because it [had] set aside a predetermined number of places for qualified minority applicants rather than using minority status as a positive factor to be considered in evaluating the applications of disadvantaged minority applicants" (438 U.S. at 378). He held that for purposes of constitutional adjudication there is no difference in the two approaches. The only difference is that in the former case the preference is obvious whereas in the latter the preference is not immediately apparent (438 U.S. at 379).

In another separate opinion, Justice Marshall recounted the history of slavery and discrimination against blacks in the country (438 U.S. at 388–394). Included in this discussion was the role played by the Court in allowing this discrimination to exist (438 U.S. at 391–394). Justice Marshall argued that because of this history of discrimination and its impact on blacks socially and economically, the task of "bringing the Negro into the mainstream of American life should be a state interest of the highest order" (438 U.S. at 396). Justice Marshall's statement, which is reminiscent of the congressional debates over Title VII, points toward redistribution.

Justice Marshall also went on to hold that the Fourteenth Amendment does not prohibit a university from remedying the cumulative effects of society's discrimination by giving consideration to race in an effort to increase the number of black doctors (438 U.S. at 397). According to Justice Marshall, the same Congress that wrote the Fourteenth Amendment passed the Freedmen's Bureau Act, which provided special relief to blacks; hence it would be difficult to believe that they intended the Fourteenth Amendment to prohibit race-conscious relief measures (438 U.S. at 398). Also, Justice Marshall stated that the Court itself had continually established the constitutionality of race-conscious remedial measures without direct evidence of discrimination, see *Swann v. Charlotte Mecklenberg Board of Education*, 402 U.S. 1 (1971), *United Jewish Organizations v. Carey*, 430 U.S. 144 (1977), and *Califano v. Webster*, 430 U.S. 313 (1970) (436 U.S. at 398–399). Therefore, it is proper to conclude that a university can also employ race-conscious measures to remedy past societal discrimination.

Justice Blackmun also wrote a separate opinion in which he began by lamenting the need for affirmative action and then expressed his hope that one day such programs would be unnecessary (438 U.S. at 403). Justice Blackmun observed that admissions programs for institutions of higher learning were basically a responsibility for academicians and those administrators they employ; thus it should be appropriate for them to address the issue of past discrimination, i.e., a university was a body capable of making a finding of discrimination (438 U.S. at 404).

Finally Justice Blackmun noted that it is probably impossible to arrange an affirmative action plan in a racially neutral way: "In order to get beyond racism,we must first take account of race. There is no other way. And in order to treat some persons equally, we must treat them differently. We cannot—we dare not—let the Equal Protection Clause perpetrate racial supremacy" (438 U.S. at 407).

Justice Stevens concurred in part and dissented in part and was joined in his opinion by Chief Justice Burger, and Justices Stewart and Rehnquist. Justice Stevens began by noting that there was no challenge to the California Supreme Court's order to admit Bakke and therefore the question of whether racial criteria can be used in an admissions process was not before the Court (438 U.S. at 410–411). Justice Stevens then addressed the scope of the Court's review of the issues. He argued that it was not necessary to consider whether the admissions program violated equal protection since Title VI clearly prohibited the exclusion regardless of whether or not the action carried with it racial stigma or resulted from an affirmative action program (438 U.S. at 412–414). Finally, Stevens held that the legislative history of Title VI, judicial authority, and actions by Congress support a private action under Title VI (438 U.S. at 412–421).

Bakke did not provide a coherent ruling on affirmative action. It served more to frame a debate than to resolve the question of the level of review of benign racial classifications. Only Justice Powell concluded that all racial classifications must be subject to strict scrutiny. Chief Justice Burger and Justices Stevens, Stewart, and Rehnquist did not address the equal protection issues at all, finding the program invalid under Title VI of the Civil Rights Act of 1964. On the other hand, Justices Brennan, Marshall, White, and Blackmun concluded that an intermediate test was appropriate for benign classifications.

In terms of equal protection analysis, *Bakke* is a divisive case. With no agreement on the level of review and, for that matter, the appropriate basis of the challenge, *Bakke* raised more questions than it resolved. Several scholars who have examined the implications of the case for equal protection analysis have lamented the decision. Karst and Horowitz (1979) felt that the decision was a blow to an already problematic system of analysis.[7] They noted that whereas Justice Powell stated that racial classifications must survive strict scrutiny, his analysis of the diversity interest was less than exacting. Powell did not require the university to carry the "heavy burden" of showing that diversity is a compelling interest but deferred to the university's right to academic freedom (Karst and Horowitz 1979: 12). Thus, whereas the Justice stated that he was utilizing strict scrutiny he was in fact requiring a lesser standard. In addition, Lavinsky has argued that the decision diluted the concept of strict scrutiny by distinguishing between benign and invidious racial classification (1980: 11). Karst and Horowitz also addressed this distinction. They seem to agree with Lavinsky's analysis, but they argued that Powell's distinction was illusionary since his analysis of diversity centered on the question of stigma, which is also the basis of Brennan's distinction (1979: 14–15).

Yet the failure to resolve the debate over the standard of review has not been particularly critical in the Court's decisions. Even those Justices who support an intermediate level of review have written opinions in which they upheld affirmative action on the basis of strict scrutiny (see Brennan's opinions in *U.S. v. Pardise* and *Johnson v. Transportation Agency*). On the other hand, the question of what justifies affirmative action as a remedy has shaped the Court's decisions. When analyzing affirmative action in terms of equal protection, a majority of the Court later rejected societal discrimination as a justification for remedial action. Powell's opinion suggested that racial preferences might also be justified as compelling on other than remedial grounds, but, to date, the Court has failed to uphold affirmative action on grounds other than as a remedy for a finding of past discrimination.

Bakke also provided no resolution of the question of when remedial action was justified. Justice Powell found that remedial action was only appropriate when there had been a judicial, legislative, or administrative finding of past discrimination or when a fundamental right such as freedom of speech, i.e., academic freedom, was implicated. Societal discrimination[8] was not enough to justify affirmative action since it was an "amorphous" and "ageless" concept (438 U.S. at 307). For Justice Powell, there must be identified victims of discrimination at which the remedy is directed. Justices Brennan, White, and Marshall, however, found that remedying societal discrimination was an acceptable reason for affirmative action when blacks were underrepresented and the handicap of societal discrimination impeded access by blacks to opportunities such as admission to a medical school.

Robert Sedler suggested in his analysis of *Bakke* that Brennan's acceptance of societal discrimination as a basis for affirmative action was based on "the interest of blacks as a group in having a 'fair share' of an employer's jobs" and that affirmative action was intended to serve this "substantial government interest" (1979: 149). Here Sedler has identified one of the arguments using redistributive values to justify affirmative action. Dworkin, on the other hand, argues that it is wrong to view affirmative action as a means of giving groups proportional shares (1985: 297). Instead, Dworkin argues that affirmative action is the only effective way of attacking the lingering effects of past societal discrimination. According to Dworkin: "Affirmative action tries to provide more blacks as classmates for white doctors, not because it is desirable that a medical school class reflect the racial make-up of the community as a whole, but because professional associations between blacks and whites will decrease the degree to which whites think of blacks as a race, rather than as people, and thus the degree to which blacks think of themselves that way" (1985: 295). Thus Dworkin accepts the redistributive results of affirmative action but sees it as a means, not an end. Sedler views the redistribution as an end.

Powell's rejection of societal discrimination as a basis for affirmative action seems to suggest that voluntary affirmative action is unjustified because it is not undertaken following a finding of discrimination and it is not directed to identified victims. E. Richard Larson, however, has argued in his analysis of *Bakke* that Justice Powell might accept voluntary affirmative action based on the congressional findings of identified discrimination in the legislative history of Title VII (1979: 252). Sedler agrees with Larson that there is no reason to read Powell's opinion as a ban on societal discrimination as a justification for affirmative action. Sedler notes that any legislative finding of discrimination would necessarily be a generalized finding that did not involve identification of the victims of discrimination (1979: 168).

Bakke can be viewed as the beginning of a transition by the Court from the purely compensatory view of affirmative action toward a broader redistributive view. In terms of compensation and redistribution, Justice Powell's opinion is based essentially on compensatory principles. In his discussion of a compelling interest, remedying past discrimination is only compelling when there has been a judicial, administrative, or legislative finding of discrimination and there are actual victims whose rights must be vindicated. In addition, he directly rejected a redistributive justification for benign preferences. Powell stated in his opinion that "[n]othing in the Constitution supports the notion that individuals may be asked to suffer otherwise impermissible burdens in order to enhance the *societal standing* of their ethnic groups" [emphasis supplied] (438 U.S. at 298). However, his rejection of this aspect of affirmative action did not resolve the issue.

Whereas there is some recognition of redistributive values in the *Bakke* decision, these values played only a limited role in the case. Justice Brennan's opinion shows some suggestion of a concern with the distributive effects of past discrimination, but the opinion does not emphasize this point. However, Brennan believed that an under-representation of minorities was part of proving past discrimination and he accepted the idea that remedies need not be directed at the actual victims of discrimination. Justice Marshall, however, showed a strong concern with redistribution. He emphasized that the remedial purpose of such preferences was to move blacks into the "mainstream of American society." Marshall argued that the Equal Protection Clause did not prohibit such remedial preferences and neither had the Court.

Fullilove v. Klutznick

Another case that is related to the Court's later affirmative action decisions is *Fullilove v. Klutznick,* 448 US 448 (1980), which deals with the question of race-conscious action in a remedial context and the level of scrutiny for equal protection analysis. *Fullilove* was a challenge to the "minority business enterprise" (MBE) provision of the Public Works Employment Act of 1977, which required that at least 10% of all federal funds granted for local public work projects must be used by the state or local grantee to procure services or supplies from businesses owned by minority group members. The petitioners sought both declaratory and injunctive relief, alleging that they had sustained economic injury from the enforcement of the MBE provision and the provision on its face violated the equal protection component of the Fifth Amendment and the Equal Protection Clause of the Fourteenth Amendment. The district court upheld the MBE provision and both the court of appeals and the Supreme Court affirmed. The Chief Justice delivered the opinion of the Court.

Dealing with the constitutionality of the provision, Chief Justice Burger first held that the Court should apply strict scrutiny to the use of a racial classification, at the same time including appropriate deference to Congress as a coequal branch of government (448 U.S. at 472). He then laid out a two-step inquiry. The first task was to determine whether the objectives of the legislation were within the power of Congress. The second task was to determine if the limited use of racial criteria was a constitutionally permissible means for achieving the objectives without violating the equal protection component of the Fifth Amendment.

The Chief Justice found the MBE provision to be an exercise of the Spending Power of Art. I, sec. 8, clause 1, which recognizes the power of Congress to "provide for the . . . general Welfare." He further supported the power of Congress to make such a provision on the basis of the Commerce Clause, and §5 of the Fourteenth Amendment, which allows Congress to pass legislation to enforce the equal protection clause (448 U.S. at 476, 478–489).

The next step in Burger's analysis was to determine whether the Court could use racial and ethnic criteria as a means to accomplish the constitutional objectives (448 U.S. at 480). He noted that Congress can use racial classifications if those classifications do not violate the equal protection component of the Fifth Amendment. To satisfy the constitutional requirements, the program using such criteria must be narrowly tailored to the achievement of the legislative objective (to remedy the present effects of past discrimination) (448 U.S. at 480). This follows the Court's holding in *Bakke*.

Chief Justice Burger rejected the contention that in a remedial context Congress must act in a wholly "colorblind" fashion (448 U.S. at 482). He noted that the Court had rejected this argument with regard to court-formulated school desegregation remedies, *Swann v. Charlotte-Mecklenberg Board of Education*, 402 US 1 (1971), *McDaniel v. Barresi*, 402 US 39 (1971), *North Carolina Board of Education v. Swann*, 402 US 43 (1971), when the Court held that "[j]ust as the race of students must be considered in determining whether a constitutional violation has occurred, so also must race be considered in formulating a remedy" (448 U.S. at 482). Since the remedial powers of Congress are broader than the remedial powers of the courts, it was also appropriate for Congress to use racial classifications in fashioning remedies.

Burger then disposed of the charge that the MBE program impermissibly deprived nonminority businesses of access to at least some portion of government contracting opportunities resulting from the act. The Chief Justice held that there was no constitutional defect on this basis since "sharing of the burden" by innocent parties is not impermissible when remedies are fashioned to cure the effects of prior discrimination (448 U.S. at 484), citing *Franks v. Bowman Transportion Co*, 424 US 747 (1976), *Albermarle Paper Co. v. Moody*, 422 US 405 (1975), and *United Jewish Organizations v. Carey*, 430 US 144 (1977). Because the burden on the nonminority firms in this case was light, the provision was appropriate.

Chief Justice Burger also found that the MBE program was not invalid due to underinclusiveness because it limited benefits to specified minority groups as opposed to all disadvantaged firms. Congress had not given a select minority group a preferred standing in the construction industry, but had undertaken a remedial program to place some firms on a more equitable footing with respect to contracting opportunities. He also concluded that there was no showing that Congress had effectuated invidious discrimination by excluding an identifiable minority group that had been the victim of discrimination equal to that suffered by the groups covered by the MBE provision.

The final challenge to the provision was that it was, on its face, overinclusive because it bestowed a benefit on businesses according to racial criteria that could be justified on the basis of competitive criteria or as a remedy for the present effects of past discrimination (448 U.S. at 486). Burger held that the regulations governing the program provided reasonable assurance that the application of the racial criteria would be narrowly limited to the accomplishment of Congress' remedial objectives (448 U.S. at 488). Because it survived the under- and overinclusiveness question, he found the MBE provision to be narrowly tailored.

Justice Powell concurred in the judgment of the Court but wrote "separately to apply the analysis set forth by [his] opinion in *Regents of the University of California v. Bakke,* 438 US 265 (1978)" (448 U.S. at 496). Powell held that a simple racial preference was not a compelling governmental interest, but the government does have a legitimate interest in "ameliorating the disabling effects of identified discrimination" (448 U.S. at 497). However, remedial action is compelling only if an appropriate governmental authority had found a constitutional or statutory violation and the means to achieving the remedial action is narrowly drawn to achieve the governmental purpose (448 U.S. at 498). Using this standard the Justice held that three questions must be considered: (1) whether Congress was competent to make findings of unlawful discrimination, (2) whether sufficient findings had been made to show that unlawful discrimination had adversely affected Minority Business Enterprises, and (3) whether the 10% set aside was a permissible means of addressing identifiable past discrimination.

Powell quickly disposed of the question of whether Congress could make findings of unlawful discrimination. He held that the history of the Court's review of congressional action regarding public accommodations demonstrated that Congress could make such findings, *Heart of Atlanta Motel v. US,* 379 US 241 (1964), *Katzenback v. McClung,* 379 US 294 (1964), Title VII, *McDonnell Douglas Corp. v. Green,* 411 US 292 (1973), (448 U.S. at 499). This was further supported by Congress' authority to pass legislation to enforce the provisions of the Thirteenth, Fourteenth, and Fifteenth Amendments (448 U.S at 500). Justice Powell also said that it was reasonable for Congress to conclude that private and governmental discrimination had contributed to the small number of public contracts awarded to MBE's since the legislative history included evidence which strongly supported that contention.

Powell addressed the question of whether the 10% set aside was a permissible means for remedying the present effects of prior discrimination in MBE procurement programs. First, he re-emphasized the point that Congress was not creating a preference but was taking remedial action intended to assure MBE's true equality of opportunity in the procurement of federal funds. He then indicated the standards previously used by courts in reviewing race-conscious remedies: (1) the efficacy of alternative remedies, (2) the planned duration of the remedy, (3) the relationship between the percentage of minority workers to be employed and the percentage of minority members in the population or relevant work force, and (4) the availability of waiver provisions if the hiring goal cannot be met (48 U.S. at 510–511).

Justice Powell noted that because the grant money was to be expended quickly, any remedy had to become effective immediately. Similarly, the MBE provision was not a permanent part of federal contracting requirements but concluded when the program ended. The 10% set aside was also acceptable because it was reasonably related to the percentage of minority group members in the population. Finally, the waiver provision allowed for flexibility in the application of the provision (448 U.S. at 512–514).

Justice Marshall entered a concurring opinion in which Justices Brennan and Blackmun joined. Marshall found that the MBE provision passed constitutional muster under the standard articulated by Justice Brennan and himself in *Bakke* (448 U.S. at 517). In that case, Marshall concluded that because a racial classification designed for remedial purposes is susceptible to misuse, it can be justified only by showing "an important and articulated purpose for its use," quoting *Bakke* at 361 (448 U.S. at 519). According to Marshall, " . . . the proper inquiry is whether racial classifications designed to further remedial purposes serve important governmental objectives and are substantially related to the achievement of those objectives" from *Bakke* at 359 (448 U.S. at 520). Marshall held that the MBE provision met both tests, i.e., it served the articulated purpose of addressing the present effects of past discrimination and the provison was substantially related to the achievement of that purpose (448 U.S. at 520–521).

Justice Stewart filed a dissenting opinion in which Justice Rehnquist joined. Stewart objected to the provision on the ground that the Equal Protection Clause prohibited any racial preference at all unless there had been a judicial finding of discrimination and the preference was a remedy for that discrimination (448 U.S. at 525, n. 4). He argued that the preference could not be supported as a congressional remedy since there was no evidence that Congress had discrimination in the disbursement of contractual funds (448 U.S. at 528). Stewart also argued that the other objectives of the provision, assuring minority contractors a certain percentage of funds and compensating for the effects of social, economic, and education disadvantage, were not acceptable grounds under the Equal Protection Clause since the first was a blatant preference that sought only racial balance and the second was too broad a categorization (448 U.S. at 528–530).

Justice Stevens also filed a dissent. He scrutinized what he saw as the four justifications for the provision: (1) as reparation for past injury to the class, (2) as a remedy for past discrimination against minority business enterprises, (3) as providing members of the class a share of the benefits, and (4) as a means of promoting greater minority participation in the competitive economy (448 U.S. at 536). He rejected the first justification, a remedy to groups who have suffered wrongs, because the MBE provision was overinclusive, provided benefits to those least likely to need them, and the random distribution of benefits on racial lines was not remedial but provided a justification for any kind of grant of special privilege (448 U.S. at 537–539). Stevens also rejected a remedy directed at minority business enterprises since there was no evidence that these enterprises had been discriminated against and the categories of MBEs was not narrowly tailored to identify those groups who had suffered specific acts of discrimination (448 U.S. at 539–541).

Justice Stevens rejected on its face any claim that a certain group of congressional members could assure that benefits were directed at their constituents (448 U.S. at 542). This is clearly a rejection of a distributive argument. He noted that it would be permissible for Congress to encourage participation by MBEs if such encouragement entailed eliminating barriers (448 U.S. at 543). Stevens, however, argued that the provision did not remove any barriers such as unfamiliarity with bidding procedures, difficulties in obtaining financing, or past discrimination (448 U.S. at 546). Finally, Stevens rejected Justices Stewart and Rehnquist's argument that the Fourteenth Amendment required color blindness, but found that the provision was not narrowly tailored since it was both underinclusive and overinclusive (448 U.S. at 552).

In *Fullilove* the Court was once again split on the appropriate level of review for noninvidious racial classifications. Chief Justice Burger, Justices Powell, White, Stewart, Stevens, and Rehnquist held that the Court must use a compelling interest/narrowly tailored test, while Justices Marshall, Brennan, and Blackmun held that the Court must use the important interest/substantially related standard. Even more significant is the fact that even those Justices who called for the compelling interest test could not agree on the analysis. Justices Stewart and Rehnquist took the position that the Fourteenth Amendment prohibited racial classifications of any kind unless justified as a remedy to the victims of discrimination. Chief Justice Burger and Justices Powell and White argued that racial set-asides were acceptable under the Equal Protection Clause when they were designed to remedy past discrimination. Justice Stevens argued that remedying past discrimination could support a racial classification, but the set-aside was not narrowly tailored and thereby did not survive strict scrutiny. The split over the level of review clearly shows that a majority of the Court favored strict scrutiny of all racial classifications, invidious or benign. Yet, the inability of these Justices to provide a consistent analysis prevents *Fullilove* from resolving the debate of the constitutionality of affirmative action.

The opinions in *Fullilove* also indicated that remedies for discrimination need not be directed only toward the victims of discrimination. Burger dismissed the overinclusiveness challenge that the provision benefitted enterprises that were not the actual victims of discrimination. Powell found that the provision was related to the percentage of minorities in the population and was thus acceptable. This might seem to suggest that Justice Powell had repudiated his *Bakke* opinion, but it is not. Powell simply deferred to Congress' power to make a finding of discrimination. Yet, by doing so, he accepted the redistributive nature of that finding and rejected the argument that a remedy need be directed at identified victims. Justices Stewart, Rehnquist, and Stevens, however, felt that the only way a purpose could be deemed remedial was if it was limited to the actual victims of discrimination. Thus, for these three Justices, any racial classification must be compensatory in order survive strict scrutiny.

Thus the Court's movement toward agreement on strict scrutiny as the appropriate standard of review is offset by its inability to provide a consistent analysis under that standard. This group was evenly divided over the correct outcome under that standard. The result is that *Fullilove* did little to settle the constitutionality of affirmative action. At most, it held that Congress could utilize racial preferences to remedy past discrimination. The questions of voluntary and court-ordered action remain to be resolved.

The Title VII and equal protection cases discussed above establish the frameworks from which the Court's affirmative action cases are analyzed. In terms of remedies, the early Title VII cases are strictly compensatory. However, the theories of discrimination outlined in these cases also provide the foundation upon which affirmation action is based. There is a recognition that distributive imbalances can identify the existence of discrimination, and this leaves the door open for solutions that attempt to remedy these distributive imbalances. The equal protection cases show a Court leaning heavily toward strict scrutiny, but a number of Justices seemingly are willing to support affirmative action as a remedy to discrimination. There is a recognition of distributive values in both *Bakke* and *Fullilove*, but these values are not overtly recognized until the Court's affirmative action decisions, which are the subject of the next chapter.

NOTES

1. Jurisdiction is the authority of a court to hear a case; jurisdictional authority is granted by Congress (Ball 1987: 4).
2. The writ of certiorari is an order by the Supreme Court to the lower court to send up the records of the case for review. Cases can also go to the Supreme Court on an Appeal as of Right if any part of the statute is ruled unconstitutional by one of the lower courts.
3. The Court had heard *Defunis v. Odegaard*, 416 U.S. 312 (1974), which involved affirmative action in higher education, but had held the case moot.
4. It should be noted that this holding assumed that nonapplicant incumbent employees were the actual victims of discrimination.
5. The Court first heard the issue in *Defunis v. Odegaard*, 416 U.S. 312 (1974), but ruled the case moot and thus did not address the issues. However, in a separate opinion, William O. Douglas argued that whereas Defunis had been discriminated against in admissions, the use of LSAT scores in the admissions process also discriminated against blacks since the test was culturally biased.
6. Title VI prohibits discrimination in federally funded programs.
7. Karst and Horowitz's article argued that the different levels of scrutiny used in equal protection analysis allows the Court to avoid the substantive issues raised by racial and other classifications.
8. Societal discrimination is discrimination that is not attributed to the actions of a particular employer but is the result of "broad social factors and attitudes" (Dowd 1980: 297). Societal discrimination might be considered a fourth type of discrimination covered by Title VII, but the Court has been and remains seriously divided over the concept with regards to Title VII, so it has not been included as a type of discrimination. However, the concept is a central issue in several affirmative action cases.

4

The Affirmative Action Cases

The statutory and constitutional doctrine in the affirmative action cases appears unstable. Each case produces multiple opinions and often the Court's decision rests on a plurality of opinions. Yet, each successive decision, whether a Title VII or an equal protection challenge, is shaped by those preceding it. Hence, the cases are analyzed in chronological order. A longitudinal analysis also permits an examination of the changing composition of the Court and its effect on affirmative action decisions. This chapter analyzes the constitutional and statutory questions raised while showing how distributive and compensatory values have influenced the answers to these questions.

UNITED STEELWORKERS V. WEBER: RECOGNITION OF TITLE VII'S REDISTRIBUTIVE PURPOSE

United Steelworkers of America, AFL-CIO-CLC v. Weber, 443 U.S. 193 (1979), presented a challenge to the affirmative action plan voluntarily established by a collective bargaining agreement between the employer, Kaiser Aluminum and Chemical Corporation, and the union, the United Steelworkers of America. The affirmative action plan reserved 50% of the openings in an in-plant craft training program for blacks until the percentage of black craftworkers in the plant approximated the percentage of blacks in the local labor force. During the first year, 13 employees were selected for the training program; seven were black and six were white. Because several of the black employees had less seniority than Weber and some of the other whites who were not admitted to the program, Weber challenged the affirmative action plan on the grounds that it violated sections 703(a) and 703(c) of Title VII of the Civil Rights Act of 1964.[1] The district court entered a judgment in favor of Weber. The circuit court affirmed. The Supreme Court granted certiorari and reversed.

The Steelworkers' Brief first addressed whether §703(j) prohibited a voluntary affirmative action and dispensed of it quickly. According to the Steelworkers, the only limitation under §703(j) adhered to the government. The courts, Congress, or the executive could not "require" that employers or unions grant racial preferences in an effort to eliminate a racial imbalance. Nothing in the section forbade an employer from doing so (Brief for Petitioners, Steelworkers, No. 78–432: 15). The Brief then carefully reviewed the legislative history of Title VII and in several instances identified a redistributive goal on the part of Congress. For example, the Steelworkers argued that "[t]he impetus for the action was the economic deprivation suffered by blacks and other minorities throughout the Nation—a deprivation which Congress believed attributable in significant part to employment discrimination . . . " (Brief for Petitioners, Steelworkers, No. 78-432: 17). Later the Steelworkers contended:

> The Congress which enacted Title VII knew that the Title could not, standing alone, materially reduce the economic distress of blacks and other minorities which was the impetus for its enactment. . . . This point was reiterated throughout the debate on Title VII.
>
> Congress did not, of course, require that employers or unions provide preferential access for disadvantaged minorities to training programs. But it would be ironic if a law triggered by a Nation's guilt over centuries of racial injustice constituted the first prohibition of private endeavors to accelerate the elimination of the vestiges of that injustice (Brief for Petitioners, Steelworkers, No. 78–432: 83–84).

These statements highlight an effort on the part of the union to move the Court away from the issue of compensation for injuries toward a broader reading of the purposes of the Title.

The Brief for Kaiser stressed the broader reading of the Title more explicitly:

> Title VII relief is meant not only to compensate or make whole individuals, but also "to achieve equality of employment opportunities and remove barriers that have operated in the past to favor . . . white employees over other employees" [citing *Griggs*, *Franks*, and *Albemarle*] This 'prophylatic' objective—which this Court has called "the primary objective of Title VII"—is a partner to the goal of making whole individual victims of discrimination, but it reaches beyond the person to the class. Compensation of an individual for harm he suffered does not assure persons of his race equal access to employment opportunities. Disadvantage to the group lingers long after the injury to the individual has been

enjoined and paid for. (Brief for Petitioner, Kaiser, No. 78–432: 40).

The Brief then made a specific redistributive argument for affirmative action:

> cases [such as *Contractors Association of Eastern Pennsylvania v. Schultz, Secretary of Labor*, 442 F.2d 159 (CA3) (1971)] implicitly recognized that racial employment goals by their nature are not concerned with redressing injury to individuals but with changing the composition of the workforce. They reflect an awareness that overcoming conditions that operate to the disadvantage of an identifiable group or class frequently requires the presence of that group in the workforce in significant numbers. Until that situation exists others may be deterred from applying or even seriously considering the possibility of doing so (Brief for Petitioner, Kaiser, No. 78–432: 41–42).

According to Kaiser, the government's interest in the achievement of the goals of equal opportunity had been expressed by Congress in Title VII and the executive branch in the federal contract compliance programs. These goals included both "the full utilization of minorities and women throughout the workforce" and "narrow[ing] the economic gaps between white and minority and male and female workers" (Brief for Petitioners, Kaiser, No. 78–432: 42).

The Brief for respondent Weber, on the other hand, took a compensatory and "color-blind" view of Title VII, which centered on the argument that the operation of the quota "present[ed] a classic case of discrimination against whites" and that discrimination against whites was as illegal under the title as discrimination against blacks (Brief for Respondent, No. 78–432: 29–30). Weber further indicated that the sole purpose of the quota was to achieve a racially balanced work force, not to remedy past discrimination as the Steelworkers and Kaiser suggested (Brief for Respondent, No. 78–432: 30).

Weber's Brief also contested that the quota was truly remedial since it was based on discrimination by society at large, not discrimination against individuals. The plurality in *Bakke* had rejected societal discrimination as a justification for affirmative action, but the Brennan group had not. Using a compensatory argument against the petitioners' redistributive argument, the Brief for Weber concluded:

> No attempt was made to provide a "remedy" to any individual victims of discrimination by Kaiser. None of the individuals preferred under the racial quota was ever subject to employment

discrimination by Kaiser. No attempt was ever made to determine whether any of the preferred minority employees had suffered discrimination at the hands of society. The racial quota embodied a policy of race discrimination against white individuals to achieve the general advancement of minority class. This policy is unlawful under Title VII (Brief for Respondent, No. 78–432: 31).

Weber provided an even more explicit rejection of the petitioners' redistributive argument:

> It may be attractive and arguably benign for government planners or corporation and union executives to decree a societal transformation through preferences based on race, but this new discrimination nonetheless has its own victims, no better off than the preferred class, who are called upon to endure curtailment of opportunity, suffer the economic effects of discrimination, and stomach the elimination of merit as a ground of advancement (Brief for Respondent, No. 78–432: 90).

Weber's Brief also contended that the legislative history of Title VII did not permit the voluntary use of racial quotas "to achieve the advancement of minority groups"; that the quotas cannot be validated on the basis of executive orders; and that the use of racial quotas could lead to increased racial animosity, enhance stereotyping of minorities, undermine the merit system [although this case involved advancement on the basis of seniority], and increase white resentment of the equal rights movement (Brief for Respondent, No. 78–432: 32–33).

The United States and the EEOC submitted an amicus brief that presented evidence in support of the petitioners' reading of Title VII. According to this brief, when Congress was considering the amendments to Title VII in 1971 and 1972, several amendments introduced to restrict federal agencies from ordering the use of numerical relief such as goals suffered defeat (Brief for U.S. and EEOC, No. 78–432: 33). Citing the debates in Congress, this brief cited several relevant remarks:

> Senator Javits, the co-floor leader for the bill in the Senate, noted that the amendment would terminate "the whole concept of affirmative action as it had been developed under Executive Order 11246 and *as a remedial concept under Title VII* [emphasis supplied], 118 Congressional Record 1664 . . . Senator Williams, the other co-floor leader, stated that a prohibition against numeri-

cal relief" would strip Title VII . . . of all its basic fiber, 118 Congressional Record 1676 . . . . The House Committee wrote in its report "Affirmative action is relevant not only to the enforcement of Executive Order 11246 but it is equally essential for more effective enforcement of Title VII in remedying employment discrimination" House of Representatives Report No. 92–238, 92d Congress, 1st Session 16 (1971) . . . (Brief of U.S. and EEOC, No. 78–432: 34).

Finally, the Brief for the U.S. and the EEOC addressed the question of limiting numerical relief to the identified victims of discrimination. The Brief noted that if an employer were to identify individual victims, it would be required to admit unlawful discrimination and make itself liable for backpay to those victims, thereby effectively eliminating any incentive for employers to attempt voluntary compliance (Brief for U.S. and EEOC, No. 78-432: 52).

Justice Brennan, joined by Justices Stewart, White, Marshall, and Blackmun, delivered the opinion of the Court upholding the Kaiser plan. Blackmun filed a concurring opinion. Rehnquist filed a dissent, joined by Burger. Powell and Stevens took no part in the case.

Justice Brennan first established the limits of the question before the Court. According to him, because the Kaiser-USWA plan implicated no state action the case did not present an equal protection challenge. Because the plan was voluntarily adopted, the only question under Title VII was whether it forbids private employers and unions from voluntarily agreeing upon bona fide affirmative action plans that grant racial preferences (443 U.S. at 200).

Weber had argued that Title VII prohibited all race-conscious affirmative action plans (443 U.S. at 201). Brennan rejected this argument because "an interpretation of the sections that forbade all race-conscious affirmative action would 'bring about an end completely at variance with the purpose of the statute'" (443 U.S. at 202). To identify the purpose of the statute, Justice Brennan examined the legislative history of Title VII as well as its historical context and found a congressional concern with "the plight of the Negro in our economy" and the need to integrate blacks "into the mainstream of American society" (443 U.S. at 202). According to Brennan, the legislative history also showed that Congress felt the essence of the problem was opening employment opportunities for blacks "in occupations which have traditionally been closed to them" (443 U.S. at 203). He also indicated that the legislative history stressed the use of voluntary resolution of discrimination (443 U.S. at 204).

Justice Brennan concluded:

> Given this legislative history, we cannot agree with respondent that Congress intended to prohibit the private sector from taking effective steps to accomplish the goal that Congress designed Title VII to achieve . . . *It would be ironic indeed if a law triggered by a Nation's concern over centuries of racial injury and intended to improve the lot of those who had "been excluded from the American dream so long,"* 110 Cong. Rec. 6552 (1964) (remarks of Senator Humphrey) constituted the first legislative prohibition of all voluntary, private, race-conscious efforts to abolish traditional patterns of racial segregation and hierarchy[emphasis supplied] (443 U.S. at 204).

In a footnote Brennan noted that the problems cited by Congress in the legislative history (a black unemployment rate twice that of whites) remained and had actually deteriorated since the passage of Title VII (443 U.S. at 204).

Brennan reinforced his arguments with further evidence from the legislative history. The opponents of Title VII raised two concerns: they argued that the act would be interpreted to *require* employers with racially imbalanced work forces to grant preferential treatment to racial minorities and that employers would grant preferential treatment even if not required to do so (443 U.S. at 205). In response Justice Brennan concluded that if Congress meant to prohibit all race-conscious affirmative action it could have done so by providing that Title VII would not "require *or* permit" preferential treatment. Yet, Congress did not do so (443 U.S. at 205).

Brennan closed with a short explanation of why the Kaiser affirmative action plan was permissible:

> The purposes of the plan miıror those of the statute. Both were designed to break down old patterns of racial segregation and hierarchy. Both were structured to "open employment opportunities which have traditionally been closed to them." . . . At the same time, the plan does not unnecesarily trammel the interests of white employees. The plan does not require the discharge of white workers and their replacement with new black hires . . . Nor does the plan create an absolute bar to the advancement of white employees . . . Moreover, the plan is a temporary measure; it is not intended to maintain a racial balance, but simply to eliminate a manifest racial imbalance . . . (443 U.S. at 208).

Four standards for an affirmative action plan derived from this. These are as follows: (1) an affirmative action plan should be designed to open employment opportunities in traditionally segregated positions,

(2) the plan must not unnecessarily trammel the interests of white employees, (3) the plan must not absolutely bar the advancement of whites, and (4) the plan must be temporary. These standards are now used to judge both voluntary and court-ordered affirmative action under Title VII.

Whereas Justice Brennan did not address the question of past discrimination on the part of the employer as a justification for voluntary action, Justice Blackmun felt it was necessary to consider that question in his concurring opinion. Blackmun suggested that it would be possible to decide this case from the "arguable violation" approach articulated by Judge Wisdom in *Alexander v. Gardner-Denver Co.*, 415 US 31, 44 (1974).[2] An arguable violation is present when an employer can show that it practiced discrimination in the past and there are statistical disparities in its work force. However, Blackmun felt that the Court's use of a broad "traditionally segregated job categories" approach was more appropriate in this case for three reasons. First, the Court's approach avoided the difficulty inherent in the "arguable violations" approach of showing a past violation of Title VII, which would make the employer liable to blacks when no incentive exists for it to do so (443 U.S. at 213). Also, this approach allowed an employer to redress discrimination that was outside the bounds of Title VII. Finally, this approach prevented Title VII from being interpreted to "lock in" the effects of segregation and discrimination (443 U.S. at 215).

Rehnquist submitted a lengthy dissent in which he chastised the Court for its interpretation of Title VII. He charged that the Court had distorted the legislative history and interpreted §703(j)'s prohibition on preferential treatment out of existence (443 U.S. at 231). According to Justice Rehnquist, no plainer language could be found than that of §§703 (a) and (c), which prohibited discrimination in employment by employers and unions. This language, coupled with §703(j)'s prohibition of preferential treatment, was enough, in Rehnquist's view, to show that the Court had reached the wrong conclusion. However, like Brennan, Rehnquist turned to the legislative history to support his interpretation of Title VII. He argued that Congress did intend to prohibit voluntary affirmative action plans (443 U.S. at 232–253). He based this reading on the statements of both the opponents and the advocates of Title VII that racial balance would not be equated with discrimination[3] and that the title would not be interpreted to require preferential treatment. Congress knew they were passing color-blind legislation. However, Justice Rehnquist's reading ignored the 1972 amendments to Title VII upon which the Steelworkers had relied (443 U.S. at 253–255). He concluded with the charge that the Court, instead of relying on the standard tools of statutory interpretation, i.e., the words of the statute and its legislative history, had substituted its own vision of the "spirit" of Title VII in order to reach its conclusion (443 U.S. at 253–254).

Analysis

The briefs in this case show the full-blown development of the redistributive/compensatory split between the advocates and opponents of affirmative action. Both the Steelworkers and Kaiser argued that Title VII had two purposes: (1) compensating identified victims of discrimination and (2) achieving equal opportunity and the removal of barriers to access. Kaiser suggested that the achievement of equal opportunity required the removal of barriers and the alteration of the composition of the work force so that it more closely resembled the distribution that would have resulted in the absence of discrimination. The Steelworkers emphasized the need to "materially reduce the economic distress of blacks," which would necessarily require a redistribution (Brief for Petitioner, Steelworkers, No. 78–432: 83–84). Weber, on the other hand, took a compensatory view of the title. The quota was unlawful because there had been no official finding of discrimination and that even if the quota were remedial, none of the blacks who benefited from the quota had ever been discriminated against and thus deserved no compensatory preference.

The decision in *Weber* involved three questions with regard to affirmative action: (1) whether Title VII prohibits voluntary affirmative action, (2) on what basis voluntary action can be supported, and (3) what type of action is permissible. The first two questions turn on the issue of statutory interpretation. Both Justices Brennan and Rehnquist have been criticized for their reading of the legislative history of Title VII and §703(j). Edwards argues that their reliance on the legislative history is "misplaced" because the 1964 debates on the title were silent on the question of voluntary preferential remedies (Edwards 1980: 743–746). That is, Justice Brennan cannot conclude that voluntary action is permissible under Title VII and Justice Rehnquist cannot conclude that it was prohibited. Brennan might have found better support for voluntary affirmative action using the 1972 debates, which considered the question of affirmative action for the first time. According to Edwards, the 1972 debates were primarily concerned with affirmative action under EO11246 so that these debates are not dispositive with respect to voluntary action (1980: 749). However, the Brief of the United States and the EEOC cited above showed that Congress also recognized that affirmative action was an essential ingredient to the enforcement of Title VII.

Others also disagree with both Rehnquist's and Brennan's reading of the legislative history to the extent that both attempted to make a "hypothetical head count" on the permissibility of voluntary affirmative action (Neuborne 1979: 553). The Congress simply never considered the question so there were no heads to count. Indeed, the legislative history is mute on the question of voluntary affirmative action. Yet, whereas this fact may prevent the Court from reaching any conclusions about voluntary affirmative action in terms of congressional intent, it does not absolve the Court of its responsibility for dealing with the issue.

Justice Brennan's opinion, however, is not without any basis for the decision that §703(j) permits voluntary action. His use of the legislative history is actually extraneous to his true argument, which derives from the purpose of the statute. Brennan clearly stated in his opinion that he was working from this starting point. This method of statutory interpretation resembles Dworkin's coherence theory of statutory interpretation under which a statute is interpreted to advance the principles that furnish the best political justification of the statute (Dworkin 1985: 327). According to Dworkin, Brennan's justification for Title VII was economic equality and the economic status of blacks, and (with certain limitations) voluntary affirmative action advances that purpose (1985: 328).[4] Justice Brennan reasoned that §703(j) supports the principle that the government should be prevented from intervening in "traditional management prerogatives" and prohibiting voluntary affirmative action would violate that principle (Dworkin 1985: 327).

Others have suggested alternate paths that the Justice could have taken to support voluntary affirmative action. Neuborne argued that the purpose of Title VII was remedial and that Brennan's use of the "traditionally segregated job categories" approach supported this remedial purpose (1979: 555–556). Because whites in traditionally segregated job categories had received unjust enrichment from past discrimination, it is appropriate to implement a preference that equitably "redistribute[s] the involuntary benefit attributable to past racial discrimination" (Neuborne 1979: 549). Similarly, Edwards felt that Justice Brennan's opinion could have been strengthened if he had emphasized the remedial purpose of the title. He noted that if voluntary action is viewed as a remedial measure it does not fit the type of discrimination the Court has held to be prohibited by §§703(a) and (c), i.e., invidious discrimination, and, therefore, the Justice could have argued that voluntary preferences were not violative of Title VII (1980: 750–754).

Reliance on the remedial purpose of Title VII to support the *Weber* decision does not mean that voluntary affirmative action is compensatory. In *Bakke* and *Fullilove* the Court held that for an action to be remedial it must be based on a judicial, legislative, or administrative finding of discrimination, not societal discrimination. Societal discrimination is not attributable to a particular employer but is the result of "broad social factors and attitudes" and is identified through general racial disparities (Dowd 1980: 297; Boyd 1980: 15).[5] Under the concept of societal discrimination, there is no identification of the perpetrators of the discrimination or the actual victims of discrimination. Therefore, a remedy based on societal discrimination is not directed toward identified victims (Boyd 1980: 15). Neither is the remedy compensatory. The remedy is redistributive as it is directed at eliminating the results of past discrimination—racial disparities.

Some scholars have suggested that in *Weber* the Court expanded the definition of remedial to include this concept of societal discrimination. Dowd (1980) suggested that this is not actually a major shift in the Court's definition of the types of discrimination actionable under Title VII. According to Dowd, the Court implicitly accepted societal discrimination as discrimination under Title VII in its prior definitions. Adverse impact and disparate impact theories of discrimination are not based on intent but on racial disparity (Dowd 1980: 322–323). To that extent, such definitions contemplate the assumption that discrimination is not necessarily due to discriminatory actions of an employer, but can be the result of other factors.

Yet Justice Brennan does not argue that voluntary affirmative action is acceptable because it remedies societal discrimination. He bases his argument on the principles of economic equality (the elimination of the economic distress of blacks) and "traditional management prerogatives." Still, the principle of economic equality supports redistribution without the concept of societal discrimination. However, Brennan had clearly accepted societal discrimination as a basis for voluntary action in *Bakke* and it can be reasonably inferred from his opinion that he would not be uncomfortable with the concept. Justice Blackmun, however, was uncomfortable with the concept. He would have preferred the "arguable violations" approach since it would require a heavier burden of proof to justify voluntary action, but for pragmatic reasons he rejected that approach. Boyd suggested that this refusal to base the decision explicitly on societal discrimination convinced Stewart to join Brennan's opinion (1980: 41–46).

Justice Brennan refused to detail the parameters of permissible affirmative action, but he gave four reasons why the Kaiser plan was acceptable: (1) it opened traditionally segregated job categories, (2) it did not unnecessarily trammel the interests of white employees, (3) it did not bar white employee advancement or require their replacement with black workers, and (4) it was temporary in that it was designed to eliminate a racial imbalance, not maintain one (443 U.S. at 208). These standards are consistent with those established in *Carter v. Gallagher*, 452 F.2d. 315, 330 (CA8), cert. denied, 406 U.S. 950 (1972), which involved a court-ordered quota (Edwards 1980: 758; Boyd 1980: 21–23). Thus the Court did not stray far from the parameters of court-ordered affirmative action when outlining the parameters of voluntary action. These standards operationalize a redistribution while protecting the interests of whites.

Boyd argued that all these standards revolve around the concept of racial imbalance. A "traditionally segregated job category" can be identified by the existence of a racial imbalance (Boyd 1980: 21). A quota does not unnecessarily trammel the interests of white employees or bar their advancement if it is designed to eliminate a racial imbalance (Boyd 1980: 22). A temporary plan seeks to eliminate racial imbalances, not maintain them, and thus ends when the racial imbalance is eliminated (Boyd 1980: 23). Thus, each of the questions raised in *Weber* is answered with some reference to racial imbalances in the work force.

Indeed, the *Weber* decision clearly turns on the question of racial imbalances. The predicate for voluntary action is racial imbalance, even if it is only due to societal discrimination. The parameters of voluntary affirmative action are judged in terms of the objective of eliminating racial imbalances. This emphasis on imbalance shifts the attention from compensatory to distributive issues. Voluntary affirmative action is acceptable as a means of eliminating imbalances with none of the prerequisites for the application of the compensatory principle, the identification of a perpetrator of an injury and a victim to whom compensation is owed. Instead, the concern is with the existence and elimination of maldistribution in the work force. Whether the elimination of the imbalance is achieved with quotas or goals, the intended result is redistribution.

The assumption behind this conclusion is that a racial imbalance shows the existence of discrimination. This assumption, of course, is open to challenge. It is not, however, an unreasonable assumption when discrimination is as pervasive a phenomenon as it has been in this country. Indeed, Congress clearly considered the poverty and high unemployment of blacks to be the result of discrimination. Racial imbalance is simply the empirical manifestation of this poverty and high unemployment. Hence, the existence of racial imbalance is equated with the existence of discrimination.

The hypothesis that is derived from this assumption is that the elimination of racial imbalance will assist in the elimination of discrimination. Although it may not follow directly that the elimination of the racial imbalance will bring an end to discrimination, the hypothesis does have some validity. Dworkin, Wasserstrom, and Segers argue that in the long run redistribution will alter present social reality. That is, in the trades, unions, and other positions where blacks have been excluded, whites who will be working with blacks will come to view blacks as persons instead of simply as blacks. Blacks will also see that they have the ability to compete in a fair competition with whites, thus reducing social tensions. The presence of blacks in the positions of power and prestige will further reduce social tensions that result from their exclusion. These considerations are sufficient for some to justify redistribution. Others, of course, believe that redistribution cannot be justified because of the burdens it places on innocent whites. The parameters set by the Court for affirmative action attempt to deal with this problem. That is, the burden on whites must not result in whites being fired to make room for blacks or prevent whites from advancing their employment status because of the operation of a quota or goal.

AFFIRMATIVE ACTION AND SENIORITY: TWO STEPS BACK WITH *STOTTS* AND *WYGANT*

Weber signaled a shift in the Court's reading of Title VII to distributive concerns. Two cases in 1985 and 1986 seemed to step back from that decision; however, both these cases, *Stotts* and *Wygant*, involved seniority. Unlike the make-whole cases such as *Franks* and *Teamsters* in which seniority was compensation to identified victims, *Stotts* and *Wygant* involved affirmative action that affected the operation of bona fide seniority systems. Whereas the Court has been willing to grant retroactive seniority to the victims of discrimination, these cases show that a majority of the Court is not willing to allow seniority systems to be bypassed or altered in the name of affirmative action. Initially, the cases appear to go beyond seniority. In them, four of the justices even argued that Title VII forbids court-ordered affirmative action altogether. However, subsequent holdings have read these cases as simply establishing seniority as a limit on affirmative action.

Firefighters Local Union No. 1784 v. Stotts

Firefighters Local Union No. 1784 v. Stotts, 467 U.S. 561 (1983), was a challenge to a court of appeals decision upholding an order enjoining the City of Memphis from following its seniority system in determining layoffs. In 1977 Carl Stotts, a firefighting captain, filed a class action suit charging the Memphis Fire Department with a pattern or practice of making hiring and promotion decisions on the basis of race in violation of Title VII. In 1980 the district court issued a consent decree that was designed to remedy the hiring and promotion practices that excluded blacks (467 U.S. at 565). The city agreed to promote 13 specific individuals, to provide backpay to 81 employees of the department, and to adopt a long-term goal of increasing minority representation in each job classification of the Fire Department. The city did not admit to "any violations of law, rule or regulation with respect to the allegations," a standard practice in consent decrees (467 U.S. at 565). Finally, the plaintiffs waived any additional relief except the enforcement of the decree and the district court "retained jurisdiction 'for such further orders as may be necessary or appropriate to effectuate the purposes of this decree'" (467 U.S. at 565–566).

In early May 1981 the city announced a reduction in force due to a budgetary deficit (467 U.S. at 566). Layoffs were to be based on the "last hired, first fired" rule of the city's seniority plan. At the respondent's request, the district court entered a temporary restraining order forbidding the layoff of any black employees (467 U.S. at 566–567). Later, the district court granted a preliminary injunction against the layoffs. The district court had found that although the consent decree did not deal with layoffs and though the seniority system was not intended to discriminate, the proposed layoffs would have a discriminatory effect (467 U.S. at 567). The court also found that the seniority system was not bona fide. The city then developed a modified plan that resulted in demotion or layoff of nonminority employees with more seniority than the minority employees (467 U.S. at 567).[6] The court of appeals affirmed, holding that the district court had erred in holding that the seniority system was not bona fide, but acted properly in modifying the decree to prevent minority employment from being disproportionately affected by the layoffs (467 U.S. at 568).

The Firefighters' brief argued that the district court had impermissibly modified the consent decree and that the modification of the consent decree was flawed because it was not limited to making whole the actual victims of discrimination (Brief for Petitioner, Firefighters, No. 82–206: 10–11). Unlike *Weber*, which involved voluntary action, *Stotts* involved the power of the Court to order relief. According to the Firefighters, the courts have only one role with regard to Title VII:

> As this Court explained in *Franks*, 424 U.S. at 764 n. 21, the Congress that "added the phrase speaking to 'other equitable relief' in §706(g) . . . indicated that 'rightful place' was the intended objective of Title VII and the relief accorded thereunder," and the Court understood the portion of the section-by-section

> analysis . . . to be "emphatic confirmation that the federal courts are empowered to fashion such relief as the particular circumstances as the case may require *to effect restitution, making whole insofar as possible the victims of racial discrimination* . . . Id. at 764 [emphasis in brief] (Brief for Petitioner, Firefighters, No. 82–206: 36).

This statement exemplifies the emphasis placed by petitioners on the compensatory aspects of Title VII. The Brief excludes references to the broader purposes of Title VII articulated by the Court in *Weber*. The second petitioner, the Memphis Fire Department, relied on similar arguments. The Fire Department reasoned that the district court had exceeded its authority both in modifying the consent decree and with respect to Title VII, which exempted bona fide seniority systems unless they were discriminatory (Brief for Petitioner, Memphis Fire Department, No. 82–206: i–ii).

The respondents emphasized the procedural argument that the injunction was only preliminary (Brief for Respondent, No. 82–206: 16–17). The only question was whether the district court had abused its discretion "in entering a decree to protect the status quo" (Brief for Respondent, No. 82–206: 19). According to the respondent, the relief was appropriate because the layoff would have violated the consent decree in two ways. First, the consent decree required the city to raise minority representation as quickly as possible, but the layoffs would have "reduced minority representation and delayed the attainment of the mandated employment levels [percentages comparable to the civilian labor force]." Second, the purpose of the decree was to "remedy any disadvantage that may have resulted from past hiring and promotional policies" and the layoffs would have "perpetuated discrimination" (Brief for Respondent, No. 82–206: 20–21).

Respondent also argued that the injunction did not require the city to use a race-conscious layoff plan. The city had selected a race-conscious plan on its own initiative and the union had never appealed the order of the court that approved of the city's plan (Brief for Respondent, No. 82–206: 21–22).[7] The respondent also addressed the question of whether the consent decree violated §706(g) and §703(h) of Title VII because it adversely affected the seniority rights of whites without a prior finding that the beneficiaries of the decree were actual victims of discrimination (Brief for Respondent, No. 82–206: 22–23). The argument presented rested on a distinction between the consent decree as voluntary action by the employer and relief ordered by a court (Brief for Respondent, No. 82–206: 23). To identify the victims of discrimination in consent decrees, the employer would have to "take to trial legal or factual claims" that would stifle the voluntary dispute resolution, which was the preference of Congress in enacting Title VII (Brief for Respondent, No. 82–206: 23, 89).

The Respondent did not emphasize the broad interpretation of Title VII taken by the Court in *Weber*. The emphasis on the voluntary nature of a consent decree, however, was clearly an attempt to apply the principles of *Weber* and not the compensatory principles articulated in *Franks* and *Teamsters*. That is, they wanted to shift the argument from one of make-whole relief to one of voluntary remedial action. However, one of the amicus briefs did cite *Weber* directly (Brief of the Officers of Justice et al., No. 82–206: 9). According to this brief:

> Municipalities such as Boston and Memphis who enter into consent decrees to remedy the effects of past discrimination should not be given the opportunity to negate their obligations in the event of layoffs by employing seniority systems which destroy the effects of the consent decree. If such practices are permitted then Title VII's relief is illusionary at best. For as the *Weber* Court pointed out, "unless blacks [are] able to secure jobs which have a future [cite omitted], the integration of blacks into the mainstream of society will not be achieved . . . . "
>
> Strong, firm, and unyielding adherence to the concept of full integration of the work force and the workplace requires that the courts be permitted to modify consent decrees in ways which do not result in the decimation of the advances made by minorit[ies] (Brief of Officers of Justice et al., No. 82–206: 9–10).

The opinion of the Court was announced by Justice White in which he held that the modification of the consent decree was unjustified. Chief Justice Burger and Justices Powell, Rehnquist, and O'Connor joined the opinion of the Court. Justices O'Connor and Stevens submitted concurring opinions. Justice Blackmun dissented and was joined in his opinion by Justices Brennan and Marshall. The dissents by Justices Brennan, Marshall, and Blackmun are consistent with their positions in *Weber*. Chief Justice Burger and Justice Rehnquist were also consistent with their positions in *Weber*. Justices Powell and Stevens had not participated in *Weber*, and Justice O'Connor was not on the Court when *Weber* was decided.

The first substantive consideration in Justice White's opinion was whether the district court's injunction could be justified either as an effort to enforce the consent decree or as a valid modification of the decree (467 U.S. at 573).[8] Regarding whether the injunction was an effort to enforce the consent decree, White held that "the scope of the consent decree must be discerned within its four corners . . . " (467 U.S. at 574). The consent decree did not mention layoffs or demotions or any intention to depart from the seniority plan. If there had been any intention to include these in the decree, it could have been done explicitly. Therefore, the injunction could not be justified as an enforcement of the consent decree (467 U.S. at 574–575). Second, Justice White considered whether the injunction carried out the purposes of the decree. The injunction did not serve the purposes of the decree because the decree involved only hiring and promotion practices and not the seniority system. The decree's remedy did not include the displacement of white employees with greater seniority than black employees (467 U.S. at 575–576).

Justice White's final consideration was whether the district court could modify the consent decree in the manner it had. The court of appeals had held that the priority given to voluntary settlement in Title VII actions permitted a consent decree that encroached on seniority systems. White rejected the claim that the "settlement" theory was applicable since there had been no settlement regarding the seniority system (467 U.S. at 576–578). The court of appeals also held that the injunction was justified on the basis of the assertion that the district court could enter an order overriding the seniority provisions if the allegations in the complaint were proved. White held that this approach overstated the trial court's authority under Title VII to disregard seniority when fashioning a remedy after finding a pattern or practice of discrimination (467 U.S. at 578–579). *Teamsters v. United States*, 431 US 324, 352 (1977), and the legislative history of Title VII required that retroactive seniority only be awarded to individuals who have been the actual victims of discrimination. Because those blacks who had been retained had not shown that they had been discriminated against, the district court had exceeded its authority with regard to the seniority system (467 U.S. at 579–583). Finally, the Justice rejected the contention that the district court had not ordered any more than would be permissible in adopting an affirmative action program because the city did not voluntarily adopt the plan since the decree was issued over the city's objections (467 U.S. at 583).

Justice O'Connor concurred on the ground that the district court's injunction was an abuse of its discretion. According to O'Connor, a consent decree cannot bar the use of seniority or require the maintenance of racial balances if layoffs became necessary nor can a district court unilaterally modify the decree to adjust racial balances or to provide retroactive relief "that abrogates legitimate expectations of the employees and applicants" (467 U.S. at 586–587). The district court can use its remedial powers only to prevent future violations and to compensate identified victims of discrimination (457 U.S. at 587–588). However, Justice O'Connor did not preclude all remedial awards of retroactive seniority. She went on to note that such relief could have been granted if the respondents had litigated the issue as such, but because they had not done so the injunction was improper (467 U.S. at 5888–5889).

Justice Stevens also concurred, but he based his opinion solely on the procedural issue of administering the consent decree, not on Title VII (467 U.S. at 590–591). Indeed, Stevens believed that Justices White's and O'Connor's reasoning regarding Title VII could only be advisory. Regarding the injunction, Justice Stevens argued that there were two ways the actions of the district court could have been justified. First, the district court could have indicated that it was enforcing the terms of the decree it was interpreting (467 U.S. at 591). The second justification would be that the district court entered the injunction "based on the likelihood that it would modify the decree" because of "changed circumstances" (467 U.S. at 592). According to Stevens, the district court failed to show either justification.

Justice Blackmun dissented and was joined in his opinion by Justices Brennan and Marshall. Blackmun's dissent attacked the Court's interpretation of the district court's actions. He began by showing how the Court had departed from precedent in its analysis of the preliminary injunction. According to him, the question before the Court was "simply whether the issuance of the injunction, in light of the applicable standard, constituted an abuse of discretion." The Court did not apply the legal standards for assessing a preliminary injunction, but instead applied the standard used for permanent injunctions—whether the city's proposed layoffs violated the consent decree (467 U.S. at 601–602). That issue was never resolved in the district court because the city did not ask for a final decision on the merits.

According to Justice Blackmun, the Court acted contrary to its unanimous decision in *University of Texas v. Camenisch*, 451 US 390 (1981), which held the determination of a party's entitlement to a preliminary injunction is a separate issue from the determination of the merits of the parties' legal claim. Therefore, the only consideration before the Court would be the "propriety of the preliminary injunctive relief" (467 U.S. at 602–604). The Court focused on the district court's power to "enter an injunction requiring white employees to be laid-off" (467 U.S. at 605). Blackmun suggested that this analysis began from an incorrect premise since the injunction did not require the city to lay off white employees but only prohibited the city from conducting layoffs in accordance with its seniority system "insofar as it will decrease the percentage of blacks . . . presently employed" in certain job categories (467 U.S. at 605). The choice of the modified layoff plan remained the city's. The true question in the case was whether the district court's authority under the consent decree allowed it to prohibit the layoff of more than a certain number of blacks, not whether the district court could require the city to lay off whites (467 U.S. at 606).

Justice Blackmun then considered whether the district court had the authority to issue a permanent injunction. According to the court of appeals and Blackmun, "if respondents can show that changed circumstances justified modification of the decree, the district court would have authority to make such a change" (467 U.S. at 607). Section 17 of the decree gave the district court the authority to enforce the terms and purposes of the decree. One such purpose of the decree required the city "to raise the black representation in . . . the fire department to levels approximating the black proportion of the civilian labor force in Shelby County, App. to Pet. for Cert. in No.82–229, p. A69" (467 U.S. at 607). Respondents claimed that the proposed layoffs would adversely affect blacks significantly out of proportion to their representation and thereby "violate[d] the spirit of the . . . consent decree" (467 U.S. at 608). Blackmun believed that this claim was important enough to be considered in a trial, but that the Court's treatment prevented the respondents from substantiating the claims.

Similarly, Blackmun challenged the Court's holding that the district court's injunction was improper because the decree did not specifically mention layoffs. It was the district court's duty to determine the intent of the decree and the district court should be granted deference to interpret the general terms of the decree (467 U.S. at 609). The Justice also considered whether there was a justification for modifying the decree. According to Blackmun, the Court held in *Chrysler Corp. v. US*, 316 US at 562, that "the test for ruling on a plaintiff's request for a modification of a consent decree is 'whether the change serves to effectuate . . . the basic purpose of the original consent decree' " (467 U.S. at 611). However, in this case the Court evaluated the propriety of the preliminary injunction by considering the type of relief the district court could have awarded if the respondent's had litigated their Title VII claims and had prevailed on the merits. Justice Blackmun observed that it is not clear that that was the correct question since a consent decree is voluntary action, but even if it is was, the Court gave the wrong answer (467 U.S. at 611).

According to Blackmun, if the respondents had prevailed at trial, the remedies available would be those provided by §706(g) (467 U.S. at 612). Under this section the courts had distinguished between individual relief and race-conscious class relief. To receive individual relief, the citizen is required to show that she was a victim of discrimination. Race-conscious relief, in contrast, may be ordered "to remedy the present class-wide effect of past discrimination or to prevent similar discrimination in the future" (467 U.S. at 613). Citing eleven cases and referring to *Bakke*, Justice Blackmun indicated that "the Courts of Appeal were unanimously of the view that race-conscious relief can also be appropriate under section 706(g)" (467 U.S. at 612–613, n. 10).

Blackmun then noted that in this case the respondent's request for the preliminary injunction did not include a request for individual awards, and that the district court did not make any such awards. It only "required the city to conduct its layoffs in a race-conscious manner" (467 U.S. at 613–614). As such, it was within the reach of Title VII. The Court had concluded, however, that the respondents could not have obtained race-conscious relief under Title VII even if the case were taken to trial.

Justice Blackmun put special emphasis on the Court's application of *Teamsters* (467 U.S. at 614–615). That case involved both race-conscious class relief and individual relief. According to the Justice, *Teamsters* and *Franks* established the two stage procedure now followed by the Court in Title VII cases. Under this procedure, the first stage of a trial involves a determination of whether the city or other political structure had engaged in unlawful discrimination. The second stage provides the individual members of the class the opportunity to show that they were the victims of discrimination. According to Blackmun, if the respondents were to prevail at trial, seniority relief would be available to them under *Franks* and *Teamsters*. Finally, he expressed the view that the Court's reading of the legislative history of Title VII was incomplete (467 U.S. at 618–620). The legislative history of §706(g) indicates that Congress supported a narrow interpretation of relief. However, the Court ignored the legislative history of the 1972 amendments to Title VII, which supports the view that Congress endorsed the remedial use of race under Title VII.

Analysis. The distinction between a compensatory or distributive reading of the purpose of Title VII is evident in the briefs of this case. Those opposed to the modification made the compensatory argument that seniority relief could only be granted to the actual victims of discrimination. Indeed, they suggested, and apparently convinced the Court, that the only relief available under §706(g) is make-whole relief. Those in support of the modification emphasized the power of the courts to modify consent decrees when the operation of the decree operated against its broad purposes by perpetuating the effects of past discrimination. The respondents also argued that to identify the victims of discrimination would make an employer liable and thus frustrate Title VII's emphasis on voluntary action, including consent decrees.

The decision in *Stotts* has been controversial not only because of its holding, but also because of its legal analysis. It has been suggested that the Court made two significant errors in its legal analysis. First, the Court analyzed the injunction as if it were a court-ordered remedy under Title VII rather than as a preliminary injunction that involved only one particular layoff in limited number of firefighter positions (Botts 1985: 765). If the Court had analyzed the modification of the decree as the preliminary injunction that it was, the appropriate review would have been to determine if the district court had abused its discretion. Because the case was based on a consent decree in which there is no finding of discrimination, the remedial powers of a Court were not applicable (Botts 1985: 766). Justice Stevens in his concurrence and Justice Blackmun in his dissent noted that the abuse of discretion standard would be appropriate. By examining the modification as if it were a court-ordered remedy resulting from a finding of Title VII violation, however, the Court not only misstated the facts of the case but also placed the respondent in a position of being scrutinized in a context for which they were not prepared (Hernandez 1986: 368–369). That is, the respondent had litigated and was arguing in terms of voluntary action, not in terms of court-ordered relief. Additionally, by examining the decree as if it were a court-ordered remedy instead of voluntary action, the Court was able to reach conclusions that it otherwise would have been unable to draw. That is, it took the opportunity to rule on §706(g) despite the fact that the case did not actually involve that section.

Even if one accepts the Court's argument that the question is the Court's powers under §706(g), it has been suggested that the legal analysis is still in error because of the Court's application of *Teamsters* (Botts 1985: 766; Hernandez 1986: 371). The application of *Teamsters* is considered inappropriate because the decision there was concerned with individual relief after a finding of discrimination. In such a case, only the victims of discrimination are entitled to relief. *Stotts*, as Blackmun noted, was based on classwide race-conscious relief in which there was no need for a finding of discrimination. Neither was there a request for individual relief as there had been in *Teamsters* (Botts 1985: 766; Hernandez 1986: 371). Thus *Stotts* should have been distinguished from *Teamsters*. Others, however, have found no fault with the application of *Teamsters*. *Teamsters* held that "mere membership in the disadvantaged class is insufficient to warrant a seniority award" and thus *Stotts* simply extended this logic to consent decrees (Fallon and Weiler 1984: 9).

Whereas the decision in *Stotts* is fraught with problems, together the majority and dissenting opinions clearly show the compensatory/distributive split in the Court. Chief Justice Burger and Justices White, Rehnquist, Powell, and O'Connor limited court-ordered relief to make-whole relief, which compensates the identified victims of discrimination. They rejected any remedy that does not directly compensate such individuals. Justice Stevens concurred in the judgment but rejected the majority's reading of Title VII. Justices Blackmun, Marshall, and Brennan would not limit remedies to compensation of the identified victims of discrimination. They did not reject the redistributive purpose of the Title, which is the primary justification for affirmative action relief (see Fallon and Weiler, 1985).

The majority opinion in the case seems to be a clear rejection of redistributive values as underlying affirmative action. The majority held that affirmative action is not an appropriate remedy for discrimination since it is not compensatory. Yet the implications are greater than simply a limitation of the remedies available under Title VII. Cox (1985) has noted that this holding could affect the Court's definition of discrimination as well. If affirmative action predicated on racial imbalance is not an appropriate remedy for discrimination, then imbalance may not be an appropriate definition of discrimination (Cox 1985: 816). The next step for the Court might be to conclude that discrimination based on racial imbalances is not discrimination at all. This would effectively limit violations of Title VII to instances of disparate treatment of identified victims and remedies to make-whole relief. The elimination of racial imbalances through a redistribution would therefore no longer be remedial and would be unacceptable under Title VII.

The broader reading of *Stotts* has not stood the test of time. As shown below, the *Stotts* decision was reinterpreted by the Court in two decisions in 1986. A different majority held that *Stotts* was nothing more than a seniority case. Affirmative action, which alters seniority systems on the grounds that the operation of the seniority system perpetuated the effects of past discrimination, is indeed constrained by §703(h). That is, redistributive goals must give way if they conflict with the operation of a bona fide seniority system. This view is still consistent with *Teamsters*. However, the expansive reading of *Stotts*, i.e., that Title VII forbids affirmative action, has not held up. Affirmative action that does not attempt to alter a bona fide seniority is acceptable under Title VII.

Wygant v. Jackson Board of Education

Wygant v. Jackson Board of Education, 476 U.S. 267 (1985), also challenged a seniority based affirmative action issue, and again the Court majority took a more compensatory approach. *Wygant* involved a collective bargaining agreement between the school board and a teacher's union. Attempting to integrate its schools and increase the number of minority teachers on its staff, the school board in 1972 recognized that layoffs would eliminate gains made in increasing minority representation and moved to negotiate an agreement that would protect the new minority employees (476 U.S. at 270–271). The union and the board agreed on a provision that held that if it became necessary to lay off teachers, those with the most seniority would be retained, except at no time would there be a greater percentage of minority employees laid off than the current percentage of minorities employed at the time of the layoff (476 U.S. at 271).

The agreement was litigated in the state courts, which validated it on the grounds that although the board was not guilty of discriminatory hiring practices, the agreement attempted to remedy the effects of societal discrimination (476 U.S. at 270–272). In 1976–1977 and again in 1981–1982, layoffs took place and nonminority teachers with more seniority than minority teachers were laid off. The displaced nonminority teachers filed suit charging that the provision violated the Equal Protection Clause, Title VII, and 42 U.S.C. §1983. On cross motions for summary judgment, the district court dismissed the plaintiff's claims (476 U.S. at 272). Regarding the equal protection challenge (the only claim on which petitioners sought review before the Supreme Court) the district court held that a racial preference did not have to be based on a prior finding of discrimination and was permissible as an attempt to remedy societal discrimination by providing "role models" for minority schoolchildren (476 U.S. at 272). The Sixth Circuit Court of Appeals affirmed (476 U.S. at 273).

Petitioners argued that the preference violated the Equal Protection Clause in two ways: it was based on improper racial comparisons and had no remedial purpose (Brief for Petitioners, No. 84–1340: 9). The Court had never used race as a remedy in the absence of "judicial, administrative, or legislative findings of constitutional or statutory violations, *Fullilove v. Klutznick*, 448 U.S. 448, 497 (1980)" (Brief for Petitioners, No. 84–1340: 9). Also, the respondent's racial preference was not designed to remedy the effects of past discrimination but "was designed to protect minority teachers from lay offs for the stated purpose of achieving 'parity' between the percentages of minorities in the teaching staff and the percentages of minorities in the student body" (Brief for Petitioners, No. 84–1340: 10). Petitioners also suggested that this was an improper basis of comparison. Citing *Hazelwood School District v. U.S.*, 433 U.S. 299 (1977), they argued that the proper comparison was not the percentage of minorities in the student body but the percentage of qualified minority teachers in the relevant labor market (Brief for Petitioners, No. 84–1340: 10). The petitioners also rejected the role model theory on two grounds. The first was that "students do not have a constitutional right to attend a school with a staff of any particular racial composition . . . " (Brief for Petitoner, No.

84–1340: 11). Second, there was no evidence to support the use of a racial preference on the basis of this model and that the lower courts had accepted it without legal or evidentiary support (Brief for Petitioners, No. 84–1340: 11).

The respondents' argument suggested a strong reliance on *Weber*. The Brief emphasized the fact that the school board had voluntarily undertaken its desegregation efforts at a time when neighboring school districts were being ordered by the federal courts to take specific action (Brief for Respondent, No. 84–1340: 16). The Brief also argued that the school board was the proper body to make a determination of past discrimination and had not exceeded its authority to remedy it (Brief for Respondent, No. 84–1340: 16). The Brief also observed that because the layoff provision had been collectively bargained, it was sufficiently tailored to avoid dismantling the board's efforts to desegregate while "providing for the sharing of the burdens of layoffs among minority and nonminority teachers without stigmatizing an individual or group as inherently inferior" (Brief for Respondent, No. 84–1340: 16).

The United States submitted an amicus brief in support of the petitioners. It presented the Reagan administration's stand on affirmative action in its fully developed form. There was no concession that affirmative action should be anything but a compensatory policy that grants make-whole relief to the victims of discrimination. The United States argued that under the Equal Protection Clause a governmental action based on race must be strictly scrutinized, a quota can never be justified even if it is supposedly benign, and the only principle consistent with the Equal Protection Clause is the compensation of the identified victims of discrimination (Brief for the United States, No. 84–1340: 6).

The United States did not support the argument that the layoff provision was justified as a "cure" for the underrepresentation of minority teachers (Brief for the United States, No. 84–1340: 25). The Brief observed that the Fourteenth Amendment proscribed quotas for this purpose. Here, the United States attempted to distinguish this case from *Weber* on three grounds. First, because *Weber* did not involve state action, it did not involve an equal protection challenge. Second, there was no showing that the percentage of minorities in the relevant work force exceeded the percentage on the faculty, i.e., there was no evidence of discrimination. Last, in this case the racial preference resulted in the discharge of innocent nonminority employees (Brief for the United States, No. 84–1340: 25–26, n. 42).

The United States also argued that the provision could not be justified as a means of remedying "societal discrimination" since it granted preferences to all members of a group and not just the victims of discrimination. According to the Brief, "[w]hen benefits do not correspond to any identified prior wrong and are not directed to the victims of such a wrong, they cannot . . . be termed compensatory or remedial" (Brief for the United States, No. 84–1340: 26). In addition, such prefences are not "precisely tailored" to remedy discrimination unless they meet the standards stated above, i.e., they correspond to an actual violation of the law and they compensate identified victims (Brief for the United States, No. 84–1340: 27–28). The United States also suggested that the layoff provision could not be justified as compensation to victims since there had been no finding of discrimination by the board or the courts. Additionally, the United States argued that a school board was not comparable to other legislative bodies since it did not have fact-finding authority (Brief for the United States, No. 84–1340: 29).

Several briefs in support of the respondents deserve attention for their analysis of seniority. Two briefs challenged the petitioners' contention that seniority systems must be based on the last-fired, first-fired rule (Brief for the Mexican American Legal Defense and Education Fund, No. 84–1340: 17; Brief for the National School Board Association, No. 84–1340). Once this premise is rejected, the public employer and unions should be able to establish a seniority system that will serve their purposes without it automatically being labeled a preference (Brief for the Mexican American Legal Defense Fund, No. 84–1340: 17). The Civil Rights Commission and Department of Civil Rights of Michigan also submitted a brief in which they pointed out that the state had similar layoff provisions and a decision to strike them down would affect the entire state government work force and seriously threaten the state's efforts to remedy discrimination (No. 84–1340: 18–19).

One final Brief for the Respondents addressed the role of seniority systems in remedying the effects of past discrimination. The states of Michigan, California, Louisiana, Nebraska, New Mexico, and Wisconsin and the California Fair Employment and Housing Commission presented a two-part argument. First, the Brief argued that "a public employer's layoff plan that retains underrepresented minorities furthers the compelling state interest of eliminating the effects of past discrimination in public employment and providing a model for the community" (Brief for California et al., No. 84–1340: 5). When Congress amended Title VII in 1972 to include state and local government, it did so because of clear evidence that discrimination in public employment was more pervasive than in the private sector and had thus prevented blacks from being represented in the public sector work force (Brief for California et al., No. 84–1340: 5–6). Therefore, a congressional determination of discrimination in employment and a determination of minority underrepresentation should establish a remedial purpose sufficient to satisfy the compelling interest test (Brief for California et al., No. 84–1340: 7).

In addition, when Congress amended Title VII to include state and local governments, it stated that public jobs are highly visible and the failure of such agencies to eliminate "the vestiges of discrimination" would negate the government's claim to represent all people equally (Brief for California et al., No. 84–1340: 7). This being so, the public sector should have the same array of techniques for eliminating the vestiges of discrimination as the private sector (Brief for California et al., No. 84–1340: 7). The Brief also noted, following the Court's decision in *Weber,* that to require a finding of a constitutional or statutory violation by public employers would be contrary to the congressional policy of encouraging voluntary compliance (Brief for California et al., No. 84–1340: 9).

The second part of the argument urged that a collectively bargained layoff provision such as the one in this case was narrowly tailored to its remedial purpose (Brief for California et al., No. 84–1340: 11). First, it contended that the tests for affirmative action plans are functionally equivalent under Title VII and the Equal Protection Clause. In several cases the courts had upheld race-conscious measures under both the Constitution and Title VII (Brief for California et al., 1985: 13–14).[9] It followed, therefore, that the factors established in *Weber* were the appropriate standards for testing the validity of an affirmative action plan.

The Brief then proposed that the layoff plan met these standards because (1) it was "designed to break down old patterns of racial segregation and hierarchy" and to "eliminate conspicuous racial imbalance in traditionally segregated job categories" (443 U.S. at 208–209), (2) the provision did not "unecessarily trammel the interests of the white employees" (443 U.S. at 208) because white and minority employees shared the burden of layoffs since minorities could be laid off if the layoffs do not decrease the proportion of minorities, (3) the provision did not "erode any legitimate interest of white employees" since they do not have a constitutionally protected right or contractual interest in a last-hired, first-fired layoff rule, and (4) the provision was temporary because there was no automatic renewal of the provision at the termination of the agreement (Brief for California et al., No. 84–1340: 15–16).

The argument concluded with the proposition that a collectively bargained agreement such as this should be presumed to be narrowly tailored since it is subject to change at regular intervals and because such agreements are the result of a voluntary, democratic process in which the union is charged with representing the interest of white employees (Brief for California et al., No. 84–1340: 17). Indeed, the Court had already established that "[s]ignificant freedom must be afforded to employers and unions to create differing seniority systems," *California Brewer's Association v. Bryant*, 444 U.S. 598, 608 (1980) (Brief for California et al., No.84–1340: 17).

Justice Powell announced the judgment of the Court reversing the lower courts. He delivered an opinion in which Chief Justice Burger and Justice Rehnquist joined and in which Justice O'Connor joined in part. Justices O'Connor and White wrote separate opinions concurring in the judgment. Justice Marshall, with Justices Brennan and Blackmun joining, filed a dissent. Justice Stevens filed a separate dissent. This line-up of the Court is the same as in *Stotts* except that Justice Stevens reversed his position and joined the dissenters.

Justice Powell began his opinion by holding that any racial classification challenged under the Equal Protection Clause must be subject to strict scrutiny by the Court, including classifications that operate "against a group that historically has not been subject to governmental discrimination", i.e., whites (476 U.S. at 273–274). This followed Powell's opinion in *Bakke*. Under this standard there are two tests: (1) the classification must serve a compelling governmental interest and (2) the means chosen by the state must be "narrowly tailored to the achievement of that goal [*Fullilove v. Klutznick*, 448 U.S. at 480 (1980)]" (476 U.S. at 274).

Powell then addressed the lower court holding that "the Board's interest in providing minority role models . . . as an attempt to alleviate the effects of societal discrimination was sufficiently important to justify the racial classification . . . " (476 U.S. at 274). He rejected this holding. The Court had never held that societal discrimination alone was enough to justify a racial classification, but had required *some showing* of prior discrimination before allowing the use of racial classifications (476 U.S. at 274). Following *Bakke*, societal discrimination was too "amorphous" a basis for imposing a racially based remedy. The concept of societal discrimination is overexpansive and "in the absence of a particularized finding, a court could uphold remedies that are ageless in their reach into the past, and timeless in their ability to affect the future" (476 U.S. at 276). Powell also noted that the Court's decision in *Hazelwood School District v. United States*, 433 U.S. 299 (1977), held that the use of statistical disparities must focus on disparities that demonstrated prior governmental discrimination. The role model theory used by the board and accepted by the lower courts did not meet this criterion. That is, the role model theory depended on disparities between the percentage of minority faculty and the percentage of minority students. *Hazelwood* held that the appropriate comparison was between the percentage of minority faculty and the percentage of qualified minorities in the relevant labor market (476 U.S. at 275). Thus the plan did not serve a compelling interest because it was not remedial or based on a finding of discrimination.

Justice Powell then addressed the question of whether the layoff provision was narrowly tailored (476 U.S. at 280–281). He noted that the Court had accepted the idea that innocent persons may be asked to share some of the burden of remedying past discrimination, but in *Stotts*, the Court had expressed concern over the burden that a preferential layoff scheme imposed on innocent parties (476 U.S. at 280–283). According to Justice Powell: "In cases involving valid *hiring* goals, the burden to be borne by innocent individuals is diffused to a considerable extent among society generally . . . [but] layoffs impose the entire burden of achieving racial equality on particular individuals, often resulting in serious disruption of their lives. This burden is too intrusive" (476 U.S. at 282–283). Powell then held that the intrusiveness of the provision resulted in the plan that was not narrowly tailored since other less intrusive means of remedying discrimination were available. That is, a plan could not be narrowly tailored because of the procedures used to develop it. Since the provision did not satisfy either part of the strict scrutiny analysis, he held that the provision violated the Equal Protection Clause.

Justice O'Connor concurred in the judgment but filed her own opinion in an effort to clarify her reading of Powell's opinion. O'Connor began with a summary of various strict scrutiny tests proposed in the opinion (476 U.S. at 284–285). Justice Powell required the compelling interest narrowly tailored test, but Justices Marshall, Brennan, and Blackmun used the important governmental interest/substantially related test (476 U.S. at 285). O'Connor stated that she preferred Powell's formulation since it was the one "consistently applied . . . in other contexts," but found little substantive difference between the two (476 U.S. at 285). According to O'Connor: "The Court is in agreement that, whatever the formulation employed, remedying past or present racial discrimination by a state actor is a sufficiently weighty state interest to warrant the remedial use of a carefully constructed affirmative action program. *This remedial purpose need not be accompanied by contemporaneous findings of actual discrimination to be accepted as legitimate as long as the public actor has a firm basis for believing that remedial action is required*" [emphasis supplied] (476 U.S. at 286). She emphasized that the Court's decision did not foreclose the possibility that other governmental interests relied on by lower courts could be "sufficiently 'important' or 'compelling' to sustain the use of affirmative action policies" (476 U.S. at 286).

Justice O'Connor then suggested that the true source of disagreement was over the degree to which the means employed fits the ends, but she observed that a plan need not be limited to remedying specific acts of discrimination for it to be narrowly tailored. Also, a public employer could undertake an affirmative action plan that furthered a legitimate remedial purpose and implemented that purpose without unnecessarily and directly trammeling the interests of white employees (476 U.S. at 287).

O'Connor agreed with the Court that remedying "societal" discrimination was not sufficiently compelling to survive strict scrutiny, but argued that to require a contemporaneous finding of discrimination by a court would undermine the emphasis Congress placed on voluntary compliance (476 U.S. at 290–291). However, she believed that the school board's reliance on statistical disparities between the percentage of minority faculty and the percentage of minority students did not provide a firm basis for its action. O'Connor did conclude, however, that the classification might survive strict scrutiny if the statistical disparities had been based on the percentages of minority faculty and the percentage of qualified teachers in the relevant labor market (476 U.S. at 294–295).

Justice Marshall dissented, joined by Justices Brennan and Blackmun (476 U.S. at 294). Marshall believed that the Court had erred in resolving the constitutional issue on a record that all agreed was insufficient. However, because the Court addressed the constitutional issue, he had to express his disagreement with its conclusions (476 U.S. at 295–296). For Marshall, the only question before the Court was whether the Constitution prohibited a union and a school board from developing an unchallenged collective-bargaining agreement that "apportion[ed] layoffs between two racially determined groups as means of preserving the effects of an affirmative action hiring policy" (476 U.S. at 300). Justice Marshall also addressed the appropriate standard of scrutiny to be used (476 U.S. at 301-303). According to Marshall, there was no agreement on that question as Justice O'Connor suggested. He stated that in *Bakke* four justices (Brennan, Marshall, White, and Blackmun) argued that because a racial classification designed to remedy past discrimination did not involve a fundamental right or a suspect classification, the appropriate test was somewhere between strict scutiny and reasonableness. That is, the plan must serve an important governmental interest and be substantially related to those objectives (476 U.S. at 301). Only one other justice (Powell) reached the constitutional issue in *Bakke* and he argued that racial classifications must be based on strict scrutiny. Marshall also noted that in *Fullilove* the Court failed to agree on the appropriate standard of review, with three justices utilizing the intermediate test and three other justices declining to adopt any particular standards (476 U.S. at 302).[10] However, Marshall concluded that the classification would survive either level of scrutiny.

Justice Marshall proposed that there was an important justification for the layoff provision that was not linked to societal discrimination but was based on the district's need to integrate the school system quickly to avoid further violence and a great deal of litigation (476 U.S. at 303). He stated that he "would hold that the state purpose of preserving the integrity of a valid hiring policy—which in turn sought to achieve diversity and stability for the benefit of *all* students—was sufficient, in this case, to satisfy the demands of the Constitution" (476 U.S. at 306).

The Justice then addressed the means chosen to achieve the state purpose. First, the layoff plan was a necessary part of an affirmative action policy since without it the efforts made to recruit minority applicants would be crippled in times of economic downturn (476 U.S. at 307). Second, Justice Powell was incorrect in concluding that the Equal Protection Clause barred race-conscious layoff plans since they involve the hardship of losing a job. He noted that under any layoff plan someone will lose a job and that any per se prohibition against layoff protection must be based on the premise that all layoff plans must follow seniority (476 U.S. at 307–308).

Marshall then cited several cases in which the Court had allowed the alteration of seniority systems to further other policy interests. In *Franks* the Court had displaced innocent workers by granting retroactive seniority (476 U.S. at 308–309). In *Ford Motor Company v. Huffman*, 345 U.S. at 339–340 (1953), the Court allowed collective bargaining agreements to go further than statutes in enhancing the seniority of certain employees to further legitimate interests (476 U.S. at 308). He also cited cases in which the court upheld collective bargaining agreements that granted enhanced seniority to veterans and union chairmen (476 U.S. at 308). Finally, the Justice cited *Weber* in which the Court specifically allowed the departure from the seniority principle to alleviate racial disparity. According to Justice Marshall:

> . . . This plan tampered with the expectations attendant to seniority, and *redistributed* opportunities to achieve an important qualification toward advancement in the company. We upheld the challenged plan under the Civil Rights Act of 1964 because it was designed to "eliminate traditional patterns of racial segregation" in the industry and did not "unnecessarily trammel the interests of white employees." [443 U.S.] at 201, 208. We required no judicial finding or employer admission of past discrimination to justify the interference with the seniority hierarchy for the sake

of the legitimate purposes at stake [emphasis supplied] (476 U.S. at 308–309).

Marshall found that protection from layoff is available as a tool for achieving legitimate interests under the Equal Protection Clause (476 U.S. at 309).

Next, the Justice addressed the question of whether the classification was a permissible means for preserving minority proportions on the teaching staff (476 U.S. at 309). The plan was narrowly tailored because (1) the burden was shared by both groups, (2) it was not used to increase minority representation, (3) the provision did not deprive individuals of an opportunity they deserved (since seniority does not involve merit or achievement), and (4) there were other more intrusive ways of reaching the goal (i.e., layoff by lottery, which would place all employees in equal jeopardy, and a freeze on minority layoffs, which would place the burden on nonminorities only) (476 U.S. at 309–311). Marshall also suggested that the provision was appropriate because it was developed with the interests of all parties being represented and had been renewed by these same interests six times (476 U.S. at 311), i.e., procedurally, the plan was narrowly tailored.

Justice Stevens also dissented on the ground that the board had a valid and legitimate interest in the integration of its faculty. The primary questions before the Court were the means (procedures) used to adopt the provision and the harm to petitioners (476 U.S. at 317–318). Stevens followed Marshall in concluding that the procedure used to adopt the provision was fair. With regard to the harm issue, he observed that any individual who is laid off suffers harm, but in this case the harm was not based on "lack of respect for their race, or on blind habit and stereotype" (476 U.S. at 318). Instead, the harm was a result of economic conditions and the contractual protections that could have been based on grounds other than race, such as protection for gifted young teachers or teachers with special skills (476 U.S. at 318–319).

Analysis. As in *Stotts*, the briefs in *Wygant* show the compensatory/redistributive split between the opponents and advocates of affirmative action. Wygant argued that under the Equal Protection Clause, a compelling interest was present only when the identified victims of discrimination were to be compensated after a Title VII violation. The amicus brief of the United States strongly emphasized this point. The United States also argued against societal discrimination as a basis for a finding of discrimination because it did not correspond to actual violations of Title VII or the Equal Protection Clause and because it did not produce a remedy that compensated the actual victims of discrimination. In other words, the United States rejected voluntary, redistributive affirmative action altogether. The school board, however, argued in support of the layoff plan in terms of *Weber* and the standards for voluntary action laid out in that decision. The respondents and amici in support of respondents argued that the 1972 amendments to Title VII equated the equal protection analysis with the statutory analysis of voluntary action. They argued, following *Weber*, that societal discrimination was enough to support the need for remedial action and the plan itself need only meet the *Weber* criteria.

This emphasis on *Weber* and the voluntary nature of the plan in this case, and in *Stotts*, permitted the respondent and amici to argue for the plan's redistributive purpose instead of arguing for the plan as compensation to identified victims of discrimination. Because the operation of the plan did not assure that identified victims were its beneficiaries (it did not even attempt to achieve this goal), it would not be possible to argue for it on the basis of compensation. Additionally, the "role model" argument is consistent with Dworkin's and Wasserstrom's argument for affirmative action as redistribution. That is, it decreases racial tensions (a goal articulated by the school board) and it permits blacks and whites an opportunity to interact as equals.

The decision in *Wygant* highlights the continuing debate over the appropriate level of review to be utilized when analyzing voluntary affirmative action plans under the Equal Protection Clause. Three justices, Marshall, Blackmun, and Brennan, supported the important interest/substantially related test. Six justices held that the plan must be analyzed in terms of the compelling interest/narrowly tailored test. Five justices, Chief Justice Burger and Justices Powell, Rehnquist, White, and O'Connor, rejected the layoff plan on the grounds it did not survive strict scrutiny. However, Justice Stevens, who also analyzed the plan in terms of strict scrutiny, found that it survived the tests and voted to uphold the plan. Yet, even the five justices who rejected the plan could not agree on what was required under the compelling interest test. Justices Powell and Rehnquist and Chief Justice Burger required a particularized finding of discrimination to support a compelling interest. That is, affirmative action must be compensatory. Justice O'Connor, on the other hand, did not require that such a finding was necessary to support a compelling interest. She felt that the voluntary nature of the plan required only a firm basis to support a remedy for past discrimination. This is reminiscent of Judge Wisdom's "arguable violation" approach from *Weber*. Justice White did not address the question of whether a particularized finding was necessary.

Justices Powell and Rehnquist and Chief Justice Burger's requirement of a finding of discrimination to support an affirmative action remedy such as that undertaken by the school board would clearly eliminate the use of voluntary action. This is also a clear rejection of the redistributive purposes of affirmative action and the concept of societal discrimination as a justification for affirmative action. For them, affirmative action can be make-whole relief only to the identified victims of discrimination. Powell, however, seemed to step back from a complete rejection of affirmative action that did not involve seniority. When he analyzed the plan under the narrowly tailored prong of strict scrutiny, Powell found that the plan was not narrowly tailored because layoffs placed too intrusive a burden on particular individuals. His statement noted, however, that hiring goals that spread the burden among society might be considered narrowly tailored.

Justice O'Connor was less strict than the others in her application of the compelling interest test. She noted that the voluntary nature of the plan was an important element when considering the nature of a finding of discrimination to support a compelling interest test. Congress had strongly urged voluntary compliance and noted that to require a judicial, administrative, or legislative finding of discrimination would effectively eliminate voluntary action as an option. She felt that an employer needed only a firm basis to support a remedy, but that the school board did not have a firm basis to support the action as a remedy because it had utilized the wrong statistical comparison. This suggests that O'Connor would be willing to accept a racial imbalance as a firm basis to support the action. This acceptance on her part of racial imbalance as evidence of discrimination suggests that she did not completely reject the concept of societal discrimination and the redistributive implications of that concept with respect to affirmative action.

Justice Marshall argued for the intermediate-level important interest test, but noted that the rationale was not based on the concept of societal discrimination. Instead, it was based on the school board's need to quickly integrate its schools. This need was based on the racial problems experienced in the schools and the board's desire to avoid the lengthy litigation experienced by its neighbors. These are essentially pragmatic justifications for the policy. Yet this rationale is not void of redistributive elements. Integration is a redistribution of the benefits of diversity and stability to those who had previously been denied these benefits. Marshall also supported the plan because it furthered the unchallenged hiring policy designed to achieve that diversity.[11] The seniority policy prevented the normal operation of the seniority system from eliminating the gains made under the hiring policy, thus perpetuating the past effects of discrimination. However, this type of discrimination was rejected by the Court in *Teamsters*.

Thus *Wygant* produced a majority in support of strict scrutiny of affirmative action. Only three members of that majority, however, limited the definition of a compelling interest to a remedy for a particularized finding of discrimination, i.e., compensation to the identified victims of discrimination. Six members of the Court allowed redistributive values to play a role in their definitions of a compelling interest. Justice O'Connor felt the voluntary nature of the plan allowed the use of racial imbalance as evidence of discrimination and consequent need for a remedy. Justices Marshall, Brennan, and Blackmun supported the plan because it prevented the seniority system from eliminating the redistribution resulting from a valid hiring policy. Justice Stevens found the need to integrate the schools (clearly a form of redistribution) to be a compelling interest to support the plan. Even though these justices utilized somewhat different redistributive values in their analyses, a majority of the Court rejected the idea that affirmative action must be limited to the compensation of specific wronged individuals.

There is another element of *Wygant* that shows the complexity and divisiveness of the affirmative action case law to this point. The Court is clearly divided over the role of voluntary action. Justices Powell and Rehnquist and Chief Justice Burger completely rejected voluntary affirmative action under an equal protection analysis.[12] The other justices, however, accepted voluntary action and allowed it to shape their analyses. O'Connor removed herself from the Powell group's rejection of voluntary action and found that the voluntary nature of the plan was significant to the equal protection analysis' definition of a compelling interest. The Marshall group and Justice Stevens all applied the *Weber* criteria to determine whether the plan was narrowly tailored or substantially related to the purposes of the plan. Thus, whereas the fact that the plan was voluntary did not save it, the voluntary nature of the plan did influence the constitutional analyses of several justices.

Moreover, *Wygant* can be viewed as another seniority case. Since *Teamsters* the trend of the Court has been to protect bona fide seniority systems from modifications intended to provide a remedy for past discrimination. This tough scrutiny of seniority cases is due probably to the explicitness of §703(h) and the fact that seniority relief places a clear burden on particular individuals. Yet the opponents of affirmative action have utilized seniority cases, particularly *Stotts*, to make more general arguments against affirmative action. The Reagan administration hoped to extend these seniority holdings to voluntary and court-ordered goals and quotas as well by using the compensatory arguments limiting relief to the identified victims of discrimination. The Court, however, did not oblige them. Instead, several months following *Wygant*, the Court upheld both court-ordered and voluntary goals that did not alter the operation of a seniority system. Several months after those cases, the Court upheld court-ordered quotas under the Equal Protection Clause. With these cases, a majority of the Court returned to the distributive issues surrounding affirmative action.

GOALS AND QUOTAS RECONSIDERED: RETURN TO REDISTRIBUTIVE AFFIRMATIVE ACTION

After *Wygant*, the Court decided *Local 28 of the Sheet Metal Workers' International Association and Local 28 Joint Apprenticeship Committee v. EEOC, City of New York and New York Department of Human Rights*, 478 U.S. 412 (1985) (hereafter *Sheet Metal Workers*), and *Local Number 93, International Association of Fighterfighters v. City of Cleveland et al.*, 478 U.S. 501 (1985) (hereafter *Vanguards*). These companion cases fall under Title VII. *Sheet Metal Workers* involved a challenge to a court-ordered remedy, and *Vanguards* involved a challenge to a consent decree, both of which involved affirmative action hiring goals.

Sheet Metal Workers v. EEOC

In *Sheet Metal Workers* a district court found the union and the apprenticeship committee in violation of Title VII for discriminating against nonwhite workers in recruitment, selection, training, and admission to the union (478 U.S. at 429). The court ordered the petitioners to cease their discriminatory practices, established a 29% hiring goal to be achieved by July 1981, and ordered petitioners to implement procedures designed to reach this goal under the supervision of a court-appointed administrator (478 U.S. at 431–432). The administrator proposed an affirmative action plan. The district court adopted the plan and the court of appeals affirmed with modifications (478 U.S. at 433). On remand, the district court revised the plan and extended the time required for meeting the hiring goal. The court of appeals again affirmed (478 U.S. at 433).

In 1982 and 1983 the district court found the petitioners guilty of civil contempt for disobeying the court's earlier orders, and imposed a fine to be placed in a special fund used to increase nonwhite membership in its union and apprenticeship program (478 U.S. at 434–435). The court also entered an amended affirmative action plan that established a 29.23% hiring goal to be met by August 1987 (478 U.S. at 437). The court of appeals affirmed all but one of the civil contempt findings and remedies, and upheld the special fund and the hiring goal under Title VII and the Constitution (478 U.S. at 439). The Supreme Court granted certiorari.

The Brief for the Petitioners argued that the contempt remedies and the hiring goal violated both Title VII and the Constitution. The hiring goal (which they called a "quota") violated Title VII on the ground that the Supreme Court had "consistently ruled that make-whole relief under the title may be awarded only to identifiable victims of past discrimination and not to an entire racial or ethnic group" (Brief for Petitioners, Sheet Metal Workers, No. 84–1656: 14). To support this contention, the Brief cited *Albemarle, Griggs*, and *Stotts*, among other cases (Brief for Petitioners, Sheet Metal Workers, No. 84–1656: 17–21). Petitioners also proposed that the legislative history of Title VII did not sanction racial preferences but only provided remedies to the actual victims of discrimination (Brief for Petitioners, Sheet Metal Workers, No. 84–1656: 14). This was supported by a reading of the 1964 debates, including a brief mention of §706(j), which states that employers are not required to grant racial preferences in order to maintain racial balance (Brief for Petitioner, Sheet Metal Workers, No. 84–1656: 21–28). The emphasis, however, was on §706(g), which deals with court-ordered relief. The last sentence of §706(g), which the petitioners interpreted as a prohibition of hiring goals, prohibits a court from ordering the hiring, reinstatement, admission to membership, or payment of backpay to anyone who was not fired or refused employment because of an act of discrimination (Brief for Petitioner, Sheet Metal Workers, No. 84–1656: 24). The petitioners also proposed that the geographical area used to determine the percentage of minorities in the relevant labor market was not equivalent to that used by the union to recruit members, thus the court order violated Title VII (Brief for Petitioners, Sheet Metal Workers, No. 84–1656: 14). This last argument is significant when statistical imbalance is utilized as evidence of discrimination. If the labor markets are not equivalent, the statistics will be of no value in identifying discrimination.

The EEOC was one of the respondents in this case and had been one of the agencies bringing the original suit. The EEOC actually switched sides during the litigation, however, and in its Brief for the Court rejected the court-ordered use of a hiring goal. The explanation for this shift was that whereas the litigation began in the mid-1970s, by the time it reached the Court, the Reagan administration had taken office and had begun its repudiation of affirmative action. The EEOC straightforwardly argued that *Stotts* prohibited the award of race-conscious relief to individuals who were not the identified victims of discrimination (Brief for Respondents, EEOC, No. 84-1656: 10–11). According to the EEOC, *Stotts* not only prohibited seniority relief to nonvictims but also prohibited all Title VII relief awarded to nonvictims (Brief for Respondent, EEOC, No. 84–1656:11).

Another respondent, the City of New York, challenged the arguments against the hiring goals made by the petitioners, the EEOC, and the United States as amicus. First, New York suggested that hiring goals were not prohibited by the part of §706(g), which prohibits the court from ordering the hiring, reinstatement, etc. of any employee who was refused employment, suspended, or discharged for reasons "other than discrimination" (Brief for Respondent, City of New York, No. 84–1656: 33–34). According to New York, this provision applied to "mixed-motive" cases where the employer had a legitimate reason for not employing the individual (Brief for Respondent, City of New York, No. 84–1656: 33).

Second, New York pointed out that the other briefs had completely ignored the legislative history of the 1972 amendments to Title VII (Brief for Respondent, City of New York, No. 84–1656: 36–38). During debates on the bill in the Senate, Sam Ervin proposed two amendments that would have prohibited the use of race-conscious relief by the courts. Both amendments were defeated by a two-thirds majority (Brief for Respondent, City of New York, No. 84–1656: 37–38). The opponents of the amendments argued they would "deprive the courts of the opportunity to order affirmative action under Title VII of the type they [the courts] had sustained in order to correct a history of unjust and illegal discrimination in employment . . . " (Brief for Respondent, City of New York, No. 84–1656: 37). By defeating these amendments, Congress affirmed the broad remedial power of the courts by amending §706(g) to include the power to order "any other equitable relief as the Court deems appropriate" in addition to the enumerated powers (Brief for Respondent, City of New York, No. 84–1656: 38).

The final respondent, the New York State Division of Human Rights, emphasized that making victims whole was not the only purpose of Title VII, a fact recognized by the Court even in the cases involving only make-whole relief. According to this brief:

> The primary purpose of Congress in enacting Title VII in 1964 was prospectively to remedy the economic disadvantages resulting from race discrimination that blacks have suffered in our economy. *Weber* at 202 . . . Congress was not, as petitioners and the Solicitor suggest . . . solely, or even primarily, concerned with the retrospective matter of remedying the injuries suffered by proven victims of discrimination. Thus, much of the Congressional debate emphasized the high rate of unemployment among blacks . . . particularly in comparison with white unemployment

> rates . . . (Brief for Respondents, NY State Division of Human Rights, No. 84–1656: 29–30).

According to the respondent, barring race-conscious relief would frustrate this "primary" purpose of the title (Brief for Respondent, NY State Division of Human Rights, No. 84–1656: 31).

The Division of Human Rights also argued that §706(g) grants the courts broad equitable authority and that the plain language of the section does not bar race-conscious relief that benefits persons who are not proven victims of discrimination (Brief for Respondent, NY State Division of Human Rights, No. 84–1656: 32–33). According to the division, the bar on relief to individuals who were not hired or were fired for reasons other than discrimination did not preclude race-conscious goals for three reasons. First, a goal does not order the admission of an individual but "directs the union to take steps to increase its overall minority membership" (Brief for Respondent, NY State Division of Human Rights, No. 84–1656: 33). Second, this part of §706(g) applies only to individuals actually refused admission. Goals are not dependent on prior rejection. Third, the sentence applies only to individuals denied membership for reasons other than discrimination and has nothing to do with prospective, classwide relief (Brief for Respondent, NY State Division of Human Rights, No. 84–1656: 33–34). The respondents also traced the legislative history of both the 1964 Act and the 1972 amendments and decisions of the Court to support its contention that §706(g) does not bar a court from ordering race-conscious relief (Brief for Respondent, New York Division of Human Rights, No. 84–1656: 34–48).

The New York respondents rejected the compensatory position of the petitioners and the EEOC on the ground that prohibiting race-conscious relief such as hiring goals would frustrate the primary purpose of Title VII: eliminating the economic disparities between blacks and whites by moving them into areas of the work force once closed to them. In the New York brief, the distributive arguments for goals are not as explicit as the compensatory arguments against them, but a distributive principle is clearly the basis of the argument for goals. They make no sense otherwise.

The City of Birmingham presented an amicus brief arguing for the hiring goals. Birmingham primarily addressed the utility of consent decrees with hiring goals.[13] It also argued that race-conscious remedies do not violate the rights of whites when they serve a redistributive purpose:

> Race-conscious remedies of the kind challenged by petitioners are not unfair to members of the historically favored race. Since

> race-conscious remedies are imposed to eradicate the effects of historical discrimination, such remedies will not unfairly injure third parties if the remedies are carefully constructed to integrate the disadvantaged class into the work force to the degree that would have occurred absent discrimination .... When a white employee has benefited by the discrimination, it is not to retard his future promotions to make way for blacks or women as long as the number of blacks or women hired does not exceed the relative number of blacks or women that would have been hired absent discrimination. The impact on the favored class member is the same whether the proven victims receive their rightful place or whether the same number of persons (potential though not proven victims) occupy their places (Brief for City of Birmingham, No. 84–1656: 24).

Here Birmingham has argued that the effect on white employees of both compensation and redistribution are the same. Thus it is useless to argue that redistribution through the use of hiring goals is inappropriate when compensation produces the same effect on white employees.

Justice Brennan, joined by Marshall, Blackmun, and Stevens, announced the judgment of the Court upholding the hiring goal. Justice Powell concurred and Justice O'Connor concurred in part and dissented in part. Justice White dissented and Justice Rehnquist, joined by Chief Justice Burger, dissented separately. The positions of Brennan, Marshall, and Blackmun, White, Rehnquist and Burger were consistent with past decisions. Justice Stevens' position as a swing vote became clear in this case. He had rejected the modification of the consent decree in *Stotts* but had argued that the Title VII holding in that case was only advisory. In *Wygant*, Stevens voted to uphold the seniority plan as a valid means of integrating the school system.

Justice Brennan began by holding that the district court had not erred in its use of statistical evidence in establishing the 29% hiring goal or in finding underutilization of minorities in the apprenticeship program (478 U.S. at 440–441). He also supported the contempt citations (478 U.S. at 442–444). The majority of Brennan's opinion addressed the Title VII challenge. As noted above, the petitioners and the EEOC argued that Title VII relief is limited to actual victims of discrimination. Brennan, and five other members of the Court, explicitly rejected this claim.

Brennan first addressed the last sentence of §706(g), which petitioners argued prohibited relief to nonvictims. According to Brennan, the petitioners' and the solicitor general's reading of the sentence "twists the plain language of the statute" (478 U.S. at 447). He held that the last sentence of §706(g) addressed only the situation where an employer can show that an individual was refused admission or fired for reasons such as the individual was unqualified or other "cause" (478 U.S. at 447). Because the hiring goal did not require the petitioners to admit individuals who had been refused admission for reasons unrelated to discrimination, §706(g) did not prohibit the hiring goals (478 U.S. at 447).

The Justice then held that race-conscious relief under §706(g) furthered the broad purposes of the statute. Those purposes included the congressional objective of opening employment opportunities traditionally closed to minorities and the Court-articulated objective of achieving equality of employment opportunities and removing barriers that had operated in the past to favor whites (478 U.S. at 448). In addition, Congress granted the courts broad power under §706(g) to fashion "the most complete relief possible" to remedy discrimination (478 U.S. at 448).

Justice Brennan then proposed that although in many cases an injunction and make-whole relief might be all that is required, there are some cases when an employer or union "engaged in . . . longstanding or egregious discrimination" and injunctive relief would not suffice as a remedy (478 U.S. at 448). According to Brennan, "[i]n such cases, requiring recalcitrant employers or unions to hire and to admit qualified minorities roughly in proportion to the number of qualified minorities in the work force may be the only effective way to ensure the full enjoyment of rights protected by Title VII" (478 U.S. at 448–449). Similarly, even if such an employer ceased its discriminatory conduct, the employer's reputation could continue to discourage minorities (478 U.S. at 449). Brennan, citing *NAACP v. Allen*, 493 F.2d. 614, 621 (CA5 1974),[14] stated that "affirmative action 'promptly operates to change the outward and visible signs of yesterday's racial distinctions and thus, to provide an impetus to the process of dismantling the barriers . . . erected by past practices'" (478 U.S. at 450).

Next, Justice Brennan considered whether the legislative history of Title VII indicated that Congress intended to limit relief under §706(g) to the victims of discrimination. He concluded that the legislative history relied on in the petitioners' and EEOC briefs against quotas did not mean to preclude hiring goals and similar relief. It was simply to "reassure opponents of the bill that it would not require employers or labor unions to use racial quotas or to grant preferential treatment in order to avoid being charged with unlawful discrimination" (478 U.S. at 453). According to Justice Brennan, these statements and the addition of §706(j) did not suggest that a court may not order preferential treatment when appropriate to remedy past discrimination (478 U.S. at 453). After providing a detailed examination of the 1964 legislative history (478 U.S. at 453–465), Justice Brennan also utilized the legislative history of the 1972 amendments to further support his conclusion. He highlighted the attempts by Ervin to include amendments prohibiting the courts from using race-conscious relief, the recognition by members of Congress that the courts had been using race-conscious remedies, and the addition in §706(g) of the phrase "and any other equitable relief as the court deems appropriate" (478 U.S. at 465–470).

Justice Brennan then discussed the make-whole relief cases such as *Franks*, *Albemarle*, and *Teamsters* cited by the petitioners and the EEOC as evidence that the Court itself had limited relief to the victims of discrimination. Justice Brennan noted that none of the decisions suggested that make-whole relief was the only relief available under Title VII. In fact, *Franks*, *Albemarle*, and *Teamsters* had emphasized that the courts' remedial powers should be exercised both to eradicate the effects of discrimination and to make victims whole (478 U.S. at 471). Brennan also discussed the petitioners' reading of *Stotts*. According to the Justice, the *Stotts* decision was primarily concerned with the authority of the district court to enforce the terms of a consent decree that did not deal with layoffs (478 U.S. at 471-475). The district court was found to have exceeded its authority to enforce the decree because there was no finding that the layoffs were motivated by a discriminatory purpose and §703(h) prevents a court from altering a bona fide seniority system that is not used to discriminate. According to Justice Brennan:

> Relying on *Teamsters*, we observed that a court may abridge a bona fide seniority system in fashioning a Title VII remedy only to make intentional victims of dicrimination whole, that is, a court may award competitive seniority to individuals who show that they have been discriminated against. However, because none of the firefighters protected by the court's order was a proven victim of illegal discrimination, we reasoned that at trial the District Court would have been without authority to override the city's seniority system, and therefore the court could not enter such an order merely to effectuate the purposes of the consent decree (478 U.S. at 472–473).

Justice Brennan continued:

> this limitation on *individual* make-whole relief does not affect a court's authority to order race-conscious affirmative action. The purpose of affirmative action is not to make identified victims whole, but rather to dismantle prior patterns of employment

discrimination and to prevent discrimination in the future (478 U.S. at 474).

Justice Brennan declined to read *Stotts* as a prohibition on race-conscious affirmative action since such a reading would "deprive the courts of an important means of enforcing Title VII's guarantee of equal employment opportunity" (478 U.S. at 474–475).

Brennan then noted that affirmative action would not always be the appropriate relief. A court should carefully consider its use and assure that it is tailored "to fit the nature of the violation it seeks to correct" (478 U.S. at 476). Justice Brennan held that the hiring goals in *Sheet Metal Workers* were appropriate because the court had found the union had a longstanding practice of discrimination and the record was replete with efforts to delay or prevent the affirmative relief (478 U.S. at 476–479). He also noted that the district court had found that the union's reputation had discouraged many minorities from applying and that an injunction would be insufficient. According to Brennan: ". . . because access to admission, membership, training, and employment in the industry had traditionally been obtained through informal contacts with union members, it was necessary for a substantial number of nonwhite workers to become members of the union in order for the effects of discrimination to cease" (478 U.S. at 477). His argument here returns to the standards developed in *Weber* for judging affirmative action. That is, the hiring goals are intended to break down the barriers of "traditionally segregated job categories" (478 U.S. at 477–478).

Justice Brennan also held that the goal was appropriate because it conformed to the other *Weber* standards. The goals were not intended to achieve or maintain a racial balance but served as a "benchmark against which the Court could gauge petitioners' efforts to remedy past discrimination" (478 U.S. at 478). Finally, the goals were temporary and did not unnecessarily trammel the interest of white employees (478 U.S. at 479).

Brennan then quickly dismissed the claim that the goals violated the equal protection component of the Due Process Clause of the Fifth Amendment under the strict scrutiny standard. He noted that there had been a finding of discrimination to justify a remedy as compelling and the remedy was narrowly tailored because it satisfied the *Weber* criteria (478 U.S. at 479–481).

Justice Powell issued a concurrence explaining his belief that the hiring goal did not violate Title VII or the Constitution. With respect to Title VII, Powell agreed that §706(g) did not restrict court-ordered remedies to those benefitting identified victims of discrimination and that the facts of this case supported a hiring goal. He also agreed with Brennan's reading of *Stotts* (478 U.S. at 483–484).

With regard to the equal protection challenge, Powell examined the hiring goals in terms of the four factors used by the court of appeals in *Fullilove* to judge race-conscious hiring remedies: (1) the efficacy of the alternative remedies, (2) the planned duration of the remedy, (3) the relationship between the percentage of minority workers to be employed and the percentage of minority group members in the relevant population or work force, and (4) the availability of waiver provisions if the hiring plan could not be met (478 U.S. at 484–485).[15] Powell believed that the hiring goal met all these requirements because the conduct of the union showed that an injunction would not produce compliance, the goal was temporary, the goal was directly related to the percentage of minorities in the relevant labor market, and the court had showed a willingness to accept legitimate reasons for the employers inability to reach the goal (478 U.S. at 486–488).

Justice O'Connor, as noted, concurred in part and dissented in part. She dissented from the holding that the goal and the fund order did not violate Title VII. She argued that §706 (g) should be read in light of §706(j), which prohibits employers from using racial preferences. She conceded that this might allow a limited use of goals when there is egregious discrimination, but found that in this case the goal actually operated as a rigid quota and thus was prohibited (478 U.S. at 489).

Justice White dissented. He, too, conceded that §706(g) would under some circumstances allow remedies that benefitted nonvictims, but he opposed this goal as a strict quota (478 U.S. at 499). He also would have dismissed the contempt findings (478 U.S. at 499–500). Justice Rehnquist also dissented, joined by Chief Justice Burger. He argued that the goal was impermissable simply because it benefitted nonvictims (478 U.S. at 500).

Analysis. The briefs in this case show the continuing compensatory/redistributive split among the opponents and advocates of affirmative action. The petitioners used a compensatory argument against the hiring goals and the contempt remedies. According to the petitioners the only relief available to a court is make-whole relief to actual victims of discrimination. This argument ignored the 1972 Amendments and cases such as *Weber* and *Fullilove* which approved race-conscious relief that was not make-whole relief.

Justice Brennan's opinion in *Sheet Metal Workers* provides an excellent illustration of a redistributive argument for affirmative action. After quickly disposing of the argument that the last sentence of §706(g) prohibited race-conscious remedies, Brennan argued that race-conscious relief was available under §706(g) because it furthered the broad purposes of the statute. These broad purposes, articulated in the early Title VII cases and *Weber*, are the distributive goals of opening employment opportunities to blacks and removing the barriers that prevent them from acquiring those jobs. The Justice also observed that in egregious cases of discrimination race-conscious remedies are necessary to eliminate "the outward and visible signs of yesterday's racial distinctions, and . . . to provide an impetus to the process of dismantling the barriers . . . erected by past practices" (54 LW at 4991). Here Brennan is making a redistributive argument. Affirmative action is deemed necessary for "breaking down the barriers" faced by minorities to higher paying jobs and toward ensuring compliance with Title VII. Injunctions will not ensure that an employer will comply nor will they help blacks and others move into the positions they would have been in without discrimination. Justice Brennan's argument reflects the arguments made by Dworkin and Wasserstrom. That is, the composition of the work force must be altered if whites are ever to learn how to live and work with blacks and if blacks are ever to believe that they are capable of successfully competing with whites for jobs.

Chief Justice Burger and Justice Rehnquist argued, as they had in other cases, that *Stotts* limited court-ordered relief to the identified victims of discrimination. As noted above, this argument rejects the redistributive characteristics of Title VII and holds that the title is compensatory only in scope. Brennan rejected this reading of *Stotts* and narrowed its holding. He argued that *Stotts* involved only the modification of a consent decree that altered a seniority system, not court-ordered hiring relief. In *Teamsters* the Court had held that a bona fide seniority system could only be altered to provide retroactive seniority to identified victims, but it did not limit a court's ability to order race-conscious relief. His justification for this reading of *Teamsters* and *Stotts* was that it would deprive the courts of the means to assure Title VII's goal of equal opportunity, a pragmatic consideration.

There was one apparent limitation on affirmative action in Justice Brennan's opinion. Affirmative action may not always be an appropriate remedy. The determinant is the extent of the violation. Justice Brennan stated that he supported affirmative action in this case because of the egregiousness of the violation and the union's continued delays in implementing the court's order. If his opinion is read so that only egregious violations of Title VII can justify affirmative action, this is a severe limitation, especially in cases where the violation is based on racial imbalance alone. Egregiousness is not defined. A future Court might require more than racial imbalance as evidence of egregiousness. Yet Justice Brennan suggested that egregious violations are not the only violations that might support affirmative action.

Justices O'Connor and White dissented from Brennan's opinion (O'Connor only in part). Both justices supported the holding that race-conscious remedies were available under §706(g), but both felt that the goal operated as a quota and was therefore prohibited. Justice White argued that requiring the union to achieve the membership goal in times of economic recession was tantamount to a court order to displace nonminority workers with minorities. This would be a violation of the *Weber* standards. O'Connor agreed with this analysis.

Justice O'Connor's and Justice White's concern about goals is related to Justice Brennan's limitation of goals to cases of egregious discrimination. The goals in this case were to be met within a relatively short time period or the union would again be subject to fines. This fact brought White and O'Connor to see the operation of the goals as a quota. It may be this same characteristic of the goals that prompted Justice Brennan to hold that such strict goals be limited to egregious violations. All three Justices suggest that more flexible goals, i.e., goals with waiver provisions and a reasonable time period to reach them without threats by the court, would be acceptable under Title VII in cases where the violations are not as egregious. These flexible goals might be more consistent with the standards established in *Weber*. Flexible goals would be less likely to adversely affect the interests of white employees or bar their advancement.

The equal protection analysis in this case is somewhat more consistent among the Justices than in the previous equal protection cases. Brennan analyzed the case under strict scrutiny to indicate to the Court that affirmative action can survive strict scrutiny. He held that the district court's finding of discrimination met the compelling interest test and the relief was narrowly tailored because the union had continually indicated that it would not cease its discriminatory practices in the face of any other relief, i.e., injunctive or make-whole relief. Justice Powell used the criteria from *Fullilove* and reached the same conclusion. Justices O'Connor, White, and Rehnquist and Chief Justice Burger did not reach the equal protection issue because they believed the case could be disposed of on statutory grounds, a standard of justices who practice judicial restraint.

Sheet Metal Workers is a definite assertion by at least four members of the Court of redistributive arguments for affirmative action. Justices Powell, O'Connor, and White, all moderates, supported the use of affirmative action but only under limited circumstances and when the relief is carefully tailored to achieve a remedial purpose. Only Justice Rehnquist and Chief Justice Burger were completely opposed to affirmative action under Title VII and they were opposed because they accept the compensatory paradigm. The next case, *Firefighters v.*

Cleveland, a companion case to *Sheet Metal Workers*, reveals approximately the same split by the Court.

Local Number 93, International Association of Firefighters v. Cleveland

Local Number 93, International Association of Firefighters v. Cleveland, 478 U.S. 501 (1985) (hereafter *Vanguards*), the companion case to *Sheet Metal Workers*, involved a Title VII challenge by Local Number 93 of the International Association of Firefighters representing the majority of the city's firefighters, to a consent decree between the City of Cleveland and the Vanguards of Cleveland, an organization of black and Hispanic firefighters employed by the city (478 U.S. at 504). In 1980 the Vanguards had filed a complaint on behalf of a class of blacks and Hispanics consisting of firefighters already employed, applicants for employment, and all future black and Hispanic applicants. The complaint charged the city with discrimination on the basis of race in its hiring, promotion, and assignment of firefighters (478 U.S. at 504–505). Having already lost several rounds of litigation involving other city departments, the city entered into negotiations with the Vanguards (478 U.S. at 506). Early in 1981 Local 93 sought to intervene in the negotiations as a party plaintiff and upon approval by the district court submitted a three-page memorandum. In the memorandum, Local 93 did not allege any causes of action or assert any claims against the city or the Vanguards. It simply expressed the view that promotions should be based on competence, not racial quotas, and asserted that Local 93 had an interest in maintaining a well-trained force that required promotions based on competency (478 U.S. at 507). Finally, Local 93 asked for relief in the form of an injunction requiring the city to make promotions on the basis of the examination system already being used (478 U.S. at 507).

Negotiations between the city and the Vanguards continued and a proposed consent decree was submitted to the Court in late 1981 (478 U.S. at 507). The proposal reserved a fixed number of promotions for minorities for several ranks and set promotion goals for three of them. The proposal also required the city to forego the use of seniority points in making promotions. The plan was to be in effect for nine years (478 U.S. at 507–508). Early in 1983 the Court held a hearing to consider the proposed decree, but reserved judgment due to objections by Local 93. The Court required the city and Vanguards to consider the union's objections and told the union to be more specific in its objections (478 U.S. at 508).

In April 1982 the Court held a second hearing and suggested the plan be revamped. The parties then met for 40 hours of negotiation and agreed to a revised decree, but the union rejected the proposal (478 U.S. at 409). In January 1983 the city and Vanguards presented another revised decree to the court, which expanded the number of promotions for all firefighters (with a certain number still reserved for minorities), retained the use of examinations, established goals for promotions to be made on the basis of the examinations restored the use of seniority points, and shortened the life of the decree (478 U.S. at 510). Local 93 was given the opportunity to object to this proposal and did so by maintaining its objection to any racial quotas. The union still failed to state any legal claims against the city or the Vanguards (478 U.S. at 510–511). The district court adopted the consent decree and the court of appeals affirmed. On writ of certiorari, the union challenged the decree as an impermissible remedy under §706(g) (478 U.S. at 514–515).

In its Brief, the petitioner proposed that because the consent decree was adopted over the objection of the union, it was not truly voluntary action but was more like court-ordered relief (Brief for Petitioners, Local Number 93 of the International Association of Firefighters, No. 84–1999: 9–10). Following the arguments made in *Sheet Metal Workers*, the petitioner argued further that court-ordered relief that benefited the nonvictims of discrimination was impermissible under *Stotts* and 706(g). Petitioner also challenged the relief on equal protection and due process grounds (Brief for Petitioner, Local Number 93 No. 84–1999: 10–11). The United States presented an amicus brief in support of the petitioner that made the same arguments.

The City of Cleveland argued that the district court had not abused its discretion in approving the "prospective race-conscious relief" in the consent decree as a means of ameliorating the effects of historical discrimination (Brief for Respondent, City of Cleveland, No. 84–1999: 12). The city argued that whereas the union had a right to be heard, it had no right to veto the settlement. The city also noted that the court had given the union several opportunities to be heard (Brief for Respondent, City of Cleveland, No. 84-1999: 12). With respect to the petitioner's equal protection challenge, the city argued that the Equal Protection Clause did not prohibit race-conscious relief designed to eliminate the effects of discrimination. The city also argued that §706(g) did not limit the court's power to use race-conscious relief (Brief for Respondent, City of Cleveland, No. 84–1999: 12).

The Vanguards argued that the consent decree was a reasonable, voluntarily adopted, race-conscious remedy that was narrowly tailored to achieve the goal of remedying judicial findings of past discrimination and preventing future discrimination (Brief for

Respondent, Vanguards, No. 84-1999: 11). As such, the decree "falls comfortably within the limits of acceptable race-conscious affirmative action set forth in *Bakke, Weber,* and *Fullilove*" (Brief for Respondent, Vanguards, No. 84-1999: 11). The plan should be viewed as voluntary. Since the union had not challenged voluntary plans, the Court should affirm. With regard to the Title VII challenge, the Vanguards argued that even if the decree was considered a court order, Congress has authorized the courts to use numerical remedies to correct past and prevent future discrimination. Because the decree was consistent with the statutory objectives of Title VII, the decision of the court of appeals should be affirmed (Brief for Respondent, Vanguards, No. 84–1999: 11).

The Vanguards discussed the goal of eliminating the effects of discrimination in the work force:

> In many situations, non-victim-specific relief is the only effective vehicle for achieving a work force which bears any reasonable resemblance to the work force which would have existed but for the employer's long-standing discriminatory practices. Where discrimination has created an all-white . . . work force . . . , the significant practical limitations of make-whole remedies often mean that affirmative action is the only way to eliminate this vestige within a reasonable time period. If unlawful discrimination were always detected and remedied immediately, then merely placing identified-proven victims into their rightful place would produce a work force whose racial composition was not affected by discrimination . . . [D]irect victims cannot always be identified . . . (Brief for Respondent, Vanguards, No. 84–1999: 35).

Other briefs addressed this claim regarding the efficacy of affirmative action. The Washington Legal Foundation argued that affirmative action "fails to achieve the leveling and redistributionist effects that are the real goals of its proponents" (Brief for Washington Legal Foundation, No. 84–1999: 18). The Brief argues that economic studies have shown that affirmative action has had little effect on the differences between black and white income levels and that the studies show that income differences are smallest in industries least affected by preferential policies.[16]

On the other hand, California and several other states cited studies that indicated that affirmative action had increased employment opportunities for minorities and "helped break down racial stereotypes, improved employee morale, streamlined personnel policies, and . . . expanded business" (Brief for California et al., No. 84–1999: 26, citing

Heany, "Busing, Timetables, Goals, and Ratios: Touchstones of Equal Opportunity, 69 *Minnesota Law Review*, (1985): 803).

The Affirmative Action Coordinating Center and others also submitted a Brief that also addressed the redistributive goal of affirmative action:

> Where lawful remedies are restricted under Title VII solely to identifiable victims, the result will be token or isolated minority group representation.... Where minority representation is limited to token representation, the likelihood is high the minority worker will be and remain isolated in his/her job ... [increasing the] potential for poor job performance. Thus, group remedies are demonstrably more efficient because they (a) will not leave only token minority representation in a work force, (b) will provide a community context for minority workers to develop within, and lastly, (c) will actually further equal opportunity since they will retard victim isolation which leads to poor performance (Brief for Affirmative Action Coordinating Center, National Conference of Black Lawyers, the National Lawyers Guild, and The Center for Constitutional Rights, No. 84–1999: 41–42).

Justice Brennan delivered the opinion of the Court in which Justices Marshall, Blackmun, Powell, Stevens, and O'Connor joined. Chief Justice Burger and Justices White and Rehnquist dissented. This was essentially the same line-up of the Court as in *Sheet Metal Workers*, with the exception that O'Connor concurred in full.

Whereas the briefs addressed the broad issues of affirmative action, the decision dealt narrowly with the nature of a consent decree. Brennan began by noting that Congress preferred the use of voluntary measures to comply with Title VII and that under *Weber* these measures could include race-conscious relief that benefited individuals who were not the identified victims of discrimination (478 U.S. at 515–518).

Justice Brennan first addressed the question of whether consent decrees were limited by §706(g). The petitioners argued that a consent decree should be treated as a court order and thus be subject to the limitations of that section. He noted that consent decrees were not treated by the courts as judicial orders, but it was nevertheless necessary to determine if Congress intended to include consent decrees in the limits of §706(g) (478 U.S. at 517). He examined the legislative history and held that the purpose of §706(g) was to limit what a court could order employers and unions to do, not to restrict what an employer and union could agree to do voluntarily (478 U.S. at 521).

Brennan further concluded that a consent decree was a voluntary agreement reached through negotiation outside of litigation and thus not subject to the limits of §706(g).

Brennan next considered the question of whether a court could approve a consent decree that provided greater relief than what could be ordered after trial (478 U.S. at 524). He began with the observation that the Court had permitted race-conscious relief orders. He went further and noted that because a consent decree involves both the relevant statute *and* the consent of the parties, it did not follow that a court could not enter a decree which the court could not have ordered after trial (478 U.S. at 525). He stressed, however, that such a decree could be subject to a challenge on the grounds that it conflicted with the relevant statute or constitutional provision (in this case §703 or the Equal Protection Clause) (478 U.S. at 526–528). Finally, the Justice considered whether the decree could be entered over the objection of the union. He concluded that the objections of an intervenor cannot be ignored, but that in this case the union was given all the process it was due (478 U.S. at 528–530).

Justice White's dissent claimed that a court cannot enter a decree that violates Title VII, which this decree did (478 U.S. at 531–532). According to White, the Court had only allowed "racially discriminatory hiring or promotion practices favoring actual or putative employees of a particular race" as a remedy for prior discriminatory practices (478 U.S. at 532). That is, there must be a predicate upon which to base the remedy. If there is no finding of discrimination, a court cannot order race-conscious relief. Therefore, a court cannot enter a consent decree that provides for race-conscious relief without a finding of discrimination. White urged that the Court had concluded that the general rule in Title VII is to enjoin discriminatory practices and to grant relief to the identified victims of discrimination. Race-conscious relief is reserved for egregious cases of discrimination (478 U.S. at 533). According to the Justice, the consent decree exceeded what is permissible under Title VII.

Justice Rehnquist, joined by Chief Justice Burger, dissented and took the majority to task for its reading of *Stotts*. Rehnquist read *Stotts* to hold that only the identified victims of discrimination can be granted seniority relief (478 U.S. at 536).[17] Rehnquist also disputed the majority's interpretation of a consent decree that allowed the lower court to enter a decree with relief broader than would be allowed under the statute (478 U.S. at 536–540). According to the Justice, §706(g) does indeed limit a court to providing relief only to the victims of discrimination. He urged that this reading is supported by both the statute and the legislative history cited in *Stotts* (478 U.S. at 540–544). Rehnquist conceded that an argument from the legislative history could support either his or Justice Brennan's reading of the statute but contended that the words of statute clearly support his reading (478 U.S. at 5447).

Analysis. The briefs in *Vanguards* also highlight the distinction between compensatory and redistributive readings of Title VII and voluntary action under Title VII. The briefs supporting affirmative action emphasized the redistributive justifications of the policy. They argued that compensation is not an effective remedy but that a redistribution is because it integrates the work force. The result is eliminating the effects of discrimination and removing many of the social and psychological barriers placed before minorities. These arguments are the same as those made by Dworkin and Wasserstrom in favor of affirmative action. Eliminating the effects of discrimination means, of course, restructuring the work force so that it more closely approximates the form it would have had absent centuries of discrimination. The union rejected this redistributive aspect of the policy and argued that Title VII is purely compensatory. The argument is that race-conscious relief has no positive value since it does not compensate the identified victims of discrimination and has a negative value of discriminating against nonminorities.

Vanguards is a narrow decision because it does not actually deal with substantive questions but primarily deals with the use of consent decrees. The Court held that consent decrees are a form of voluntary action and are not subject to the limits of §706(g). This suggests that if substantive challenges were made to a consent decree, the Court would apply the *Weber* criteria. It has already been noted above that the decision in *Weber* was based on redistributive arguments for the policy. The dissenters argued that a consent decree is court-ordered relief and, therefore, is subject to the limits of §706(g). Being subject to that section, the dissenters argued the only relief available was injunctive and make-whole relief. This, however, is the argument that was rejected by a majority of the Court in *Sheet Metal Workers*.

Title VII is a statute and its interpretation ultimately raises deeper issues about the nature of statutory interpretation. *Vanguards* is a particularly good illustration, given the different approaches to statutory interpretation taken by Justices Brennan and Rehnquist. Brennan found that the words of §706(g) were not clear on whether the section applied to consent decrees. Section 706(g) states that "[n]o order of the Court shall *require* . . . [emphasis supplied]." Its clearest concern was thus with the coercive aspects of a judicial decree. Consent decrees, however, have both contractual and judicial features and, Brennan found, it is not clear whether the statutory language encompasses them as well. Since the words were unclear, he turned to the legislative history. Brennan read the legislative history as permitting voluntary race-conscious relief. He argued that Congress had emphasized voluntary action in order to limit governmental intrusion into the managerial prerogatives of employers and unions. The section, therefore, should not be read to limit voluntary action.

Again, Justice Brennan employed Dworkin's coherence theory of statutory interpretation, which holds that a statute should be interpreted to further the best political justification of the statute. Brennan argued that one of the broad policy purposes articulated in the legislative history was a preference for voluntary action. When taken in conjunction with the decision in *Weber* in which he held that race-conscious remedies were consistent with Congress' purpose of moving blacks into the "mainstream of society," the consent decree in Vanguards furthers the political purposes of Title VII.

Justice Rehnquist found no ambiguity in the words of §706(g). He argued that the language covered all court orders, consensual or not. He cited legislative history to support the proposition that §706(g) limited consent decrees, but admitted that Justice Brennan's reading of the legislative history was equally supportive of his proposition that consent decrees were not covered by §706(g). This being the case, Rehnquist argued, the words of the statute should control its interpretation. Since he found the words were clear, he argued that the section should be applicable to consent decrees.

There is disagreement among scholars regarding methods of statutory interpretation. The Legal Realists, for example, contend that the meanings of statutes are never plain or unambiguous (Radin 1930: 866–868). Thus Rehnquist's view that the words of Title VII plainly include consent decrees is disingenuous at best. The Realists would agree with Justice Rehnquist, however, that the discovery of intent in the legislative history can produce opposite conclusions. The Realists would also argue against Justice Brennan's arguments regarding the purpose of the statute since purpose can be synonymous with intent, but even if it is not, it is still difficult to identify the purpose of a statute (Radin 1930: 875–876).

Dworkin has noted objections to his theory of interpretation as well (Dworkin 1982: 165). The primary objection is that it is based on natural law and thus inappropriately reads in values (Dworkin 1982: 165). Yet, this objection is exactly why the theory is preferable to a more perfunctory one. Title VII cannot be easily read on a plain meaning theory, or even an intent theory, because of the broad ethical and policy language it contains. Beyond the specification of who was covered by Title VII, Congress simply laid down broad principles to be enforced by the courts. Congress did not even define discrimination in the title. That task was left to the courts. Thus the Court must decide what principles are the basis for Title VII.

All the cases examined to this point show that the Court is deeply troubled by affirmative action. In *Weber* the Court accepted affirmative action on redistributive grounds. In *Stotts* and *Wygant*, the Court appeared to reject affirmative action beyond the compensatory paradigm. In *Sheet Metal Workers* and *Vanguards*, the Court upheld affirmative action, again on redistributive grounds. The best reconciliation of these holdings is that the moderates on the Court, who clearly determine which way the Court will go, place limitations on affirmative action that affects seniority systems. The last cases to be considered do not involve seniority systems and the Court begins to establish some further consistency by upholding the affirmative action plans.

EQUAL PROTECTION AND COMPENSATION : *UNITED STATES V. PARADISE*

United States v. Paradise, 480 U.S. 149 (1986), involved an equal protection challenge to a court-ordered promotion quota that required the Alabama Department of Public Safety (State Troopers) to fill 50% of its promotional openings with qualified blacks. In 1972 the district court made a finding that the State Troopers had systematically excluded blacks from employment for over four decades in violation of the Equal Protection Clause (480 U.S. at 154–155). The court ordered a hiring quota and enjoined the Troopers from engaging in discrimination in its employment practices, including promotions (480 U.S. at 154–155). The district court stated the purpose of the quota:

> The use of quota relief in employment discrimination cases is bottomed on the chancellor's duty to eradicate the continuing effects of past unlawful practices. By mandating the hiring of those who have been the object of discrimination, quota relief promptly operates to change the outward and visible signs of yesterday's racial distinctions and thus, to provide an impetus to the process of dismantling the barriers, psychological or otherwise, erected by past practices. *NAACP v. Allen*, 493 F.2d 614, 621 (1974) (480 U.S. at 156).

By 1979 no blacks had been promoted to the upper ranks of the Trooper force. The court entered a partial consent decree in which the Troopers agreed to develop within a year a procedure for promotion to corporal that would not have an adverse impact on blacks, in conformance with the Uniform Guidelines on Employee Selection Procedures (480 U.S. at 157). The Troopers also agreed to develop similar procedures for the other upper ranks (480 U.S. at 158).

By 1981 no blacks had been promoted. The court entered a second consent decree in which the parties agreed that the Troopers' proposed promotional test would be administered, the results would be reviewed to determine if there was an adverse impact on blacks, the determination of a procedure would be submitted to the court if the parties did not agree, and no promotions would occur until the parties agreed or the court ruled upon the promotion method to be used (480 U.S. at 159–160). Following the examination, only five blacks were listed in the top half of the register. The Troopers declared a need to make up to 10 promotions to corporal and stated their intention to elevate between 16 and 20 more individuals to corporal before making a new list (480 U.S. at 160–161). In 1983 the court held that the test had an adverse impact on blacks and ordered the Troopers to submit a promotional plan that would not adversely affect blacks (480 U.S. at 161–162). The Troopers proposed the promotion of four blacks among the 15 new corporals, but the court rejected the proposal and ordered that for a period of time at least 50% of those promoted to corporal must be black, if enough qualified blacks were available. The court also imposed a 50% promotional quota for the other upper ranks but only if there were qualified black candidates, if a rank were less than 25% black, and if the Troopers had not developed and implemented a promotion plan that did not have an adverse impact on blacks. The Troopers were also required to submit a realistic schedule for the development of nondiscriminatory promotional procedures (480 U.S. at 163–164). The Troopers then promoted eight blacks and eight whites to corporal under the court order and submitted its proposed procedures for promotions to corporal and sergeant. At this point, the court suspended the 50% requirement for those ranks (480 U.S. at 155). The United States appealed on equal protection grounds and the court of appeals affirmed.

The briefs in this case are unusual because the United States (the Petitioners), the Troopers (the Respondent), and the Intervenor-Respondent (a class of whites who had taken the promotional examination declared to have an adverse impact on blacks) all argued against the promotion quota. The EEOC, of course, had shifted its stand on affirmative action under the Reagan administration. The only Brief in support of the quota came from amici. The United States argument can be summarized as follows: (1) A racial classification must be narrowly tailored to achieve a compelling purpose in order to satisfy strict scrutiny, (2) the quota was not narrowly tailored to remedy the Troopers' past discrimination, (3) promotion quotas cannot be used as "catch-up" measures designed to achieve racial balance, and (4) the quota unnecessarily burdened innocent persons and thus failed to satisfy strict scrutiny (Brief for Petitioner, United States, No.

85–999: iii). The Brief also argued that relief should be available only to the actual victims of discrimination (Brief for Petitioner, United States, No. 85–999: 15).

The United States argued that the district court had not ordered quotas for the purpose of remedying discrimination. According to the United States the first purpose was to "terrorize" the Troopers into compliance with its orders (Brief for Petitioner, United States, No. 85–999: 16). Another purpose was that of attaining numerical balance at each level of the Troopers (Brief for Petitioner, United States, No. 85–999: 16). According to the United States: "The one-for-one quota may have . . . been designed as a 'catch-up' quota that aimed, not simply to remedy the effects of the [Troopers'] past discrimination, but to help bring about the 'racial mix' that theoretically would have existed in the upper ranks of the [Troopers] if it had never discriminated in hiring at all" (Brief for Petitioner, United States, No. 85–999: 30). In this instance, the United States deviated from its compensatory arguments long enough to challenge the redistributive arguments for the policy. Arguing against this redistributive purpose for quotas, the United States began with the proposition that a desire to achieve racial balance is unacceptable under the Constitution. Here the United States cited Justice Powell's opinion in *Bakke* where he stated that "[p]referring members of any one group for no other reason than race or ethnic origin is discrimination for its own sake . . . 438 U.S. at 307" (Brief for Petitioner, United States, No. 85–999: 31). The United States accepted the proposition that eliminating the effects of discrimination was a proper remedial purpose under the Equal Protection Clause, but argued that "the elimination of such effects could not be equated with the attainment of racial balance" (Brief for Petitioner, United States, No. 85–999: 31).

In support of this claim, the United States cited *Sheet Metal Workers* for the holding that "race-conscious affirmative measures [should] not be invoked simply to create a racially balanced work force." Goals are intended to eliminate the effects of past discrimination (meaning the "lingering effects" such as reputation and the "old boy" network) or to serve as a benchmark for measuring efforts by the employer to eliminate discrimination (Brief for Petitioners, United States, No. 85–999: 31–33). The United States also rejected the use of quotas on the ground that they were not narrowly tailored because they placed an unnecessarily heavy burden on white employees. The quota diminished their prospects for advancement through the ranks. According to the United States, the promotion quota placed the same burdens on the whites as the layoff provisions in *Stotts* and *Wygant* since such burdens affected particular individuals with valid expectations and not society generally.

The Troopers (as respondent) made the same arguments as the United States against the quotas (Brief for Respondent, Troopers, No. 85–999). The Troopers also argued that the quota was designed only to eliminate the racial imbalances in the Troopers' ranks, not to remedy discrimination (Brief for Respondent, Troopers, No. 85–999: 23). To support this, the Troopers cited both the district court's decision and that of the court of appeals to the effect that the quota was intended to eliminate a "manifest racial imbalance" (Brief for Respondents, Troopers, No. 85–999: 23). The Troopers also observed that the courts had never made a finding of discrimination in promotions, only in hiring.

The Southern Poverty Law Center submitted a Brief in support of the promotional quotas. The Brief began by claiming that remedying the effects of the Troopers' egregious discrimination by enforcing the consent decrees was a compelling governmental interest (Brief for Southern Poverty Law Center, No. 85–999: 19). The Brief noted the Troopers' continued reluctance to develop the nondiscriminatory promotion procedures required by the consent decree. It also challenged the Troopers' claim that there had been no finding of discrimination in promotions. According to the Brief: " . . . facing new allegations of promotion discrimination, the [Troopers] chose to settle rather than litigate, entering into a consent decree mandating promotions with 'little or no adverse impact upon blacks . . . .' Told that it must finally live up to its obligations, the [Troopers] now [resist] enforcement by claiming that there was, after all, no judicial finding of promotion discrimination" (Brief for Southern Poverty Law Center, No. 85–999: 24–15). The Brief also supported the quotas because they were not imposed to achieve a racial balance but to faciliate the enforcement of the consent decree (Brief for Southern Poverty Law Center, No. 85–999: 25).

In addressing the question of whether the remedy was narrowly tailored, the Southern Poverty Law Center Brief analyzed the quota in terms of Justice Powell's criteria set forth in *Fullilove* and *Sheet Metal Workers*: (1) the necessity of the relief, (2) the flexibility and duration of the relief, (3) the relationship of any numerical goals to the relevant labor market, and (4) the impact of the relief on third parties (Brief for Southern Poverty Law Center, No. 85–999: 26). The Brief once again pointed to the Troopers' longstanding exclusion of blacks and recalcitrance in meeting the requirements of the consent decree in support of the necessity of the quotas (Brief for Southern Poverty Law Center, No. 85–999: 28–32). The quotas were temporary and in fact had already been eliminated with respect to promotions to corporal and sergeant following the Troopers submission of acceptable promotional procedures (Brief for Southern Poverty Law Center, No. 85–999: 34). The relationship of the quota to the relevant labor market was also appropriate because it was only to be applied until the work force was 25% black, the percentage of blacks in the Alabama population. According to the Brief, it was understood that it is often necessary to hire or promote at a higher rate than the established goal if it is to be achieved in the "foreseeable future" (Brief for Southern Poverty Law Center, No. 85–999: 35–36). The quota also had a limited impact on whites because it did not require the hiring of unqualified blacks. The quota applied only if there were qualified blacks and if the Troopers failed to adopt an acceptable procedure. Also, the quota did not result in the loss of future employment opportunity or the loss of a job. Moreover, it did not reduce the employees' expectations based on seniority since seniority was not a significant factor in the Troopers' promotional policies (Brief for Southern Poverty Law Center, No. 85–999: 38–41).

Justice Brennan announced the judgment of the Court upholding the promotion quota. Justices Marshall, Blackmun, and Powell joined in his opinion. Powell also wrote a concurring opinion. Justice Stevens joined in the judgment and wrote a concurrence to address Justice O'Connor's dissent. Besides O'Connor, Chief Justice Rehnquist and Justice Scalia dissented. Justice White wrote a separate dissent. White and now Rehnquist were steadfast in their opposition to affirmative action. Scalia's vote was unsurprising as his opposition to affirmative action was known at the time of his appointment. Justices Stevens and Powell were consistent with their votes in *Sheet Metal Workers* and *Vanguards*. O'Connor's dissent placed her in a clear swing position since she had voted against affirmative action in *Stotts* and *Wygant*, but had supported (at least partially) the majorities in *Sheet Metal Workers* and *Vanguards*.

Brennan first noted that the Court had not reached a consensus on the level of analysis when reviewing such classifications under the Equal Protection Clause, but that it was not necessary to deal with that question since the quota survived even the compelling interest/narrowly tailored standard of strict scrutiny (480 U.S. at 166–170). There is a compelling governmental interest in remedying past discrimination. In the Justice's words "... the pervasive, systematic, and obstinate discriminatory conduct of the [Troopers] created a profound need and a firm justification for the race-conscious relief ordered by the District Court" (480 U.S. at 167). Brennan rejected the claim that there had been no finding of discrimination in promotions because the record showed that the district court had been concerned with promotions throughout the proceedings (480 U.S. at 168). In addition, the quota was further supported by the societal interest in compliance with the judgments of federal courts (480 U.S. at 170).

Brennan then addressed the question of whether the relief was narrowly tailored. He utilized Justice Powell's analysis from *Sheet Metal Workers* which examined the necessity of the relief, the efficacy of alternative remedies, availability of waiver provisions, the relationship of the numerical goals to the relevant labor market, and the impact of relief on the rights of third parties (480 U.S. at 171). With regard to the necessity of the relief, Justice Brennan examined the purposes of the order: to eliminate the Troopers' long-standing discrimination, to ensure quick compliance with the two consent decrees, and "to eliminate as far as possible the effects of the [Troopers'] delay in producing . . . a [promotion] procedure" (480 U.S. at 171–172). Faced with Troopers' need to make 15 promotions to corporal, the district court determined that these purposes could be served only by the promotion of eight blacks and eight whites.

Brennan held that the proposal of the Troopers to promote four blacks and 11 whites was inadequate. It ignored concerns about the development of an acceptable promotion procedure (which the Troopers had failed to implement three years after the consent decree was entered) and "ignored the injury to the plaintiff class that resulted from its delay in complying with the 1972 order and the 1979 and 1981 decrees (480 U.S. at 172–173). According to Justice Brennan:

> As the Eleventh Circuit pointed out, no blacks were promoted between 1972 and 1979; the four blacks promoted in 1979 were elevated pursuant to the 1979 Decree and not as a result of the voluntary action of the [Troopers]; and finally, the whites promoted *since 1972* "were the specific beneficiaries of an official policy which systematically excluded all blacks." 767 F.2d. at 1533, n. 16. To permit ad hoc decisionmaking to continue and allow only four of fifteen slots to be filled by blacks would have denied relief to black troopers who had irretrievably lost promotion opportunities [note omitted] [emphasis in original] (480 U.S. at 173–174).

This is certainly the use of compensation as a justification for the quota relief. It was, however, not the only justification used and the Justice clearly noted in a footnote that none of the goals cited were permitted to dominate at the expense of the others in the district court's decision (480 U.S. at 174, n. 22).

Justice Brennan rejected the proposal made by the United States that the court could have imposed heavy fines to induce compliance. The Troopers had already been required to pay the plaintiff's attorney fees and costs, but that requirement had not prevented the delays experienced. Furthermore, a fine would not compensate those blacks for the delays (480 U.S. at 174–175). Brennan also held that the quota relief was flexible, temporary, and waivable (480 U.S. at 178). The relief is required only until the Troopers developed an acceptable procedure, which had in fact occurred. Because of the absence of qualified blacks for promotion to the upper ranks, the Troopers had been allowed to promote only whites. Finally, since the Troopers now appeared willing to implement procedures without an adverse impact, the relief proved effective as well (480 U.S. at 480 U.S. at 178–179).

Brennan then examined the relationship between the numerical relief and the relevant labor market (480 U.S. at 179–184). The United States argued that the 50% requirement was arbitrary since it had no relationship to the 25% labor pool in the State of Alabama. The Justice noted that the 50% figure was not the goal (the goal was 25%), but rather it represented the speed at which the 25% goal was to be achieved. According to Brennan:

> To achieve the goal of 25% black representation in the upper ranks, the court was not limited to ordering the promotion of only 25% blacks at any one time. Some promptness in the administration of relief was plainly justified in this case, and use of deadlines or end-dates had proven ineffective. In those circumstances, the use of a temporary requirement of 50% minority promotions, which, like the end date in *Sheet Metal Workers*, was crafted and applied flexibly, was constitutionally permissible (480 U.S. at 180).

He emphasized that the quota had taken into account two important purposes, the ending of the continuous delays by the Troopers and the compensation necessary because of these delays.

Justice Brennan found that the quota did not impose an unacceptable burden on white Troopers. He gave three reasons: (1) the relief was temporary and limited, (2) the quota did not require the lay off or discharge of whites (thus distinguishing the case from *Wygant*), and (3) the quota did not require the hiring of unqualified individuals (480 U.S. at 182–183). He closed the opinion with a note that a district court had broad, flexible powers to remedy past discrimination and that such remedies need not be limited to "the least restrictive means of implementation" (480 U.S. at 183–185). Whereas the relief available is limited by the burdens on the rights of the white employees, the district court had properly balanced the "individual and collective" interests involved (480 U.S. at 185–186).

Justice Powell's concurrence agreed with Brennan's analysis of the quota relief. However, Powell stated that he believed the Court had definitely decided that racial classification required strict scrutiny

(480 U.S. at 187, n. 2). He also supported the quota primarily on the ground that it served as a benchmark for judging the progress toward remedying past discrimination (480 U.S. at 186).

Justice Stevens also concurred in the Court's opinion. He wrote primarily to address Justice O'Connor's dissent in which she argued that the Court must consider whether the lower court's order was supported by a compelling governmental interest. Stevens held that O'Connor's theory was novel since that standard was usually applied to state legislative or executive action, not to actions of the federal courts (480 U.S. at 190, n.1). In any event, Stevens felt the district court had a compelling interest in remedying past discrimination (480 U.S. at 189–196).

Justice O'Connor, joined by Chief Justice Rehnquist and Justice Scalia (who had just taken Rehnquist's old seat), dissented. O'Connor believed that the court's order must serve a compelling governmental interest. She agreed that the court did have such an interest, but could not conclude that the quota was narrowly tailored (480 U.S. at 196–197). Her opinion suggested that there was only one purpose for the quota, achieving compliance with the consent decree requirement to provide a promotion procedure that had no adverse impact, but that the quota's operation did not serve that purpose and no other alternatives were consider by the district court (480 U.S. at 197–198).

Analysis. The briefs in *Paradise* show a somewhat different approach by the opponents of affirmative action. In addition to arguing that only the identified victims of discrimination should be granted relief, they also argued that the redistributive purpose of affirmative action violated the Equal Protection Clause. They argued that it is inappropriate under equal protection to equate remedying discrimination with achieving a racial balance. This obviously cuts at the heart of the redistributive argument. Yet the advocates of the quota did not emphasize the redistributive arguments as had been done in *Sheet Metal Workers*. Instead, they stressed the egregiousness of the discrimination and the fact that the Troopers had shown a great reluctance to conform with the consent decree. Therefore, there was a compelling interest to support the quota.

This change of tactics on both sides is an interesting phenomenon. The opponents had just suffered two significant defeats with *Sheet Metal Workers* and *Vanguards*, in which the Court upheld the use of affirmative action under Title VII. The shift was essential. They could not base their argument only on the grounds that race-conscious remedies were unavailable. Therefore, they argued that racial balance was not equal to remedying discrimination (the compelling interest). The advocates, on the other hand, had their arguments supported in *Sheet Metal Workers* and *Vanguards*, so they stressed the equal protection analysis. That is, they did not have to argue for the redistributive purpose of affirmative action, they only had to argue that there was a compelling interest and the quota was narrowly tailored. The Troopers' obvious recalcitrance made this a relatively easy argument to support.

Justice Brennan's opinion also showed a shift in emphasis. First, he argued that there was still a dispute over the correct level of analysis for benign classifications, but he chose to analyze the quota using strict scrutiny. The assertion that the level of analysis was still in dispute is true to the extent that at least three Justices supported an intermediate level of review. However, in Wygant, a majority of the Court had argued that strict scrutiny was appropriate. Justice Brennan's use of strict scrutiny may have encouraged Powell and Stevens to join his opinion. The case against the Troopers was strong enough to support a compelling interest and both Stevens and Powell had supported strict scrutiny of affirmative action.

Justice Brennan also altered his emphasis in holding that the quota could be considered narrowly tailored because it compensated the black Troopers who had suffered discrimination in promotions after the entry of the consent decree. This approach meant to defuse the opponents' arguments that the quota did not operate to remedy past discrimination but was redistributive. Indeed, Brennan's opinion does not depend on redistributive arguments at all. By stressing the compensatory aspects, he was able to weaken the dissenters' argument that the quota was not remedial. His avoidance of redistributive arguments in *Paradise* might also be due to the fact that the quota could be upheld without resorting to them.

There is another nonpolitical reason why Justice Brennan might have avoided redistributive arguments. When a challenge is made to court-ordered affirmative action, the finding of discrimination may be based on racial imbalance and not on particular acts. If the finding is based on an imbalance, the remedy that follows will generally be directed at eliminating that imbalance through a redistribution. Thus there is a direct relationship between the violation and the remedy. When the affirmative action is voluntary, it is generally based on racial imbalances in the employer's work force and again the remedy is directly related to the perceived violation. The quota in *Paradise* was not directly related to the composition of the work force and could not be upheld simply as a means of eliminating racial imbalance. Instead, the quota was justified on the grounds that it was the only means shown to be effective in producing rapid compliance with the consent decree.

This case is interesting because it is the first instance where the United States and others directly challenged the redistributive goals of affirmative action. Yet, instead of upholding the quota on redistributive grounds, Justice Brennan held that the quota had a compensatory purpose. This may have been for political purposes. It is more likely, however, that in this case the remedy need only be justified on compensatory grounds so Justice Brennan felt no need to go any further. Yet *Paradise* does not suggest in any terms that the Court has stepped back from using redistributive justifications for affirmative action.

AFFIRMATIVE ACTION FOR WOMEN: *JOHNSON V. TRANSPORTATION AGENCY*

Johnson v. Transportation Agency, Santa Clara County, California, 107 S.Ct. 1442 (1987), raises the question of affirmative action for women. In 1978 the Transportation Agency adopted an affirmative action plan for the hiring and promotion of minorities and women. The plan provided that in making promotions to traditionally segregated job classifications in which women were underrepresented, the agency could consider the sex of a qualified applicant (107 S.Ct. at 1442, 1444). The agency had determined that whereas women made up 36.4% of the local labor market, they composed only 22.4% of the agency's work force. In addition, these women were primarily concentrated in job categories traditionally held by women and no women held positions in the category involved in this case (Skilled Craft Worker)(107 S.Ct. at 1446).

The agency stated that its plan was intended to achieve "a statistically measurable yearly improvement in hiring, training, and promotion of minorities and women in job classifications where they were underrepresented" and that its long-term goal (which served as a benchmark by which to evaluate progress) was to attain a work force whose composition reflected the proportion of women and minorities in the local labor market (107 S.Ct. at 1447). Recognizing that the long-term goal would be affected by other short-term factors, the plan provided that short-term goals would be established and annually adjusted to serve as a guide for actual employment decisions. The plan did not set aside a specific number of positions for women or minorities but allowed the consideration of race and gender as a factor when evaluating candidates (107 S.Ct. at 1447).

In 1979 the agency announced an opening for a road dispatcher. Nine of 12 applicants were deemed qualified. Seven applicants scored above 70 on an interview and were certified as eligible. Two of these candidates were Johnson, the petitioner, and Diane Joyce (who was ultimately offered the job). Both Johnson and Joyce were considered well qualified for the job. After a second interview, the panel recommended that Johnson be promoted (107 S.Ct. at 1447–1448). In the meantime, Joyce went to the County Affirmative Action Office. She feared her application might not be given disinterested review because of differences and difficulties she had experienced with two of the interview panel members. The Affirmative Action Co-ordinator recommended to the director of the agency that Joyce be promoted since no woman had ever held the road dispatcher position. The director was authorized to choose any of the seven eligible candidates and based on the information from the second interview and the Affirmative Action Co-ordinator, he decided to promote Joyce (107 S.Ct. at 1448). Johnson filed a complaint with the EEOC and received a right-to-sue letter. The district court found the agency's affirmative action plan invalid under Title VII on the ground that it did not satisfy the *Weber* criteria of being temporary. The circuit court reversed.

The petitioner argued that a voluntary affirmative plan undertaken by a public employer must comply with the Equal Protection Clause, i.e., serve the compelling governmental interest of remedying past discrimination and be narrowly tailored (Brief for Petitioner, No. 85–1129: 16). According to the petitioner, the agency's affirmative action plan did not serve a remedial purpose. It was not based on a finding of past discrimination but purely on a "naked" statistical disparity, which is not sufficent evidence to justify the conclusion that there has been prior discrimination (Brief for Petitioner, No. 85–1129: 24). The petitioner also argued that the affirmative action plan was not narrowly tailored to avoid unnecessarily curtailing Johnson's individual rights (Brief for Petitioner, No. 85–1129: 17). According to the petitioner, the preferences granted under the plan operated effectively to bar Johnson from advancement when competing against minorities or women.[18]

Finally, the petitioner argued that the plan did not satisfy the Title VII requirements established in *Weber* (Brief for Petitioner, No. 85–1129: 17). These standards hold that the plan must (1) operate to open traditionally segregated job categories, (2) achieve a racial balance, not maintain one, (3) not bar the advancement of white employees, and (4) be temporary. These criteria, although articulated in the context of voluntary action, have been consistently applied to both voluntary and court-ordered affirmative action. According to the petitioner, the plan had no other remedial purpose but "to correct societal attitudes" (as opposed to breaking down patterns of segregation and hierarchy). It also barred the petitioner's advancement when competing against minorities and women, trammeled the petitioner's rights by denying him the promotion, and lacked an end date, i.e., was not temporary (Brief for Petitioner, No. 85–1129: 17–18).

The agency based its case on Title VII and *Weber*. First, however, the agency drew from Justice O'Connor's *Wygant* opinion to address the question of support for the use of voluntary race-conscious action. In *Wygant*, O'Connor had argued that voluntary race-conscious relief required a firm evidentiary basis and that statistical disparities would provide such a firm basis (Brief for Respondent, No. 85–1229: 16). According to the agency, the firm basis for gender conscious action was the agency's awareness of statistical disparities which showed that in several job categories women were "severely" underrepresented when compared to the local labor market and the agency was aware of its own "restrictive" employment practices that contributed to the underrepresentation of women (Brief for Respondent, No. 85–1129: 11–12).[19] Therefore, the agency had sufficient grounds for taking gender-conscious action. Also, the agency indicated that to require more than a firm basis to support gender conscious action would defeat Title VII's preference for voluntary compliance.

The agency also contended that the affirmative action plan was consistent with the standards established in *Weber* for the following reasons. First, the plan was flexible and did not impose fixed numerical preferences. The most specific affirmative action measure required by the plan was that "special consideration" be given to protected group members in underrepresented job categories (Brief for Respondent, No. 85–1229: 28). The plan had no fixed ratios and so every person had an opportunity to compete for every position. As such, this plan was similar in approach to the Harvard Plan discussed in *Bakke* (Brief for Respondent, No. 85–1129: 29).

Second, the plan was temporary despite the lack of an end date. Testimony indicated that affirmative action would be taken in those categories that were underrepresented. Once the goals were met in each category, affirmative action would cease. Similarly, the plan was meant to attain these goals, not maintain them. (Brief for Respondent, No. 85–1129: 30–31). Last, the plan did not trammel white male employees' rights because it did not require the layoff of any employees, employees did not lose seniority or salary, and employees were not foreclosed from future opportunities (Brief for Respondent, No. 85–1129: 34–37).

The United States filed an amicus brief in support of Johnson. Although the United States argued on the basis of Title VII, instead of using the standards articulated by the Court in *Weber*, they transformed these standards through their own interpretation of subsequent cases. That is, the U.S. argued that affirmative action plans must serve a remedial purpose and be narrowly tailored to further this purpose without adversely affecting innocent persons whether challenged under Title VII or the Equal Protection Clause (Brief for United States, No. 85–1129: 12–13).

The United States argued that statistical disparities attributed to societal discrimination cannot support remedial action because achieving statistical balance is nothing more than "untrammeled social engineering" (Brief for United States, No. 85–1129: 14). Since the stated purpose of the affirmative action plan was to achieve numerical balance and not to remedy past discrimination, it cannot be justified on the grounds that it served a remedial purpose (Brief for United States, No. 85–1129: 25). The United States also argued that the plan was not narrowly tailored because it was not temporary. Furthermore, it limited Johnson's right to a promotion that he legitimately expected (Brief for United States, No. 85–1129: 27–28).

The National League of Cities, National Association of Counties, U.S. Conference of Mayors, and the International City Management Association submitted an amicus brief in support of the respondent. The Brief supported the use of statistical disparities as a basis for remedial action on three grounds. First, statistical evidence is "probative of past discrimination" (Brief for National League of Cities et al., No. 85–1129: 16–17). The Brief cited *Teamsters*, 431 U.S. 324, 340 n.20 (1977), *Hazelwood School District v. United States*, 433 U.S. 299, 307–308 (1977) and other cases in which the Court held that statistical imbalance "is often a tell-tale sign of purposeful discrimination." Longstanding gross disparity between the composition of a work force and the general population may be significant (Brief for National League of Cities et al., No. 85–1129: 16–17). Thus the fact that there were no women in the skilled crafts positions provided a firm basis for taking remedial action.

Second, the Court had indicated that affirmative action may be justified on the basis of statistical evidence (Brief for National League of Cities et al., No. 85–1129: 18). The Brief cited *Weber*, *Fullilove*, and *Wygant* in support of this proposition. With respect to *Wygant*, the Brief quoted Justice O'Connor:

> "demonstrable evidence of a disparity between the percentage of qualified [minorities in the employer's work force] and the percentage of minorities in the relevant labor pool sufficient to support a prima facie Title VII pattern or practice claim by minority" applicants would provide a "compelling basis for . . . conclud[ing] that implementation of a voluntary affirmative action plan is appropriate to remedy apparent prior employment discrimination" (slip. op. 9) (Brief for National League of Cities et al., No. 85–1129: 18–19).

Last, employers would be placed in an intolerable position if they could not take remedial action on the basis of evidence that would be likely to expose them to liability to minorities. This possibility would frustrate the achievement of Title VII's goals (Brief for National League of Cities et al., No. 85–1129: 19–20).

Another amicus brief filed by California, the California Fair Employment and Housing Commission, the States of Idaho, Louisiana, Maryland, Michigan, Nebraska, New York, Oregon, and Wisconsin, and the Pennsylvania Human Relations Commission cited cases from all but one circuit court of appeals that had held that employers need not prove that it had engaged in discrimination in order to show that an affirmative action plan satisfied the remedial purpose of Title VII (Brief for California et al., No. 85–1129: 14). Most of the amici in support of the respondent also argued that the agency's affirmative action plan met the standards for voluntary affirmative action under *Weber*. That is, they all argued that the plan was remedial, temporary, flexible, and did not bar the advancement of non-minorities.

Justice Brennan delivered the opinion of the Court and was joined by Justices Marshall, Blackmun, Powell, and Stevens. Brennan began the opinion by noting that the petitioner carries the burden of establishing the invalidity of an affirmative action plan (107 S.Ct. at 1449). He held that the legality of the plan must be measured in terms of *Weber* (107 S.Ct. at 1449). According to Brennan, when Congress included public employers in Title VII in 1972, Congress expressly indicated that the Title VII principles be applied to governmental and private employers in the same way. According to the Justice: "The fact that a public employer must also satisfy the Constitution does not negate the fact that the statutory prohibition with which the employer must contend was not intended to extend as far as that of the Constitution" (107 S.Ct. at 1449, n. 6).

Brennan restated the holding in *Weber* that held that voluntary race-conscious action was permissible when it was designed to "break down old patterns of racial segregation and hierarchy," did not "unnecessarily trammel the interests of the white employees," did not "create an absolute bar to the advancement of white employees," and was a temporary measure, not designed to maintain a racial balance, but to "eliminate a manifest racial imbalance" (107 S.Ct. at 1450–1451). In addition, as Blackmun noted in *Weber*, an employer can justify its plan without "point[ing] out its own prior discriminatory practices or even the evidence of an 'arguable violation' on its part" (107 S.Ct. at 1451). Brennan stated that this case must be examined in terms of whether the plan was prompted by concerns similar to those in *Weber* and whether the effect of the plan on males and nonminorities was comparable to the effect in that case (107 S.Ct. at 1451).

The first issue, according to Brennan, was whether considering the sex of applicants for skilled craft positions was justified by a " 'manifest racial imbalance' that reflected underrepresentation of women in 'traditionally segregated job categories' " (107 S.Ct. at 1452). He first observed that when dealing with positions that require special training, the comparison should be with those persons in the labor force who possess the relevant qualifications (107 S.Ct. at 1452). On the other hand, the imbalance need not be sufficient to support a prima facie case against the employer because Title VII does not place the same restraints on a voluntarily adopted affirmative action plan as does the Constitution. Also, application of such a standard would be inconsistent with *Weber's* focus on statistical imbalance (107 S.Ct. at 1452–1453). That is, when a job category requires special training, the relevant labor market may have the same imbalance as the work force. This would prohibit an employer from taking race-conscious action. Therefore, an employer who provides training for such positions can make the comparison with the local labor market in general (107 S.Ct. at 1452, n. 10).

When examining the agency's plan, Brennan found that the agency's long-term goals were benchmarks for eliminating underrepresentation. Short-terms goals were to be established for each job category. These short-term goals were to be refined measures that took into account "turnover, layoffs, lateral transfers, new job openings, retirements, and availability of minorities, women, and handicapped persons who possess the desired qualifications or potential for placement" (107 S.Ct. at 1454). The plan also specifically stated that the goals should not be treated as quotas but as "reasonable aspirations" (107 S.Ct. at 1454).

Justice Brennan held that if the plan had not taken these various factors into consideration in the development of short-term goals but had simply compared the positions with the general labor pool, the validity of the plan could be questioned. However, this plan did not order "blind hiring" on the basis of a broad goal and thus was acceptable. Also, the clear lack of women in the job category made it reasonable for the agency to consider the sex of Joyce as one factor in making its decision. According to Justice Brennan, these facts satisfied the *Weber* requirement that the plan be designed to eliminate work force imbalances in traditionally segregated job categories (107 S.Ct. at 1455).

The next consideration was whether the plan trammeled the rights of male employees or created an absolute bar to their advancement. Noting the similarity to the Harvard plan approved in *Bakke*, Justice

Brennan held that the plan was acceptable because (1) no persons were automatically excluded from consideration, (2) the petitioners had no absolute entitlement to the position since the director was free to select any of the seven candidates deemed qualified, (3) the petitioner did not lose his job, salary, or seniority and he remained eligible for other promotions, and (4) the agency plan was intended only to attain a balanced work force, not maintain one. With respect to the last point, Brennan commented: "The Agency acknowledged the difficulties it would face in remedying the imbalance in its work force, and it anticipated only gradual increases in the representation of minorities and women. It is thus unsurprising that the plan contains no explicit end date, for the Agency's flexible, case-by-case approach was not expected to yield success in a brief period of time" (107 S.Ct. at 1456). This moderate approach placed minimal intrusion on the legitimate expectations of other employees. The plan was meant to attain a balanced work force, not maintain one. Together these factors satisfied the *Weber* criteria (107 S.Ct. at 1456–1457).

Justice Stevens concurred. He first stated that whereas he believed Title VII established an "absolute blanket prohibition" against discrimination, the Court had interpreted the title to allow actions that benefited members of minority groups for whose protection the statute had been enacted. He would adhere to the Court's construction (107 S.Ct. 1457–1459). According to Stevens:

> As construed in *Weber* and in [*Vanguards*], the statute does not absolutely prohibit preferential hiring in favor of minorities; it was merely intended to protect historically disadvantaged groups *against* discrimination and not to hamper managerial efforts to benefit members of disadvantaged groups that are consistent with that paramount purpose. The preference granted by respondent in this case does not violate the statute as so construed; the record amply supports the conclusion that the challenged employment decision served the legitimate purpose of creating diversity in a category of employment that has been almost an exclusive province of males in the past. Respondent's voluntary decision is surely not prohibited by Title VII as construed in *Weber* [emphasis in original] (107 S.Ct. at 1459).

Justice Stevens also stated that this decision did not establish the outer limits of voluntary action (107 S.Ct. at 1460). It should not be necessary for an employer to determine if its past conduct would constitute an arguable violation prior to taking preferential action. The employer should be allowed to focus on the future and other legitimate reasons for granting preferences (107 S.Ct. at 1460). That is, the Court had yet to rule on other possible justifications for affirmative action, hence this decision is not the final word.

Justice O'Connor concurred in the judgment although she believed that the Court's decision followed an "expansive and ill-defined" approach. On the other hand, the dissenters wrote as if from a clean slate, which was a "useful point of academic discussion" but contrary to the reality of affirmative action case law (107 S.Ct. at 1461). O'Connor proposed that the appropriate standard for evaluating the voluntary action of a public employer is drawn from *Wygant*—the employer must have a firm basis for believing that remedial action is needed and that a statistical disparity sufficient to support a prima facie case of discrimination under Title VII is such a firm basis (107 S.Ct. at 1462).

According to O'Connor, *Weber* had balanced two concerns of Title VII: (1) rooting out invidious discrimination against all persons, and (2) eliminating the lasting effects of discrimination against minorities. In balancing these concerns, the Court had held that Congress permitted affirmative action only as a remedial device (107 S.Ct. at 1462). She further asserted that *Wygant's* requirement of a firm basis to support remedial action was consistent with *Weber*. Therefore, it was not necessary for a public employer to show a contemporaneous finding of discrimination, but there must be evidence sufficient to support a prima facie case. Such evidence "suggests that the absence of women or minorities in a work force cannot be explained by general societal discrimination alone and that remedial action is appropriate" (107 S.Ct. at 1463).

Justice O'Connor's examination of the plan indicated her belief that if the plan was based simply on long-term goals it would be invalid because focusing only on the proportion of women and minorities in the work force is not remedial (107 S.Ct. at 1463–1464). On the other hand, a goal that takes into account the number of women and minorities qualified for the position could be deemed remedial and the agency's plan did so. O'Connor also disagreed with the dissenters argument that the decision to promote Joyce was based simply on her gender (107 S.Ct. at 1464). Finally, O'Connor said that the almost complete absence of women in skilled craft positions constituted a prima facie case of discrimination. Therefore, the plan was remedial and valid (107 S.Ct. at 1465).

Justice Scalia dissented, joined by Chief Justice Rehnquist and Justice White in Parts I and II. Scalia began with a clear attack on the redistributive goals of affirmative action. According to him, the Court "effectively replace[d] the goal of a discrimination-free society with the quite incompatible goal of proportionate representation by race and sex in the workplace" (107 S.Ct. at 1465).

Scalia examined the plan and found that it was not designed to remedy past discrimination since there had been no past discrimination. Scalia found that the plan did not even meet the objective of achieving "the state of affairs this Court has dubiously assumed would result from an absence of discrimination—an overall work force 'more or less representative of the racial and ethnic composition of the population in the community'" (107 S.Ct. at 1466). Justice Scalia continued: "... the plan did not seek to replicate what a lack of discrimination would produce, but rather imposed racial and sexual tailoring that would, in defiance of normal expectations and laws of probability, given each protected racial and sexual group a governmentally determined 'proper' proportion of each job category" (107 S.Ct. at 1467). In addition, the plan did not simply allow for consideration of gender as a "plus" factor but mandated concrete results. It informed supervisory personnel that they would be evaluated on the basis of the affirmative action results they achieved (107 S.Ct. at 1467). Finally, the Justice concluded that the decision to promote Joyce was not made on the basis of a multitude of factors but turned simply on her gender (107 S.Ct. at 1468–1469).

Next Scalia noted that the result of the Court's decision is the legal proposition that "racial or sexual discrimination is permitted under Title VII when it is intended to overcome the effect ... of societal attitudes that have limited the entry of certain races, or of a particular sex, into certain jobs" (107 S.Ct. at 1469). He argued that the *Johnson* holding contradicted the *Wygant* holding that remedying *societal* discrimination violates the Equal Protection Clause. He also argued that *Wygant* should control because there is no basis for finding that Title VII places lesser constraints on public employers than the Constitution (107 S.Ct. at 1469–1470). The *Johnson* holding also contradicted *Sheet Metal Workers* because it was not limited to cases of egregious discrimination (107 S.Ct. at 1470). Last, Justice Scalia argued that the decision inappropriately expanded the Court's interpretation of "traditionally segregated job categories" to include those that women have found undesirable (107 S.Ct. at 1471).

Scalia concluded with an argument that *Weber* should be overturned. The Justice felt that *Weber* wrongly rewrote Title VII's nondiscrimination principle and that the result has been a requirement of discrimination, not the allowance of voluntary action (107 S.Ct. at 1471–1472). This is the same argument made continuously by Chief Justices Rehnquist and Burger.

Analysis

The briefs in *Johnson* show that the opponents of affirmative action had given up attempting to argue that race-conscious remedies were not appropriate. Instead, the opponents again attempted to show that the agency's plan was not remedial. Both the plaintiff and the United States argued that the plan was not remedial because it was not based on evidence of past discrimination, but was based only on statistical disparities or societal discrimination. This is clearly an attempt to limit the definition of remedial. The advocates responded to this argument by establishing that affirmative action had been upheld on the basis of statistical disparities in *Weber, Fullilove,* and *Wygant*. The advocates stressed again that to require a specific finding of discrimination would frustrate the congressional emphasis on voluntary compliance.

The split between the compensatory and distributive purposes of affirmative action is not as clearly defined in these briefs as in the briefs from previous cases because of this shift in emphasis by the opponents. There were no arguments that the remedy must be directed only to the identified victims of discrimination. The advocates, on the other hand, stressed the applicability of *Weber*, which, as was shown above, relied extensively on distributive values. Yet this is not as essential to the advocates' briefs as the arguments that the plan satisfied the *Weber* criteria.

The majority opinion in *Johnson* relied completely on *Weber*. Justice Brennan noted that in 1972 Congress had indicated that Title VII would be applied equally to private and public employers. Thus the majority rejected any possible distinction between voluntary action by private employers and voluntary action by public employers under Title VII.[20] This holding, along with that in *Vanguards*, extended the *Weber* analysis to consent decrees and to voluntary action by both public and private employers. This increased the importance of *Weber* significantly by expanding the number of situations in which those criteria would be applicable. Since *Weber* supported a distributive justification for affirmative action, this holding gives a boost to those who support affirmative action on redistributive grounds.

As noted in the analysis of *Weber*, it is a matter of dispute whether that decision supported the concept of societal discrimination as a basis for remedial action. The matter is not adequately resolved in *Johnson* either. The majority's use of *Weber* allowed them to avoid the question. Only Justice O'Connor rejected this view. She voted, however, to support the plan on the grounds that the employer had showed there was a firm basis for its actions.[21] O'Connor held that a firm basis required that a disparity be sufficient to support a prima facie case of discrimination. This requirement meant that an employer had to show that the disparity could not be based on societal discrimination alone.

Justice Stevens' concurrence presents a justice who clearly thought the law prohibited any form of discrimination, but was unwilling to reject the Court's construction of the statute. He noted that the case law supported affirmative action to the extent that affirmative action protected minorities against discrimination and did not hinder the employer's efforts to benefit minorities by protecting them against discrimination. This argument does not seem to support a redistributive justification for affirmative action, but Justice Stevens also found that "creating diversity" in "traditionally segregated job categories" was legitimate (107 S.Ct. at 1460). This statement does support a redistributive justification.

Stevens' votes in these affirmative action cases reflect this conflict expressed above. He had argued against quotas in *Bakke* and *Fullilove* and had voted against the modification of the consent decree in *Stotts*.[22] He did, however, vote to uphold the seniority plan in *Wygant* on the same grounds as he used in *Johnson*—yet, Stevens also supported the use of goals and quotas in *Sheet Metal Workers*, *Vanguards*, and *Paradise*. The one consistency in this pattern is that Stevens supported affirmative action when a redistributive justification supported the action. He appears to favor an argument that Title VII supports both a nondiscrimination principle and a redistributive principle. When the redistributive principle is used appropriately, i.e., within the *Weber* standards, Stevens apparently thinks it is substantial enough to override the nondiscrimination principle.

Justice Scalia and Chief Justice Rehnquist explicitly rejected the redistributive justification of affirmative action. Title VII is to be limited to providing nothing more than a nondiscrimination principle and affirmative action limited to compensating the actual victims of discrimination. Scalia's argument was that affirmative action did not produce a work force whose composition reflected the absence of past discrimination. He characterized the result as "racial or sexual tailoring" to produce proportional representation of protected groups "in defiance of normal expectations and laws of probability" (107 S.Ct. at 1467). This is a restatement of the views presented by Thomas Sowell, who argues that the composition of the work force is not determined by probability but is shaped by the average age of groups in the population, availability, and cultural factors (1981: 65–66). This argument, however, misstates distributive values as they have been expressed by the Court. That is, the Court has not upheld affirmative action because it produces a particular distribution. The Court has upheld affirmative action because a redistribution both eliminates the effects of discrimination and produces a change in the work force that, in the long run, reduces racial tension. Of course, as Justice Brennan's opinion in *Paradise* suggests, redistribution also compensates those individuals who have been excluded from positions by an employer's refusal to implement remedies already agreed to by the employer.

A significant part of the *Johnson* decision is the application of the *Weber* criteria to the agency's plan. The action in *Weber* involved a 50% quota, but *Johnson* involved a plan similar to the Harvard plan discussed in *Bakke*. That is, gender was a positive factor in the decision-making process and goals were provided to measure the agency's progress. This is one of the weaker forms of affirmative action, i.e., affirmative action that involves changes in selection procedures but which does not require goals or quotas.[23] On its face, the plan would appear to satisfy the criteria, but the operation of the plan was the primary concern of the justices. Justice Brennan, of course, had no trouble with the operation of the plan. He noted that the plan eliminated imbalances in traditionally segregated job categories by allowing the consideration of gender in employment decisions. The plan did not bar the advancement of males, preclude their consideration, or deny them entitlement to a position. It was temporary and not intended to maintain a racial balance. Justice Scalia found that the plan did not satisfy the criteria. He disputed the argument that the plan eliminated an imbalance in traditional segregated job categories on the grounds that the segregation was not the result of discrimination but was due to most women's view that the job was undesirable. This view, however, ignores the fact that discriminatory attitudes may be the cause of women finding such jobs undesirable. Scalia also argued that the plan did not simply require the use of gender as a positive factor, but the goals mandated specific results. This is reminiscent of O'Connor's and White's arguments in *Sheet Metal Workers*. They both argued goals can operate as strict quotas. Yet, the Court had upheld a strict quota in *Weber*.

Justice Scalia's opinion in *Johnson* was anticipated since his views on affirmative action were well known at the time of his appointment to the Court (see Scalia 1979). When *Weber* was still in the lower courts, Scalia chastised Judge Wisdom's dissent, which supported the plan, as "an elaborate intellectual word game . . . [and] pretense or self-delusion" (1979: 150). Scalia argued that in light of federal regulations and an employer's need to avoid expensive litigation, "discuss[ing] . . . [affirmative action] . . . in the ficticious context of voluntarism not only makes any intelligently reasoned decision impossible in the particular case, but poisons the well of legal discourse" (1979: 151). Considering these strong words, it is not surprising that Scalia suggested that *Weber* be overturned. Nor is it unexpected that Justice

Rehnquist joined Scalia's opinion since he has been the strongest advocate of the compensatory justification of affirmative action.

THE STATE OF AFFIRMATIVE ACTION CASE LAW

This and the previous chapter examine the evolution of employment discrimination and affirmative action case law. In *Griggs v. Duke Power Co.*, the Court defined discrimination to include adverse impact and thereby opened the door for affirmative action remedies. The first major affirmative action decision, *Bakke*, was an equal protection challenge, and its plurality opinion showed the split in the Court over distributive and compensatory values in affirmative action plans. The different equal protection challenges heard by the Court, *Bakke*, *Fullilove*, *Wygant*, and *Paradise*, centered on doctrinal issues, i.e., the appropriate level of review, but the compensatory/distributive split was evident in these cases as well.

The major point of contention in all the Title VII cases was whether the statute was intended to remedy clear maldistributions in the work force of this country. Prior to *Weber*, the Court had considered only the compensatory purpose of Title VII, though it had recognized that Title VII had the broader purpose of achieving equal opportunity. With *Weber*, however, the Court found that the achievement of equal opportunity required more than compensating victims. It must also include the elimination of the maldistribution in the work force. Following *Weber*, the Court digressed somewhat with its *Stotts* and *Wygant* decisions which on their face rejected the redistributive values in favor of the compensatory values. In *Sheet Metal Workers*, *Vanguards*, and *Johnson*, however, the Court interpreted *Stotts* and *Wygant* narrowly, i.e., as seniority decisions, and explicitly supported the argument that the elimination of the maldistribution in the work force was necessary to break down the psychological and societal barriers erected by years of discrimination. In these decisions, the Court was using a redistributive argument supported by utilitarian justifications.

The compensatory/distributive split was evident in all the cases, but those who did not support the argument that affirmative action is redistributive did not take a direct stand against this view until *Paradise* and *Johnson*. In *Paradise* the United States argued against the redistributive purpose on the grounds that it was intended only to bring about proportional representation in the work force. In *Johnson*, the United States used stronger language and referred to affirmative action as nothing more than "untrammeled social engineering." Justice Scalia also rejected this justification for affirmative action in *Johnson*. By this time, however, a majority of the Court had already accepted the redistributive purpose as valid. Indeed, this was Justice Stevens' point in his concurrence in *Johnson*.

It is unlikely that *Johnson* will be the last word from the Court on voluntary or court-ordered affirmative action. The Court is closely split over the policy, almost all the opinions discussed above were 5–4 or 6–3 decisions with strong dissents, and Justice Powell's retirement presented Reagan with another opportunity to shape the Court in his conservative image. With the appointment of Anthony Kennedy and the Rehnquist Court agreeing to hear more affirmative action challenges, the policy may very well be limited to compensating the identified victims of discrimination.

NOTES

1. Sections 703(a) and (c) prohibit discrimination in employment on the basis of race, color, sex, religion, and national origin by employers and labor organizations, respectively.
2. Judge Wisdom concluded that because Congress intended to encourage private efforts to come into compliance with Title VII, employers and unions who committed "arguable violations" of Title VII should "be free to make reasonable responses without fear of liability to whites . . . " (443 U.S. at 211).
3. The Court, however, had already defined discrimination in this way in *Griggs*.
4. Dworkin rejected Justice Rehnquist's reading of the statute as providing only for a nondiscrimination principle since this rejects both the principle of economic equality and the remedial purpose of the statute.
5. According to Boyd, Justice Brennan's "traditionally segregated job category" approach was premised on societal discrimination since its focus was on racial disparities instead of the source of the disparities (1980: 13). Neuborne argued that Justice Brennan's "traditionally segregated job categories" are not equivalent to the concept of societal discrimination.
6. There is disagreement on this point. Respondents state that the whites who were laid off were hired on the same date as the minorities who were not laid off and that the only factor that placed them before the minorities on the layoff roll was the alphabetical order of their names.
7. By not appealing the district court's order approving of the race-conscious layoff, the city could not now legitimately challenge that order before the Supreme Court.
8. The Court's opinion and the concurring and dissenting opinions also considered the question of mootness.
9. *Kromnick v School District of Philadelphia*, 739 F.2d. 894 (3rd Circuit, 1984), cert denied, 105 S.Ct. 782 (1985); *Boston Chapter, NAACP v Beecher*, 679 F.2d. 965 (1st Circuit, 1982), vacated and remanded for mootness, 461 U.S. 477 (1984); and *Hammon v Barry*, 606 F.Supp. 1082 (D.D.C. 1985).

10. It is possible to conclude that these three justices did indeed utilize strict scrutiny.
11. Justice Powell found that a diverse student body was a compelling interest in *Bakke*. Marshall extended the concept to a diverse faculty as well.
12. Because there was no Title VII challenge, these justices were unable to reach or attempt to alter the holding on voluntary action in *Weber*.
13. Birmingham argued that under a voluntarily adopted affirmative action plan, the situation of blacks and women did not improve, but that progress was made under the consent decree since it was the only way to break through the barriers of the "archaic" civil service system (Brief for the City of Birmingham, No. 84–1656: 21).
14. *NAACP v Allen* was heard by the Court as *U.S. v Paradise*.
15. These are variations on the *Weber* standards.
16. The Brief cites Sowell, "Weber and Bakke and the Presuppositions of Affirmative Action," 26 *Wayne Law Review* (1980): 1313, 1326 and Rankin, "The Stroke of a Pen," 5 *Regulation* (1981): 16.
17. Rehnquist argued that reserving a certain number of positions for minorities violated the seniority rights of nonminorities who would be passed over for minorities with less seniority.
18. Johnson was subsequently promoted to road dispatcher despite this assertion.
19. The Brief noted that the court of appeals found this evidence to constitute a prima facie case of discrimination (Brief for Respondent, No. 85–1129: 12).
20. Public employers would still be subject to equal protection challenges.
21. Justice O'Connor's use of the firm basis rationale seems to explain her inconsistency in these cases. That is, she is consistent in her rationale, but the result is that her opinions do not always bring her down on the same side in each case.
22. Justice Stevens did not participate in *Weber*.
23. The weakest form of affirmative action was followed by the Reagan administration: the expansion of the applicant pool and training programs.

5

Affirmative Action, Policymaking, and Statutory Interpretation

This book has explored the principles used by the Court to validate affirmative action and the evidence showed that Court majorities have used redistributive principles to justify affirmative action when interpreting Title VII. The major decisions, *Weber, Sheet Metal Workers, Vanguards*, and *Johnson*, all recognized that a primary purpose of Title VII was to change the composition of the work force so that minorities and women would be more justly represented in the middle and higher levels. These decisions reflect the belief that affirmative action was necessary to achieve this goal. Compensatory values did play a role in the Court's decisions upholding affirmative action (see *U.S. v Paradise*, Chapter 4), but the Supreme Court's major justification for affirmative action remedies was redistributive.

One cannot, however, lightly ignore cases such as *Stotts* and *Wygant* where the Court rejected affirmative action. These cases, however, involved seniority systems. The words of §703(h) provided the opponents of affirmative action with an opportunity to limit affirmative action affecting legitimate seniority systems. Yet a majority of the Court, even swing justices such as Powell and O'Connor, later rejected the argument that affirmative action must be limited to the compensation of identified victims when seniority was not involved. Nevertheless, the Court's recent decisions upholding affirmative action do not put it on high ground, safe from attack or change.

Justices such as Rehnquist, Scalia, and White are opposed to affirmative action because they view it as a violation of Title VII and the Equal Protection Clause. As supporters of judicial restraint, they believe the Court's decisions have been policymaking decisions. The Court, they contend, has not simply interpreted the law but has made new law and, hence, policy. Only an argument that shows that the Court has not been making policy, but has engaged in ordinary statutory interpretation, might persuade these Justices that affirmative action based on distributive values is acceptable.

Statutory interpretation is a major part of judicial decision making today. Indeed, Radin acknowledged that Anglo-American law was becoming essentially statutory almost 60 years ago (1930: 863). Having long recognized the role of statutes in judicial decision making, legal scholars have produced theories of statutory interpretation, many of which conflict with each other. This conflict among theories of statutory interpretation stems from the different views of law articulated by the various schools of jurisprudence. Legal positivists support a theory of interpretation that is based on the discoverable intent of the legislature (Landis 1930). Legal Realists, on the other hand, argue that legislative intent is not discoverable and judges must make subjective interpretations of statutes that are limited primarily by precedent and the judge's place as a citizen in a particular society (Radin 1930: 881–882). Dworkin has developed a "natural law" theory of both constitutional and statutory interpretation that relies not on intent or the subjectivity of the judge, but on the underlying principles that justify the statute and on political morality. Irving Kaufman, a judge on the court of appeals for the second circuit, takes a pragmatic view that statutory and constitutional interpretation are a "mixture of theory and practice, art and science" that are shaped by the judge's character (1984: 1).

As the Legal Realists and Kaufman note, statutory interpretation is not an exact science. It involves making choices, but these choices do not necessarily equate with policymaking as it is generally understood. Policymaking is a political decision that "advances or protects some collective goal of the community as a whole" (Dworkin 1979: 82). The task of the judge, on the other hand, is to enforce the political rights and duties enacted in a statute (1979: 87). The judge engaged in constitutional or statutory interpretation does not justify a decision on the basis of policy; she justifies the decision on the basis of principle, i.e., the decision "respects or secures some individual or group right" (Dworkin 1979: 82). When there are competing principles involved in a statute, the judge is forced to make a choice between them. To do so, however, does not move the judge from the realm of statutory interpretation into the realm of policymaking. The judge is still enforcing the political rights of individuals.[1]

This concluding chapter shows that the Court has not been making policy by upholding affirmative action on distributive grounds. Instead, it has simply been engaged in statutory interpretation. Because the emphasis in this research is on the role of principles of justice, Dworkin's theory of interpretation is emphasized. However, the other theories mentioned above are not ignored as they provide a starting point for Dworkin's theory.

The argument to be made takes the following form. First, the legislative history of Title VII supports the proposition that the goal of the title was to eliminate the maldistribution of minorities and women in the work force. Second, the Court's early (nonaffirmative action) employment discrimination decisions recognized the distributive values present in Title VII.[2] The Court's recognition of these values in its cases defining the meaning of discrimination opened the door for affirmative action remedies. Finally, affirmative action as redistribution is consistent with distributive justice. On the other hand, affirmative action as compensation, even when limited to the identified victims of discrimination, does not completely satisfy the requirements of compensatory justice.[3] Thus, when statutory interpretation requires a choice between possible justifications, the distributive justification is superior because it provides a more coherent analysis of the underlying moral principles.

LEGISLATIVE HISTORY OF TITLE VII OF THE CIVIL RIGHTS ACT OF 1964

The argument that the Court has been making policy with its affirmative action decisions centers on the question of whether Title VII supports a distributive principle. As noted previously, this question turns on theories of statutory interpretation. In England, judges are allowed only to examine the words of the statute when interpreting it (Murphy and Pritchett 1974: 410). In the United States, however, judges usually look beyond the words when interpreting a statute. Ball notes six reasons why judges must look beyond the words of a statute: "... because legislators (1) do not write clearly, or (2) deliberately write ambiguously, (3) wrestle with complex, technical problems, (4) do not clearly identify legislative intent, (5) use complex communicative symbols, i.e., words, to express their purposes, and because, (6) as fallible public officials, they cannot address all the ramifications of a public policy issue as these emerge during the implementation phase, federal judges are obliged to practice the art of gleaning or discerning legislative purpose or intent" (1987: 5). When judges must look beyond the words of statute in order to "glean" its legislative intent, they generally turn to the legislative history.

Legal scholars have long debated the use of legislative intent (as identified in legislative history) in the interpretation of statutes. Legal Realists accept the notion that the meaning of a statute cannot be found through a simple reading of the words, but reject the argument that this problem can be resolved by identifying legislative intent (Radin 1930: 866, 870). Radin argued that legislative intent is not discoverable since the legislative process involves compromise and negotiation among many individuals who may each hold different ideas and beliefs regarding a statute (1930: 870). The legislative history cannot resolve this problem (Radin 1930: 873). Radin also argued that there is no reason why the legislative intent must be obligatory on the courts (1930: 871). The legislature's task is to "pass statutes," but it is the courts and the executive that must use those statutes to perform their functions (Radin 1930: 871). Interpretation takes place only after a statute comes into play in a certain event, not prior to that event. Thus interpretation is the responsibility of the courts and the executive, not the legislature, and legislative intent need not bind the courts (Radin 1930: 871–872).

The Legal Realists view of legislative intent has not gone unchallenged. Landis argued that legislative intent is discoverable through an analysis of the legislative history (Landis 1930: 888–889). According to Landis, when a legislator votes for a statute, he or she has concurred in the expressed views contained in the legislative history and "[a] particular determinant . . . becomes the possession of the majority of the legislature, and as such a real discoverable intent" (Landis 1930: 889). Landis also argued that sucessive drafts and amendments to statutes actually assist in discovering intent (1930: 889–890). Landis therefore concluded that because intent is discoverable, it should guide judges in the interpretive process.

The legislative history of the 1964 debates shows the presence of both compensatory and redistributive values. The compensatory values were rarely discussed in debate, but they are clearly evident in the congressional choice to provide backpay and other make-whole relief to the identified victims.[4] On the other hand, every expressed justification for the title was the need to eliminate the maldistribution of blacks and women in the work force. Even more significant is the legislative history of the 1972 amendments. Justice Rehnquist and the others who oppose affirmative action seem to ignore the amendments when arguing against the policy. The legislative history of the 1972 amendments shows that Congress was still very much concerned with the distribution of blacks and women in the work force. The justification given for the amendments was the lack of progress made in eliminating the maldistribution of the work force. At the same time, Congress was aware of executive branch affirmative action programs under EO11246 and court-ordered affirmative action remedies. The Senate overwhelming voted against amendments that would have prohibited their use. Senator Javits noted that affirmative action was a necessary tool that should be utilized to assist in the elimination of discrimination and its effects on the work force (U.S. Congress 1972: 1665). Justice Brennan noted this in his decision in *Sheet Metal Workers*, which upheld court-ordered hiring goals.

The legislative history of the 1972 amendments provides a strong argument for court-ordered and executive branch affirmative action.

It does not, however, settle the issue of voluntary affirmative action. Justices Rehnquist and Brennan reached contrasting conclusions regarding whether Congress intended §703(j) to prohibit voluntary action by employers. Rehnquist argued that the legislative history showed that Congress intended to pass color-blind legislation that prohibited discrimination against whites as well as blacks and women, i.e., reverse discrimination, preferential treatment, affirmative action. Brennan argued that the legislative history showed a congressional preference for voluntary action. Prohibiting employers from utilizing affirmative action would frustrate Congress' intention to limit government intervention in employer decision making and, at the same time, frustrate the redistributive goal of Title VII. Both Justices supported their arguments with speeches and opinions from the legislative history. Clearly, this makes it difficult to determine what was the true legislative intent.

Like Radin, Dworkin (1985) has also argued that it is not possible to resolve questions of statutory interpretation simply on the basis of identifying the legislative intent. Often it is impossible to accurately determine the intent of Congress. Dworkin suggests the use of a "coherence theory," which holds that "a statute be interpreted to advance the policies or principles that furnish the best political justification for the statute" (1985: 327).[5] According to Dworkin, a justification must be "consistent with the provisions of the statute and [find] substantial support in the political climate of the times" (1985: 328).

Dworkin notes that identifying the political justification of a statute might be as problematic as identifying the legislative intent (1985: 328; see also Radin 1930: 875). Just as Brennan argued that the political justification of Title VII was to create a redistributive policy, Rehnquist argued that the justification of Title VII was a nondiscrimination principle that limits Title VII remedies to make-whole relief. Both these arguments are consistent with the statute and the political climate of the times. Thus the choice of which justification is superior depends on deciding which one provides a "more sensitive or sounder analysis of the underlying moral principles" (Dworkin 1985: 329).

The essence of Dworkin's analysis is that no matter what theory of statutory interpretation is used, judges must still make "political judgments" (1985: 329). Political judgments, however, need not be equated with judicial policymaking. According to Dworkin:

> It is no use protesting that this procedure [the application of the coherence theory] allows judges to substitute their own political judgment for the judgment of elected representatives of the people . . . [I]f there is no institutionalized intention, no pertinent

> collective understanding, and two competing justifications, there is no such judgment. . . . [T]he protest suggests that judges have some way to decide such a case that does *not* require them to make a political judgment. But there is no such procedure, except a method that leaves a decision to chance, like flipping a coin [emphasis in original] (1985: 329).

Dworkin's conclusion applies to any theory of statutory interpretation, not just the coherence theory. A judge who reads a legislative history in search of congressional intent also makes political judgments. Indeed, the whole idea that judges are interpreting statutes implies the need for judgments of some kind.

Therefore, whereas the legislative history assists in the identification of the principles underlying Title VII, it cannot settle the question of whether Title VII supports voluntary affirmative action. There are two competing principles between which the justices must choose. That choice, however, is not dependent on a justice's ideology or personal values. The choice depends on which justification provides the "more sensitive or sounder analysis of the underlying moral principles" (Dworkin 1985: 329). However, before moving to an analysis of the principles involved, there is another aspect of statutory interpretation that must be considered.

EARLY TITLE VII EMPLOYMENT DISCRIMINATION CASES

One aspect of statutory interpretation that is essential to the argument that the Court has been engaged in statutory interpretation is the role of precedent. According to Kaufman, precedent is "the bedrock of our legal system . . . for reasons of both principle and efficiency" (1984: 11). Radin also recognizes precedent as one of the limits on the subjectivity of judges (1930: 881). Here the role of precedent is important for two reasons. First, Congress did not define discrimination in Title VII but left it to the courts. This meant that the Court would have to settle the question in its early employment discrimination cases so that the lower courts would have guidelines regarding what did and did not constitute discrimination. Thus the Court had to create precedent. Second, the role of precedent in statutory interpretation is to provide consistency for later decisions. This section shows that the Court has consistently applied its precedent to its affirmative action decisions. That is, it has followed the rule articulated in early cases, not created a new rule for these different affirmative action cases.

Affirmative action was not the first issue raised in Title VII litigation. The first issue the Court considered was the definition of discrimination, since Congress had abdicated that task. The first definition of discrimination, disparate treatment, was derived from the words of Title VII, specifically §703 (a) and (c), which prohibit employers from treating employees differently on the basis of their race, sex, national origin, or religion. However, as more cases entered the court system, the Court (and Congress) recognized that discrimination was not limited to this one particular form. Discrimination also manifested itself in more subtle and systematic ways, i.e., procedures and requirements that had an adverse impact on the entry and advancement of disadvantaged groups and procedures that perpetuated the effects of past discrimination. A new question before the Court was whether Title VII also prohibited these forms of discrimination. To decide this question the Court had to examine the underlying principles of Title VII.

Both adverse impact discrimination and the present effects of past discrimination can be derived only from the distributive values in Title VII. Congress was concerned with eliminating the maldistribution of blacks and women in the work force, but these forms of discrimination operated to maintain this imbalance by closing off opportunities to these groups. In *Griggs v Duke Power Company*, the Court held that adverse impact and present effects of past discrimination were prohibited by Title VII for that very reason (401 U.S. at 429–430 (1971)). The Court later limited the application of the present effects theory when a bona fide seniority system was involved in *Teamsters v U.S.*, 431 U.S. 324 (1977).

The definition of discrimination also shapes the scope of remedies available under Title VII. After a finding of disparate treatment, there are identified individuals or class of individuals for whom remedies such as backpay and seniority relief can be granted. Section 706(g) provided for such relief. On the other hand, adverse impact and the present effects of past discrimination manifest themselves in the form of racial or gender imbalance. The elimination of the racial imbalance is the remedial goal. If a finding of discrimination is based on these definitions, there are no identified victims who can be provided compensation in the form of make-whole relief. Therefore, the remedy cannot be directed at identified victims, but must be directed toward the racial imbalance.[6] Prior to the 1972 amendments, Title VII seemed to limit remedies to make-whole relief. However, by 1972 when Title VII was amended, Congress had recognized that discrimination was systematic and not simply the result of discrete acts of individuals (see Chapter 2). Section 706(g) was changed to include "any other equitable relief the court deems appropriate." This change removed the apparent limitation on make-whole relief and opened the door for affirmative action remedies after a finding of adverse impact.

The previous section showed that Title VII is primarily concerned with distribution. Distributive values were also recognized and utilized by the Court in its early employment discrimination cases that defined discrimination. These cases and the 1972 amendments opened the door for affirmative action remedies. Yet compensatory values are also present in both the legislative history and the earlier employment discrimination cases. With two competing justifications, it is possible that the Court was mistaken when it emphasized the distributive values over the compensatory values when it defined discrimination and the scope of remedies available. Dworkin argues that this dilemma of competing justifications for the title can be solved by determining which justification provides the more sensitive analysis.

THE PHILOSOPHICAL BASIS OF AFFIRMATIVE ACTION

This research centered on two types of justice, compensatory and distributive, and the role each played in the Supreme Court's affirmative action decisions. Distributive justice concerns the relative access to rights, benefits, and burdens among the members of a society. Compensatory justice concerns repaying individuals for particular wrongs or injustices against them by other individuals or their government. Compensatory and distributive justice have been used by scholars to both justify and oppose affirmative action policy. The Court itself has used both types of justice to uphold the policy, but in most cases distributive justice has been the principal justification given by slim Court majorities.

Chapter 1 contains the different arguments used when assessing whether justice permits or requires affirmative action. Compensatory justice is generally used to argue against affirmative action on the grounds that the policy violates the compensatory paradigm. Others have argued that affirmative action can be permitted under a compensatory paradigm when that paradigm is extended to include injuries to large groups as well as individuals. Affirmative action has also been advocated on the ground that distributive justice requires that no group should be relegated to the lower end of the socioeconomic scale. The present maldistribution requires redistribution of disadvantaged groups throughout the work force. Another argument supports redistribution as a means for reducing racial tensions and achieving true equality of opportunity. Chapter 1 makes no effort to assess the plausibility of these arguments. Indeed, that decision ultimately has been left to the Court in its interpretation of Title VII. This section shows that the distributive justification should be preferred over the compensatory justification since it provides the more sensitive analysis of principles underlying Title VII.

Compensatory justice follows a simple rule: when an individual has been injured, the perpetrator of the injury must pay an amount equal to fair compensation and the victim cannot demand as a right payment from third or unrelated parties (Goldman 1979: 67). Affirmative action goals deviate from this rule in two respects. First, the individual who benefits from the policy is not required to show that he or she has been the actual victim of discrimination. This is, of course, a major argument against affirmative action. However, this argument is only relevant on the assumption that affirmative action is compensatory. It is irrelevant to affirmative action as a redistributive policy, for a redistributive policy is not concerned with identification of individuals according to their status as victims. The individuals are identified simply through their membership in a targeted group.

Some advocates of affirmative action have argued that the compensatory principle is no longer limited in its application to identified individuals, but can be applied to groups that have suffered an injustice based on group characteristics. One form of this argument advances the proposition that all blacks have been the victims of discrimination, some directly and all others indirectly (i.e., psychologically) because of this nation's long history of slavery and Jim Crow laws. Therefore, it is not necessary to identify those blacks who have been victims of specific acts of discrimination. A similar argument can be made in support of affirmative action for women. This proposition has been criticized on the grounds that not all blacks and women have been discriminated against since there are indeed some advantaged blacks and women in society. Therefore, it is inappropriate to make reparation on the basis of group characteristics.

The second deviation from a strict compensatory model is that the burden of payment is not placed on the perpetrator, the employer, or his or her agents who practiced discrimination. Instead, the burden is placed, directly or indirectly, on other employees or the public. This is true even in cases of make-whole relief or contempt citations and fines. Backpay awards and fines increase the cost of doing business for the employer, and this cost is generally shifted to the employess or to the consumer. Thus even when affirmative action is limited to make-whole relief, in a sense it still violates the compensatory principle.

A variety of distributive principles have been proposed over the years, but the United States does not officially operate under any particular principle. The most likely candidate for an operating distributive principle in the United States is the principle of equal opportunity, which holds that all individuals have an equal chance to compete for jobs and other societal benefits. This principle allows for economic inequalities, but does not permit political inequalities (e.g., inequality in the right to vote, free speech, due process, etc.). Rawls (1971) has expressed this idea in his theory of justice as fairness. The difficulty with this distributive rule is that there is no clear concept of what shape economic inequalities might take. The congressional debate over Title VII suggested that Congress subscribed to the principle that the inequalities are just if no particular group is relegated to the lower end of the socioeconomic scale as a result of discrimination. Rawls has suggested that the shape of the economic distribution is not important as long as the political, social, and economic institutions are a fair or just system (1971: 86–87).[7]

The strongest distributive argument for affirmative action (the one used by Justice Brennan) holds that redistribution is not the end, it is the means. Dworkin and Wasserstrom both make the argument that the redistribution is not designed to achieve proportional representation or achieve equality of opportunity, but is necessary to reduce racial tension and increase, over the long run, the expectations of blacks and women through integration of the work force. Justice Brennan makes a similar argument in *Sheet Metal Workers* and *Johnson*. In these cases, imbalance is useful as a tool both for identifying the existence of discrimination and for establishing legitimate goals. It is a rough way for the courts and employers to identify the existence of discrimination and it provides a reasonable stopping point for affirmative action goals.

The rejoinder to Dworkin's and Wasserstrom's arguments for affirmative action states that affirmative action only increases racial tension because of the perception by some whites that it benefits undeserving or unqualified blacks and the perception by some blacks that affirmative action is degrading. Dworkin notes that this is not an inherent difficulty with affirmative action, but simply a short-term cost that must be paid if real progress is to be made (Dworkin 1985: 297). As long as no rights are violated, Dworkin believes the cost is acceptable.

According to Dworkin's coherence theory of interpretation, when the Court is faced with competing justifications, it should decide the case on the basis of the justification that provides a more sensitive analysis of the underlying moral principles. In this case, the Court must choose between a distributive or a compensatory justification, both of which are plainly present in Title VII. The distributive justification of affirmative action is clearly more sensitive to its underlying principle. Affirmative action is a remedy that is derived directly from the distributive goal of Title VII. It is designed to eliminate imbalance in the work force. Affirmative action does not serve a compensatory principle. It is not designed to compensate identified victims of a wrong. Thus the Court has a firm foundation for upholding affirmative action as a distributive policy under Title VII.

CONCLUSION

This research has shown that the Supreme Court has upheld affirmative action because it serves the distributive goal of moving blacks and women into positions in the work force from which they have been excluded because of discrimination, not because it compensates for specific acts of discrimination. Congress openly expressed a distributive purpose behind Title VII in the committee reports and the debates on the floor of both the House of Representatives and the Senate in 1963 and 1964. Although the statute itself was fashioned on 30 years of failed employment discrimination legislation and limited the relief available to make-whole or compensatory relief, in 1972 Congress recognized that this limited approach had not served the distributive goal set in 1964. Thus Congress amended Title VII to permit the courts to fashion broader relief. Having recognized the distributive values in Title VII, the Supreme Court defined adverse impact and the present effects of past discrimination as discrimination under Title VII. These definitions, when combined with the amendments to Title VII, paved the way for affirmative action. The compensatory arguments against affirmative action are valid to the extent that the policy does not serve compensatory principles. However, the compensatory arguments are unnecessary because affirmative action is not compensatory. It is redistributive and entirely consistent with the purposes of Title VII.

Yet the point may prove moot if the EEOC under the administration of George Bush continues to enforce Title VII as it was currently enforced by the Reagan EEOC. As noted in the first chapter, under the leadership of Clarence Thomas, the EEOC has altered its enforcement policy. This occurred following Thomas' statement, submitted to the Office of Management and Budget for inclusion in the *Regulatory Program of the United States Government*, that goals and timetables "turned [Title VII and its amendments] on their heads" by using a "fundamentally flawed" definition of discrimination based on statistical evidence (U.S. Congress 1986: 11). Today instead of seeking affirmative action relief, either in the courts or in the conciliation process, the EEOC has required its employees to seek the following compensatory remedies:

1. A requirement that all employees of the discriminating employer be notified of their right to be free of unlawful discrimination (including a requirement that the employer post in the workplace a notice that indicates that the notice is part of an agreed or ordered remedy).
2. A requirement that corrective, curative, and preventative action be taken to ensure that future discrimination will not occur, including changing discriminatory policies, removing the discriminatee from the perpetrator of the discriminatory conduct, and expunging adverse materials in the plaintiffs employment files.
3. A requirement that each identified victim of discrimination be unconditionally offered placement in the position (or a substantially equivalent position) that the person would have occupied absent discrimination even if that placement results in the displacement of another employee.
4. A requirement that each identified victim be made whole for any loss of earnings resulting from the discrimination, i.e., backpay.
5. A requirement that the employer cease from engaging in the unlawful employment practice found or conciliated in the case (U.S. Congress 1986: 8–9).

In addition, EEOC staff have reported that goals and timetables are no longer encouraged or permitted as a remedy.

During the 1987–1988 term in a plurality opinion, the Supreme Court upheld the use of statistical evidence in Title VII when it extended the application of adverse impact analysis to hiring and promotion systems that utilize subjective criteria (see *Watson v Ft. Worth Bank and Trust*, 108 S.Ct. 2777 (1988)). The endorsement of adverse impact analysis would seem to show some support for affirmative action. However, in January 1989, the Court struck down an MBE set-aside established by Richmond, Virginia. The plan was challenged on equal protection grounds and the Court held that the city had failed to justify the plan as a remedy for past discrimination in contracting (*New York Times*, January 24, 1989: 12). For the first time, a majority of the Court held that affirmative action-type plans require the application of strict scrutiny; thus, a plan must serve a compelling governmental interest such as identifiable past discrimination. This suggests that with the addition of Anthony Kennedy, the Court is less likely to continue its support for affirmative action.

If the Bush EEOC continues to avoid affirmative action remedies and the Court rejects affirmative action under Title VII absent a showing of identificable discrimination, then the future of affirmative action is quite dim. Only Congress would have the power to reinstate affirmative action as an effective tool of social and economic change.

Just as Congress passed the Civil Rights Restoration Act to overturn the Court's interpretation of Title IX of the Education Amendments of 1972 in *Grove City v Bell,* 465 U.S. 555 (1984), it can also enact legislation supporting the use of affirmative action remedies by the EEOC and the courts. In essence, the legal battle over affirmative action that has been waged in the courts and analyzed in this book may move back to the political arena where it began.

NOTES

1. There are some constraints on a judge when she chooses between two competing principles to justify a decision. These constraints are discussed in the next section.
2. These cases involved the definition of discrimination, a task that Congress purposefully left to the Court (see Chapter 3).
3. This is, of course, why affirmative action is easy to criticize in terms of compensatory justice.
4. There were other types of relief available including injunctive relief and penalties and fines; see Chapter 2.
5. Dworkin's theory of interpretation has been critized as a natural law theory that inappropriately brings in values. See, e.g., John Mackie, (1984). The Third Theory of Law. In Marshall Cohen, ed., *Ronald Dworkin and Contemporary Jurisprudence.* Totowa, NJ: Rowman and Allenheld. For Dworkin's response to these charges, see the same and Ronald Dworkin, (1982), "Natural" Law Revisited. *University of Florida Law Review,* 34: 165–188.
6. This does not mean that affirmative action is an attempt to achieve proportional representation in the work force. Instead, affirmative action facilitates the elimination of imbalance, i.e., the manifestation of discrimination, by increasing opportunities for the disadvantaged groups. As these groups move into better positions, the barriers that once prohibited their advancement can be broken down. Blacks and whites and men and women can learn how to work together and racial and gender tensions can be reduced. Other blacks and women who once felt they were locked out increase their own expectations and goals. Eventually the scope of the prejudices and procedures that blocked the advancement of disadvantaged groups are reduced or even eliminated.
7. This is Rawls' pure procedural justice. Rawls goes on to argue that until pure procedural justice is achieved, distribution is a matter of imperfect procedural justice (1971: 198). Inequality of opportunity is acceptable under imperfect procedural justice if that inequality is to the advantage of the least advantaged in society.

References

Allen, William B., Drew S. Days III, Benjamin Hooks, and William Bradford Reynolds. 1985. Is Affirmative Action Constitutional? *Regulation*, 9: 12+.
Anderson, James. 1979. *Public Policy Making*, 2nd ed. New York: Holt, Rinehart, and Winston.
Aristotle. 1925. *The Nicomachean Ethics*. David Ross, trans. New York: Oxford University Press.
Ball, Howard. 1980. *Constitutional Powers*. St. Paul: West Publishing Co.
———. 1986. *Justice Downwind: America's Atomic Testing Program in the 1950's*. New York: Oxford University Press.
———. 1987. *Courts and Politics: The Federal Judicial System*, 2d ed. Englewood Cliffs, NJ: Prentice-Hall, Inc.
———. 1988. The U.S. Supreme Court's Glossing of the Federal Tort Claims Act: The Impact of Statutory Construction on Military Veteran's Court Actions for "Corrective Justice" From *Feres* (1950) to *Broudy* (1985). *Western Political Quarterly*, 1988.
Barker, Lucius, and Twiley Barker, Jr. 1982. *Civil Liberties and the Constitution*, 4th ed. Englewood Cliffs, NJ: Prentice-Hall, Inc.
Berger, Morroe. 1968. *Equality By Statute*. New York: Doubleday.
Botts, Sherman. 1985. Has the Court Put the Fire Out on Court Ordered Affirmative Action? *Firefighters Union Local No. 1784 v Stotts*, 104 S.Ct. 2576 (1984). *Creighton Law Review*, 18:737–769.
Boxill, Bernard. 1984. *Blacks and Social Justice*. Totowa, NJ: Rowman and Allenheld.
Boyd, William. 1980. Affirmative Action in Employment. *Iowa Law Review*, 66:1–61.
Bureau of National Affairs. 1973. *The Equal Employment Opportunity Act of 1972*. Washington, DC: Bureau of National Affairs.
Burstein, Paul. 1985. *Discrimination, Jobs, and Politics*. Chicago: The University of Chicago Press.
Cohen, Marshall, ed., *Ronald Dworkin and Contemporary Jurisprudence*. Totowa, NJ: Rowman and Allenheld.
Cox, Paul. Some Thoughts on the Future of Remedial Race and Gender Preferences and Title VII. *Valparaiso Law Review*, 19: 803–828.
Dowd, Nancy. 1980. *Bakke* and *Weber*: The Concept of Societal Discrimination. *Loyola University (Chicago) Law Journal*, 11:297–326.
Dworkin, Ronald. 1979. *Taking Rights Seriously*. Cambridge: Harvard University Press.

———. 1982. "Natural" Law Revisited. *University of Florida Law Review*, 34: 165–188.

———. 1985. *A Matter of Principle*. Cambridge: Harvard University Press.

Dye, Thomas. 1971. *The Politics of Equality*. New York: Bobbs-Merrill.

———. 1981. *Understanding Public Policy*, 4th ed. Englewood Cliffs, NJ: Prentice-Hall, Inc.

Edwards, H.T. 1980. Affirmative Action or Reverse Discrimination: The Head and Tail of *Weber*. *Creighton Law Review*, 13: 713–767.

Fallon, Richard H., and Paul C. Weiler. 1984. *Firefighters v Stotts*: Conflicting Models of Racial Justice. *Supreme Court Review*, 1984:1–68.

Foster, James, Mary Segers and Bette Novit Evans and Mary C. Thornberry. 1983. *Elusive Equality: Liberalism, Affirmative Action and Social Change in America*. Port Washington, NY: Associated Faculty Press.

Frazier, Edward Franklin. 1974. *The Negro Church in America*. New York: Schochen Books.

Fullinwider, Robert. 1980. *The Reverse Discrimination Controversy: A Moral and Legal Analysis*. Totowa, NJ: Rowman and Littlefield.

Goldman, Alan. 1979. *Justice and Reverse Discrimination*. Princeton, NJ: Princeton University Press.

Goldman, Sheldon. 1987. *Constitutional Law: Cases and Essays*. New York: Harper and Row.

Gross, Barry, ed. 1977. *Reverse Discrimination*. Buffalo, NY: Prometheus Books.

Hernandez, Berta. 1986. Title VII v Seniority: The Supreme Court Giveth and the Supreme Court Taketh Away. *American University Law Review*, 35: 339–386.

Jacobs, Joanne. April 13, 1987. Women Win in Court, But at What Cost? *Salt Lake Tribune*.

Karst, Kenneth, and Harold Horowitz. 1979. The *Bakke* Opinion and Equal Protection Doctrine. *Harvard Civil Rights-Civil Liberties Law Review*, 14: 7–29.

Kaufman, Irving R. 1984. The Anatomy of Decisionmaking. *Fordham Law Review*, 53: 1–22.

Kluger, Richard. 1975. *Simple Justice*. New York: Random House.

Landis, James. A Note on "Statutory Interpretation." *Harvard Law Review*, 43: 886–893.

Larson, E. Richard. 1979. Race Consciousness in Employment after *Bakke*. *Harvard Civil Rights-Civil Liberties Law Review*, 14: 215–264.

Lavinsky, Larry. 1980. The Affirmative Action Trilogy and Benign Racial Classifications: Evolving Law in Need of Standards. *Wayne Law Review*, 27:1–34.

McDowell, Gary. April 7, 1987. Ruling on Affirmative Action Turns Fairness Upside Down. *Salt Lake Tribune*.

Murphy, Walter F., and C. Hermann Pritchett. 1974. *Courts, Judges and Politics*, 2d ed. New York: Random House.

Nagel, Thomas. 1973. Equal Treatment and Compensatory Discrimination. *Philosophy and Public Affairs*, 2:349–363.

Neuborne, Burt. 1979. Observations on *Weber*. *New York University Law Review*, 54: 546–559.

New York Times. "Excerpts from Court Opinions in Voiding of Richmond's Contracting Plan." January 24, 1989.

Nickel, James. 1977. Preferential Policies in Hiring and Admissions: A Jurisprudential Approach. In Barry R. Gross, ed., *Reverse Discrimination*. Buffalo, NY: Prometheus Books.

Oberschall, Anthony. 1973. *Social Conflict and Social Movements*. Englewood Cliffs, NJ: Prentice-Hall, Inc.

Podhoretz, Norman. April 3, 1987. Court Passes into Lawlessness. *Salt Lake Tribune*.

Radin, Max. 1930. Statutory Interpretation, *Harvard Law Review*, 43: 863–885.

Rawls, John. 1971. *A Theory of Justice*. Cambridge: Harvard University Press.

Ripley, Randall, and Grace Franklin. 1984. *Congress, the Bureaucracy, and Public Policy*, 4th ed. Homewood, IL: Dorsey Press.

Schlei, Barbara, and Paul Grossman. 1983. *Employment Discrimination Law*, 2nd ed. Washington, DC: Bureau of National Affairs.

Schwartz, Bernard, ed. 1970. *Statutory History of the United States: Civil Rights: Part II*. New York: Chelsea House.

Schulke, Flip, and Penelope McPhee. 1986. *King Remembered*. New York: Pocket Books.

Sowell, Thomas. 1981. Affirmative Action. *Across the Board*, XVIII: 65–72.

———. 1984. *Civil Rights: Reality or Rhetoric?* New York: Morrow.

Stokey, Edith and Richard Zeckhauser. 1978. *A Primer for Policy Analysis*. New York: W.W. Norton.

Supreme Court Records and Briefs. 1979. *United Steelworkers v Weber*. 78–432. Washington, DC: Congressional Information Service (microform).

———. 1985. *International Firefighters v Stotts*. 82–206. Washington, DC: Congressional Information Service (microform).

———. 1986. *International Firefighters v Cleveland*. 84–1999. Washington, DC: Congressional Information Service (microform).

———. 1986. *Johnson v Transportation Agency*. 85–1129. Washington, DC: Congressional Information Service (microform).

———. 1986. *Sheetmetal Workers v EEOC*. 84–1656. Washington, DC: Congressional Information Service (microform).

———. 1986. *United States v Paradise*. 85–999. Washington, DC: Congressional Information Service (microform).

Sutherland, Arthur, Jr. 1971. Civil Rights, Congress, and the Constitution—1963. In *Civil Rights and The South*. New York: DeCapo Press.

Tribe, Laurence. 1988. *American Constitutional Law*. 2ed. Mineola, NY: The Foundation Press.

Uniform Guidelines on Employee Selection Procedures. *Federal Register*, Vol. 43, No. 166 (August 25, 1978).

United States Code Congressional and Administrative News. 1965. St. Paul, MN: West Publishing.

United States Commission on Civil Rights. 1971. *Federal Civil Rights Enforcement Effort—1971*. Washington, DC: Government Printing Office.

———. 1977. *Federal Civil Rights Enforcement Efforts—1977.*Washington, DC: Government Printing Office.
U.S. Congress. 1964. *Congressional Record.* Vol. 110.
———. 1972. *Congressional Record.* Vol. 118.
———. 1985. House, Committeee on Education and Labor, *Oversight Hearings on EEOC's Proposed Modification of Enforcement Regulations, Including Uniform Guidelines on Employee Selection Procedures.* 99th Cong. 1st sess. (99-63), 2 October.
———. 1986. House, Committeee on Education and Labor, *Investigation of Civil Rights Enforcement by the Equal Employment Opportunity Commission.* 99th Cong. 2d sess. (99-Q), May.
———. 1987. House, Committeee on Education and Labor and Committee on the Judiciary, *Affirmative Action in the Workforce.* 100th Cong. 1st sess. (100-49), 8 October.
WGBH. June 17, 1986. *Frontline.*
Wasserstrom, Richard. 1980. *Philosophy and Social Issues: Five Studies.* Notre Dame: University of Notre Dame Press.
Whalen, Barbara, and Charles Whalen. 1985. *The Longest Debate: A Legislative History of the 1964 Civil Rights Act.* Washington, DC: Seven Locks Press.
Williams, Juan. February, 1987. A Question of Fairness. *Atlantic.*

Cases Cited

Bolling v Sharpe, 347 U.S. 497 (1954)
Boston Chapter, NAACP v Beecher, 679 F.2d. 965 (CA1) (1982), vacated and remanded for mootness, 461 U.S. 477 (1984)
Brown v Board of Education, 347 U.S. 483 (1954)
Califano v Webster, 430 U.S. 313 (1970)
California Brewer's Association v Bryant, 444 U.S. 598 (1980)
Carter v Gallagher, 425 F.2d. 315 (CA8), cert. denied, 406 U.S. 950 (1972)
Chambers v Florida, 309 U.S. 227 (1940)
Chrysler Corp. v U.S., 316 U.S. 556 (1941)
Contractors Association of Eastern Pennsylvania v Schultz, Secretary of Labor, 442 F.2d. 159 (CA3) (1971)
Ford Motor Corp. v Huffman, 345 U.S.—(1953)
Franks v Bowman Transportation Co., 424 U.S. 747 (1976)
Fullilove v Klutznick, 448 U.S. 448 (1980)
Griggs v Duke Power Company, 401 U.S. 424 (1971)
Grove City College v Bell, 465 U.S. 555 (1984)
Hammon v Barry, 606 F.Supp. 1082 (DDC)(1985)
Hazelwood School District v U.S., 433 U.S. 299 (1977)
Heart of Atlanta Motel v United States, 379 U.S. 241 (1964)
International Brotherhood of Teamsters v United States, 431 U.S. 324 (1977)
International Firefighters, Local 93 v Cleveland, 478 U.S. 501 (1986)
International Firefighters, Local 1784 v Stotts, 467 U.S. 561 (1983)

Johnson v Transportation Agency, Santa Clara County, California, 107 S.Ct. 1442 (1987)
Katzenbach v McClung, 379 U.S. 294 (1964)
Korematsu v United States, 323 U.S. 214 (1944)
Kromnick v School District of Philadelphia, 739 F.2d. 894 (CA3)(1984)
Local 28, Sheet Metal Workers v EEOC, 478 U.S. 421 (1985)
McDaniel v Barresi, 402 U.S. 39 (1971)
McDonnell Douglas Corp. v Green, 411 U.S. 292 (1973)
McLaurin v Oklahoma Board of Regents, 339 U.S. 637 (1950)
Missouri ex.rel. Gaines v Canada, 305 U.S. 337 (1938)
NAACP v Allen, 493 F.2d. 614 (CA5)(1974)
NLRB v Jones and Laughlin Steel Corp., 301 U.S. 1 (1937)
North Carolina Board of Education v Swann, 402 U.S. 43 (1971)
Pearson v Murray, 182 Atlantic Reporter 590 (1936)
Plessy v Ferguson, 163 U.S. 537 (1896)
Oatis v Crown Zellerbach Corp., 1 FEP Cases 328 (CA5) (1972)
Quarles v Phillip Morris Inc., 279 F.Supp. 505 (1968)
Regents of the University of California v Bakke, 438 U.S. 268 (1978)
San Antonio v Rodriguez, 411 U.S. 1 (1973)
Shapiro v Thompson, 294 U.S. 618 (1969)
Slaughterhouse Cases, 16 Wallace 36 (1873)
Swann v Charlotte-Mecklenberg Board of Education, 402 U.S. 1 (1971)
Sweatt v Painter, 339 U.S. 629 (1950)
United Jewish Organizations v Carey, 430 U.S. 144 (1977)
United States v Carolene Products Co., 304 U.S. 144 (1938)
United States v Darby, 312 U.S. 100 (1940)
United States v Iron Workers Local No. 86, 443 F.2d. 544 (CA9) (1971)
United States v Paradise, 480 U.S. 149 (1986)
United Steelworkers of America, AFL-CIO-CIC v Weber, 443 U.S. 193 (1979)
University of Texas v Camenisch, 451 U.S. 390 (1981)
Watson v Ft. Worth Bank and Trust, 108 S.Ct. 2777 (1988)
Wygant v Jackson Board of Education, 476 U.S. 267 (1985)

Index

About the Author

KATHANNE W. GREENE is Assistant Professor of Political Science at the University of Southern Mississippi, Hattiesburg.